nona A. Butterworth

In Order To Serve

In Order To Serve

Christ Church Cooks II

Published by
Christ Episcopal Church Women
to benefit Seeds of Hope

First Edition

Printed in the United States of America
By
Jostens Graphics
Winston-Salem, North Carolina

Original art by Nona Butterworth and Risden L. McElroy

Library of Congress Catalog Number 96-85725

ISBN 0-9653460-0-5

To order books, contact:

Christ Episcopal Church
The Good News Shop
1412 Providence Road
Charlotte, North Carolina 28207
704-333-0378

Foreword

In Order To Serve is more than a collection of recipes. Service to God and others is at the heart of our mission, and this book gives us the opportunity to weave the recipes into artwork and spiritual messages about service. The proceeds will support many outreach missions, initially benefiting our Seeds of Hope project.

This is the Episcopal Church Women's second parish cookbook. The first cookbook, Christ Church Cooks, was published in 1974. Twenty thousand copies were printed. The ordering information stated that a copy could be shipped for seventy-five cents and beautifully wrapped for an additional twenty-five cents. The first cookbook made no mention of food processors, microwave ovens, or gas grills. Beef fondue was an entertaining staple, and readers were urged "to cheat and use pastry shells". Times have changed; nevertheless, the old cookbook is a classic, and some favorite recipes have been included in *In Order To Serve.*

In Order To Serve is the work of many hands. We especially wish to thank The Reverend Henry Nutt Parsley, our rector of ten years, and Benjamin Hutto, our organist and choirmaster, for the pastoral advice and spiritual food they added to the beginning of each chapter. We are also grateful to all of the clergy and our Senior Warden, Anne Tomlinson, for the words of wisdom they provided in the chapter titled "Meals To Share With Others". Lastly, we thank our parishioners Nona Butterworth and Risden L. McElroy for their most beautiful illustrations of Christ Church.

May you find *In Order To Serve* delicious and inspiring. Bon Appetit!

Cookbook Committee

Editors
Kate Buckfelder
Susan Plott
Mimi Rees

Recipe Formatting
Jane Bruce
Gail Carr
Meredith Forshaw
Ann Linde

Committee Chairmen
Ross Andresen
DeeDee Dalrymple
Judy Dubose
Judy Gaines
Cynthia Gass
Anita Griffin
Susan Hamilton
Sue Head
Mary Jenrette
Lulie Mallard
Celia Marshall
Evaline Marshall
Camille Salisbury
Fran Stroud
Lisa Tomlinson
Anne Zollicoffer

Advisors
Carolyn Coleman
Margaretta Leary
Anne Tomlinson

Design and Graphics
Liz Lea
Mary Davis Smart
Melissa Tolmie

Artists
Nona Butterworth
Risden McElroy

Writers
Rachel Haynes
Marty Hedgpeth
Ben Hutto
Henry Parsley
Fred Paschall
Lisa Saunders
Brian Suntken
Anne Tomlinson

The Cookbook Committee thanks the many people who contributed their time and talents to *In Order To Serve.*

Table Of Contents

Appetizers

Being Called To Serve

In Order To Serve

1. Being Called To Serve

Lord, bless this food to our good health and our lives in your loving and faithful service; through Jesus Christ our Lord.
[SCOTTISH GRACE, ADAPTED]

...let the greatest among you become as the youngest,
and the leader as one who serves . . .
I am among you as one who serves.
[LUKE 22:26-27]

Serving is one of life's privileges. The service of guests at table is perhaps civilization's most ancient expression of hospitality. I think of Abraham and Sarah serving a quickly prepared feast to three strangers by the oaks of Mamre and "entertaining angels unawares." I think of Martha preparing supper in Bethany while Mary kept Jesus company. And of the risen Christ breaking bread at table in Emmaus.

"There is a call to us," Dorothy Day wrote, "a call of service - that we join with others to try to make things better in this world." Serving others at table is a parable of the larger call of service God gives to each of us. Neighbors need us. The poor need us. The world needs us. What matters in life is not what we have but what we give. Which is why the Lord said, "The greatest among you will be your servant."

An old saying goes, the servant is served by his serving. As we nourish the lives of others, our souls are fed. In giving, we receive.

Jesu, Jesu, fill us with your love
show us how to serve
the neighbors we have from you.
GHANAIAN FOLK HYMN [Hymn 602, refrain]
tr. THOMAS STEVENSON COLVIN (b.1925), Protestant minister; missionary

THE REVEREND HENRY NUTT PARSLEY, JR., RECTOR

10

CHEESE BISCUITS

Yield: 80 to 100 wafers
Jo Rankin

1   stick butter, softened
2   cups grated sharp
     cheddar cheese
1 1/2 cups flour, sifted
1/2 teaspoon salt
1/4 teaspoon cayenne pepper
1   tablespoon caraway seed

† Cream butter and cheese. Combine flour, salt and pepper together and add to cheese mixture. Add caraway seed if desired.
† Form into two long rolls about 1 1/2 inches in diameter. Wrap in wax paper and chill until firm.
† Preheat oven to 350°.
† Slice thin and bake about 10 minutes.
† Store in tin can when cool.

Rolls keep indefinitely in refrigerator and can be baked as needed. Recipe can be doubled. Omit caraway seeds and place a pecan on top if desired.

CROWD PLEASER

Yield: 20 cups
Nan Allison

1   cups butter
2 1/2 teaspoons garlic salt
3   tablespoons Worcestershire
     sauce
5   cups Honey Comb cereal
5   cups Crispix corn chex
1   cup melba rounds
1   cup cashew nuts
5   cups Cheese Nips
2   cups tiny pretzels
1   cup peanuts

† Preheat oven to 250°.
† Melt butter in a roasting pan and add remaining ingredients, mixing well.
† Bake for 60 minutes, stirring every 15 minutes.
† Store in airtight containers.

Mixture may be frozen.

COLD ARTICHOKE DIP

Yield: 31/2 cups
Lisa Seaton

2 (13.75 oz.) cans artichokes, drained
2 cups mayonnaise
1 (.75 oz.) package Italian dressing mix

† Blend ingredients in food processor until smooth. Chill overnight.
† Serve with salsa and tortilla chips or with vegetables.

CHEESE DOLLARS

Yield: 21/2 dozen
Sara Lowe

2 cups grated sharp cheddar cheese, softened
2 sticks margarine, softened
2 cups flour, sifted
3/4 teaspoon salt
1/2 teaspoon cayenne pepper
1 1/2 cups crispy rice cereal
    chopped pecans, optional

† Preheat oven to 350°.
† Combine cheese and margarine until creamy. Add flour, salt and cayenne pepper blending well.
† Add cereal and form into small balls about the size of a quarter.
† Press with fork and bake 15 minutes. Do not let them get too brown.

BLACK BEAN SALSA

Yield: 6 cups
Gayle Gilbert

2 15 ounce cans black beans, rinsed and drained
1 (11 or 17 ounce) can whole kernel corn, drained
2 large tomatoes, seeded and chopped
1 large or 2 small avocados, peeled and chopped
1/2-1 purple onion, chopped

MARINADE:
1/8-1/4 cup chopped fresh cilantro
3-4 tablespoons lime juice
2 tablespoons olive oil
1 teaspoon salt
1/2 teaspoon black or garlic pepper
1 tablespoon red wine vinegar
    avocado slices and fresh cilantro for garnish

† Combine first 5 ingredients in large bowl.
† Prepare marinade using remaining ingredients and combine with black bean mixture. Cover and chill overnight.
† Garnish and serve with tortilla chips.

BLACK BEAN MEXICAN DIP

Yield: One (9 inch) pie
Jeanne Kutrow
Henrietta Palmer

1 (15-ounce) can black beans, drained
1 (10-ounce) can tomatoes with chilies, drained
1/2 cup sour cream
4-5 green onions, chopped
1 cup grated cheddar cheese
1 cup grated Monterey Jack cheese

† Preheat oven to 350°.
† Combine beans and tomatoes with sour cream and onions and place in pie plate.
† Sprinkle with cheeses and bake uncovered for 30 minutes.
† Serve with tortilla chips.

BLACK-EYED PEA DIP

Yield: 6 cups
Marcia Gilbert

4 cups black-eyed peas, drained
Jalapeño peppers to taste, chopped
1 medium onion, chopped
1-2 cloves garlic, minced
1 (4-ounce) can chopped green chiles, undrained
1/2 pound shredded sharp cheddar cheese or sharp processed cheese spread
8-10 tablespoons butter

† Combine black-eyed peas and next 3 ingredients in a blender. Process until smooth.
† Heat cheese and butter in a double boiler until cheese melts. Add black-eyed peas mixture; cook until thoroughly heated.
† Serve with tortilla chips.

A tradition on New Years Day

CAROLINA CAVIAR

Yield: 12 servings
Susan Smart

1 pound fresh black-eyed peas
2 cups zesty Italian dressing
1 1/2 cups finely chopped onions
1/2 cup diced jalapeño peppers
2 cups diced red bell peppers
1 tablespoon minced garlic

† Cook peas according to package directions and drain. Pour Italian dressing over peas. Cool.
† Add remaining ingredients and refrigerate 24 hours.
† Serve at room temperature with tortilla chips.

CAPONATA

Yield: 6 to 7 cups
Nancy Hemmig

2   large eggplants, diced
2   large onions, chopped
2   bell peppers, chopped
3   stalks celery, chopped
1/2   cup olive oil
1   (6-ounce) can tomato paste
1   (8-ounce) can tomato sauce
5   cloves garlic, chopped
1   (10-ounce) jar salad olives, drained
1   (7 3/4-ounce) jar black olives
1/4   cup sugar
1/3   cup vinegar
    Salt and pepper to taste
    Tabasco sauce to taste
    Oregano to taste

† Sauté eggplant, onions, peppers and celery in olive oil until soft, stirring constantly.
† Add remaining ingredients and cook 35 to 40 minutes. Pack into sterilized jars and chill 24 hours before serving.
† Serve on crackers.

May be frozen and thawed before serving.

CLAM DIP

Yield: 10 to 12 servings
Anne Dooley

2   (8-ounce) packages cream cheese, softened
4   (6.5-ounce) cans minced clams, drained
1   cup mayonnaise
4   drops Tabasco sauce
4   shakes Worcestershire sauce
1   medium onion, grated
1   tablespoon lemon juice
    Paprika for garnish

† Combine all ingredients and refrigerate overnight.
† Dust with paprika and serve with corn chips.

MOTHER'S CHARLESTON CRAB DIP

Yield: 2-21/4 cups
Susan Fitch

1/4-1/2 cup mayonnaise
1   3-ounce package
    cream cheese
1/2-1 tablespoon horseradish
1   cup freshly picked crabmeat
4   tablespoons French dressing
1/2   small onion, minced

† Mix all ingredients and chill.
† Serve with saltine crackers.

SMOKEY CHEESE DIP

Yield: 3 cups
Marsha Rich

3-4 strips bacon
1/3   cup sliced almonds
3/4   cup mayonnaise
1 1/2 cups grated sharp cheese
1   tablespoon sliced
    green onions
1/4   teaspoon salt (optional)
1   tablespoon parsley flakes

† Cook and crumble bacon.
† Combine and mix lightly remaining
   ingredients.
† Serve with crackers.

DANIEL'S NACHO FEAST

Yield: One (9 x 12 inch) pan
Daniel Fitch

1   24 ounce can chili with beans
    Restaurant style corn chips
1/2   cup grated Monterey Jack
    cheese
1   cup grated cheddar cheese

† Warm chili in small saucepan.
† Line pan with corn chips and cover
   with beans.
† Add grated cheeses and broil
   until cheese melts.

HUMMUS

Yield: 4 Servings
DeeDee Dalrymple

1   12 ounce can chickpeas
2   tablespoons sesame oil
1/4-1/2 cup lemon juice
1   clove garlic
3   tablespoons water
    Olive oil (optional)

† Purée chickpeas in food processor.
† Blend in remaining ingredients.
† Serve with pita bread cut into triangles.

A little olive oil added before serving adds taste and will help blend if hummus is made ahead of time.

ROASTED RED PEPPER AND GARLIC DIP

Yield: 8 to 10 servings
Janie Sellers

2   red bell peppers
2   cloves garlic, minced
1   (8-ounce) package cream
    cheese, softened
2   tablespoons fresh lime juice
3   tablespoons finely chopped
    basil
1   tablespoon parsley
1/2 teaspoon salt
1/4 teaspoon freshly ground
    white pepper

† Roast whole red peppers by broiling six inches from heat until blackened on all sides. Let peppers sit 10 minutes then drain and pull off skins. Cut in half and remove stem, seeds and ribs.
† Place peppers in food processor and add remaining ingredients. Process until creamy.
† Serve with breadsticks or vegetables.

VIDALIA ONION DIP

Yield: 4 to 6 servings
Henrietta Palmer

1   cup chopped Vidalia onions
1   cup mayonnaise
1/2   cup grated cheddar cheese
1/2   cup grated Swiss cheese

† Preheat oven to 325°.
† Combine all ingredients and place in greased pie pan. Bake for 30 minutes.
† Serve with crackers.

HOT CANAPÉ SPREAD

Yield: 8 to 10 servings
Mary Cathey

2   (8-ounce) packages cream cheese, softened
1   (8-ounce) carton sour cream
4   tablespoons chopped bell pepper
4   tablespoons finely chopped onion or scallions
3   (2.25-ounce) jars chipped beef, shredded
2   tablespoons chopped pimiento
    Cracked pepper to taste
1/2   cup crushed walnuts

† Preheat oven to 325°.
† Combine all ingredients except walnuts in food processor.
† Spread in shallow baking dish and top with walnuts. Bake for 30 minutes.
† Serve with corn chips.

SAUSAGE HORS D'OEUVRE

Yield: 6 to 8 servings
Ann Carmichael

1   pound country sausage
1   (10-ounce) can diced tomatoes with chiles
1   (8-ounce) package cream cheese

† Preheat oven to 350°.
† Cook sausage and drain well. Add drained tomatoes and cheese to hot sausage. (May be frozen at this point.)
† Bake uncovered for 20 minutes.
† Serve with corn chips.

BRIE CHEESE WITH CHUTNEY

Yield: 4 to 6 servings
Dot Osher

1   (13.2-ounce) round
    Brie cheese
1   (8-ounce) jar chutney,
    preferably with lots of nuts

† Preheat oven to 350°.
† Split Brie horizontally. Place in baking
  dish with chutney between the cheese
  layers.
† Bake until bubbly and brown on top.
† Serve with wheat crackers.

FAVORITE CHEESE BALL

Yield: 1 ball
Paula Freeman

2   (8-ounce) packages
    cream cheese
1   (151/4-ounce) can crushed
    pineapple, well drained
1   cup chopped pecans
1   bell pepper, chopped
1   small onion, finely chopped

† Combine all ingredients and shape into
  a ball. Chill overnight.
† Serve with crackers.

This may also be served in half of a hollowed-out fresh pineapple.

FOUR CHEESE PÂTÉ

Yield: One (9-inch) round
Nancy Ehringhaus

3   (8-ounce) packages cream
    cheese softened, divided
2   tablespoons milk
2   tablespoons sour cream
3/4 cup chopped toasted pecans
1   (41/2-ounce) package
    Camembert cheese,
    softened
1   (4-ounce) package blue
    cheese, crumbled and
    softened
1   cup grated Swiss cheese
    Pecan halves for garnish

† Line a pie plate with plastic wrap
  and set aside.
† Combine one package cream cheese
  with milk and sour cream. Beat at
  medium speed until smooth. Spread
  in pie plate and sprinkle with pecans.
† Blend remaining ingredients on medium
  speed until smooth. Spoon into pie plate
  and spread to edge. Cover with plastic
  wrap and chill. May chill up to one week.
† Invert onto serving plate and pull away
  plastic wrap. Garnish with pecans.
† Serve with apple wedges.

CRANBERRY RELISH

Yield: 2 pints
Jean Spratt

1 cup sugar
1 small or medium onion, chopped
1 whole clove
1 teaspoon cinnamon
1/2 cup vinegar
1 teaspoon ginger
Dash of red pepper flakes
1/3 teaspoon salt
1/2 cup water
1/3 cup brown sugar
1 cup seedless raisins
2 cups cranberries, washed and picked over

† Boil all ingredients, except brown sugar, raisins, and cranberries, until sugar is melted.
† Add remaining ingredients. Boil until cranberries burst.
† Cool and refrigerate for 2-3 hours before serving.
† Serve as relish or over cream cheese with crackers.

May be sealed in small jars or refrigerated.

PÂTÉ

Yield: 6-8 Servings
Janie Sellers

1 pound chicken livers, fat removed
3 tablespoons chopped onion
1 Granny Smith apple, peeled and chopped
21/2 sticks unsalted butter, softened, divided
1 teaspoon dry mustard
1/4 teaspoon salt
1/4 teaspoon grated nutmeg
Dash of cayenne pepper
Dash of ground cloves

† Cover livers with water and bring to boil. Simmer 30 minutes and cool in liquid, then drain.
† Sauté onions and apple in 1 teaspoon butter over medium heat about 5 minutes.
† Combine livers with 2 sticks of butter, onion and apple mixture, and remaining ingredients. Blend in food processor until smooth.
† Pack into a container which will tightly hold the pâté. Pour 3 tablespoons clarified butter (see below) on top and refrigerate. Make at least 1 day ahead.
† When serving, scrape clarified butter off top. Invert and serve with French bread rounds.

To clarify butter, melt butter over low heat. Remove and set aside for 5 minutes. Use spoon to carefully remove and discard the foamy butterfat on top. Pour off the clear liquid which is the clarified butter, cool and refrigerate. Discard any solids left on bottom.

CRAB AND MANGO PACKETS

Yield: 36 appetizers
Chef Ed Steedman, Marais

2-3 tablespoons mayonnaise
3 tablespoons ketchup
1 tablespoon cognac
   Dash of Tabasco
1 head lettuce
3 mangoes, peeled and diced
1 pound backfin or
   lump crabmeat
36 toasted bread rounds
   Salmon caviar for garnish

† Combine mayonnaise, ketchup, cognac
   and Tabasco to make cocktail sauce.
† Remove lettuce leaves one by one
   and blanch very quickly in simmering
   salted water. Remove immediately to
   bowl of ice water until cool. Remove
   and place flat on towels to dry.
† Mix mangoes and crabmeat with small
   amount of cocktail sauce.
† Spread remaining cocktail sauce on toasted
   bread rounds. Make individual balls with
   lettuce and fill with crabmeat mixture,
   placing one on each round. Garnish
   with salmon caviar.

SALMON MOUSSE

Yield: 4 to 8 servings
Elizabeth Clark

1 (1/4-ounce) envelope gelatin
2 tablespoons lemon juice
1 small onion, sliced
1/2 cup boiling water
1/2 cup mayonnaise
1 (1-pound) can salmon,
   drained
1/4 teaspoon paprika
1 teaspoon dried dill
1 cup heavy cream
   Salt to taste

† Place gelatin, lemon juice, onion and
   water in blender. Blend on high 40
   seconds.
† Add mayonnaise, salmon, paprika,
   and dill. Blend on high.
† Gradually pour in cream and blend for
   30 seconds. Add salt to taste.
† Pour into 4-cup oiled ring mold. Chill.
† Serve with crackers.

SHRIMP MOLD

Yield: About 3 cups
Gail Carr

1   (12-ounce) bottle chili sauce
1/2 cup ketchup
1   teaspoon sugar
2   tablespoons grated onion
2   (1/4-ounce) envelopes
    unflavored gelatin
1   tablespoon Worcestershire
    sauce
1-2 teaspoons prepared
    horseradish
3   tablespoons lemon juice
4   drops Tabasco sauce
2   (5-ounce) cans tiny shrimp

† Blend all ingredients except shrimp in top
  of double boiler until gelatin dissolves.
† Add shrimp to ingredients. Pour into
  lightly oiled mold. Chill. (Will fill a
  31/2-cup mold 2/3 full).
† Serve with buttery round crackers or
  wheat crackers.

SEA ISLAND SHRIMP MOLD

Yield: 25 Servings
Camille Salisbury

1   can she-crab soup
1   8 ounce package cream
    cheese, softened
2   (1/4-ounce) envelopes
    unflavored gelatin, prepared
1   cup mayonnaise
1   cup finely chopped celery
1   tablespoon lemon juice
4   green onions, finely chopped
1   teaspoon curry powder
1   pound cooked shrimp, peeled
    and chopped
    Dill, olives, capers, and
    pimientos for garnish

† In a saucepan, heat soup and cream
  cheese until creamy. Add prepared
  gelatin.
† Blend in remaining ingredients and
  spoon into a fish mold that has been
  sprayed with nonstick cooking spray.
† Chill at least 4 hours. Unmold on tray
  and garnish.

PESTO-LAYERED TORTA

Yield: one (2-cup) mold
Holli Wear

1 (8-ounce) package cream cheese, softened
1/2 stick butter (not margarine), softened
4 tablespoons Parmesan cheese
1/4-1/2 cup thick pesto, drained
1/4-1/2 cup sun-dried tomatoes

† Beat cream cheese and butter together with Parmesan.
† Place tomatoes in food processor and process until moderately smooth.
† Line 2 miniature loaf pans or other containers with coffee filter. Place a sprig of basil or rosemary in bottom of container.
† Spread some of cream cheese mixture into bottom of the pan. Spread some of pesto on top. Add another layer of cream cheese mixture, then layer of sun-dried tomatoes. End with a layer of cream cheese mixture.
† Cover top with plastic wrap. Pick up container (unless it is glass) and hit a few times on counter to settle the ingredients.
† Refrigerate until ready to serve.
† Remove from container and peel off coffee filter.
† Serve with warm crusty bread.

Layers of pesto and tomatoes can be thick or thin. Just use enough so layers are visible when served. Layers of chopped olives or smoked salmon can also be substituted.

VEGETABLE SANDWICHES

Yield: 20 to 28 party sandwiches
Peggy Tyson

2 medium cucumbers, chopped
1 bell pepper, chopped
2 small onions, chopped
2 small carrots, chopped
4 ripe tomatoes, chopped
1 envelope unflavored gelatin
1 cup mayonnaise
1 teaspoon salt

† Blend cucumbers, pepper and onions. Add carrots and tomatoes. Drain, saving 3 tablespoons of juice.
† Soak gelatin in juice and dissolve over water. Add to vegetables and fold in mayonnaise and salt.
† Store in refrigerator overnight.
† Spread on bread when ready to serve sandwiches or store in refrigerator overnight.

ASPARAGUS ROLL-UPS

Yield: 100 to 125 pieces
Marcia Gilbert

3 ounces blue cheese, crumbled
1 (8-ounce) package cream cheese, softened
1 egg
1 (24-ounce) loaf white bread
2 (15-ounce) cans asparagus spears
2 sticks butter, melted

† To make filling, combine cheeses and egg into a spread.
† Remove crusts from bread and roll thin with a rolling pin.
† Spread filling on bread and lay asparagus spear on bread and roll jelly-roll style. Dip in melted butter, place on cookie sheet and freeze.
† Slice each spear into 3 bite-size sections and refreeze until ready to use.
† Bake on cookie sheet for 20 minutes at 425°.

CUCUMBER SANDWICHES

Yield: 100 sandwiches
Nan Allison

2 tablespoons Worcestershire sauce
1/4 cup fresh dill, minced or 1 1/3 tablespoons dried
2 drops Tabasco sauce
3 tablespoons lemon juice
1/4 teaspoon salt
3 green onions, minced
1 clove garlic, minced
2 8-ounce packages cream cheese, softened
50 slices white bread
6-8 cucumbers, thinly sliced, unpeeled
2 bunches dill for garnish

† Combine first seven ingredients in food processor. Add cheese in small amounts and blend. Refrigerate for 20 minutes.
† Cut bread into desired shapes. Spread a thin layer of cheese mixture on bread and top with slice of cucumber and garnish with dill.

JALAPEÑO SQUARES

Yield: 12 to 24 squares
Lynn DeLoache

4 cups grated Colby cheese
4 cups grated cheddar cheese
4 eggs, beaten
1 (5-ounce) can evaporated milk
1/2 (12-ounce) jar jalapeño slices, rinsed

† Combine cheeses.
† Mix eggs and milk.
† In 9x13-inch casserole, spread half of cheese. Top with jalapeño slices and sprinkle with remaining cheese.
† Pour egg mixture over cheese and let sit at least 6 hours.
† Preheat oven to 350°.
† Bake 1 hour. Cool 10 minutes before slicing. Drain on paper towels.

May be frozen.

MUSHROOM PUFFS

Yield: 40 to 50
Marcia Gilbert

PASTRY:
1 (3-ounce) package cream cheese, softened
1 stick butter, softened
1 1/2 cups flour

† Combine cream cheese and butter. Blend in flour. Chill 30 minutes.
† On floured board, roll out chilled dough until very thin. Cut into 3-inch rounds.

FILLING:
1 small onion, minced
3 tablespoons butter
1/2 pound mushrooms, minced
1/4 teaspoon thyme
1/2 teaspoon salt
   Pepper to taste
1/4 cup sour cream

† Preheat oven to 450°.
† Sauté onion in butter. Add mushrooms and cook 3 minutes. Add seasonings.
† Sprinkle flour over sautéed mixture. Blend in sour cream and cook until thickened. Do not boil.
† Place less than one teaspoon of filling on each round. Fold edges over and press together with fork. Prick and bake on ungreased cookie sheet 12 to 15 minutes.

Freezes well. Allow extra time for baking.

PEPPERONI CHEESE BITES

Yield: 4 dozen
Anne Scott

1 (10-ounce) package sliced pepperoni
1 package frozen chopped spinach, thawed and well drained
2 cups ricotta cheese
1 1/2 cups Parmesan cheese
1 1/4 cups chopped mushrooms
1/2 cup chopped onion
1 teaspoon oregano
1/2 teaspoon salt
2 eggs
1/4 cup sour cream

† Preheat oven to 375°.
† Place one pepperoni slice in bottom of small muffin tins sprayed lightly with nonstick cooking spray. Cut remaining slices into 48 wedges for garnish.
† Combine spinach with remaining ingredients. Spoon on top of slices.
† Bake 20 to 25 minutes or until lightly browned.
Cool 10 minutes and remove from tins.
Top each with sour cream and pepperoni wedge.

May be frozen up to 3 months. Thaw in refrigerator and bake at 350° for 10 minutes.

ROSEMARY EYE OF ROUND

Yield: 8-10 servings per pound
Hope Parrott

Eye of round beef roast (see Note)
1 teaspoon seasoned salt
1 teaspoon garlic salt
1 tablespoon black pepper
1 teaspoon dried rosemary, crushed, or 1 tablespoon fresh
1 tablespoon vegetable shortening

† Combine seasoning ingredients. Rub entire surface of meat with seasoning mixture 24 to 48 hours before cooking. Wrap in foil and refrigerate.
† Allow meat to reach room temperature before cooking.
† Preheat oven to 300°.
† Brown meat in melted shortening. Place in shallow pan and bake 15 minutes per pound for rare, 20 minutes per pound for medium.
† Cool and refrigerate for 12 to 24 hours before slicing very thin.
† Serve on party size rolls.

Size of roast will vary. Seasoning ingredients may be increased in order to cover very large roast.

TOMATO AND OLIVADA CROSTINI

Yield: About 50
Linda Minor

1   (16-inch) baguette
1-11/2 cups Parmesan cheese
2   (28-ounce) cans whole
       Italian tomatoes
1/4 cup olive oil
1   clove garlic, mashed
1/2 teaspoon sugar
       Salt and pepper to taste
1/2-3/4 cup black olive paste

† Preheat oven to 350°.
† Cut baguette into 1/4-inch slices.
   Arrange bread on 2 baking sheets and
   sprinkle half with Parmesan cheese.
   Toast until crisp and golden 8 to 10
   minutes.
† Drain tomatoes in colander. Squeeze
   out liquid and blot with paper towels.
   Chop tomatoes.
† Combine tomatoes with remaining
   ingredients except olive paste.
† Put a heaping teaspoon tomato mixture
   on each Parmesan crostino and top
   with 1/4 teaspoon olive paste.
† Spread each plain crostino with
   1/2 teaspoon olive paste and top with
   heaping 1/2 teaspoon tomato mixture.

MARINATED SHRIMP

Yield: 10 to 12 servings
Christ Church Cooks I

5   pounds cooked shrimp,
       peeled and deveined
1   cup vegetable oil
1/2 cup vinegar
11/4 cups finely minced celery
21/2 tablespoons finely minced
       bell pepper
4   tablespoons grated onion
1   clove garlic, minced
5   tablespoons minced parsley
3/4 cup horseradish mustard
11/2 teaspoons salt
1/4 teaspoon pepper
4   tablespoons paprika

† Combine all ingredients, except shrimp.
† Pour over shrimp and marinate in
   refrigerator 24 hours.

ORIENTAL CHICKEN WONTONS

Yield: about 25
Jan Richards

1/2 pound ground raw chicken
   or pork
1/2 cup grated carrot
1/4 cup finely chopped celery
   or water chestnuts
1 tablespoon soy sauce
1 tablespoon dry sherry
2 teaspoons cornstarch
2 teaspoons grated gingerroot
1/2 (16-ounce) package wonton
   wrappers
2 tablespoons margarine
   or butter, melted

† Cook chicken or pork until no pink remains. Drain. Blend in next six ingredients.
† Preheat oven to 375°.
† Spoon 1 tablespoon of filling onto wonton wrapper. Lightly brush edges with water.
† To shape wonton, carefully bring two opposite points of the square wrapper up over the filling and pinch together in the center.
† Carefully bring two remaining opposite points to the center and pinch together. Pinch together edges to seal.
† Place wontons on greased baking sheet. Brush with margarine and bake 8 to 10 minutes until lightly brown and crisp.
† Serve with plum or sweet and sour sauce.

May be frozen.

SILVER SPOON WINGS

Yield: 6 to 8 servings
Mimi Rees

2-3 pounds chicken wings

MARINADE:
1/2 cup sugar
1/2 cup water
1/2 cup dark soy sauce
1/4 cup pineapple juice
2 tablespoons vegetable oil
1 teaspoon grated fresh
   ginger
1/2 teaspoon garlic powder

† Cut wings at the joints. Discard tips.

† Combine ingredients and pour over wings. Cover and refrigerate at least one day.
† Preheat oven to 350°.
† Remove chicken from marinade and bake 40 minutes on cookie sheet until tender. Baste with marinade while cooking.

Notes:

Soups And Salads

Preparing To Serve

II. Preparing To Serve

*Blessed Lord Jesus, let not our souls be busy inns that have no
room for you and yours; but quiet homes of prayer and praise
where you may find fit company, where the needful cares of
life are wisely ordered and put away, and wide spaces kept for
you.*

[PRAYERS ANCIENT AND MODERN, ADAPTED]

The service of others must include the service of oneself. That means the care
of our own souls. If we do not feed our inner self and nurture our relationship
with God, chances are we will have little to give to others. This is what Jesus
meant by the salt losing its savor. That happens when we become diluted, too
over-committed. God wants us to be salty servants.

Care of the soul begins in taking time to be quiet and still. The soul cherishes
silence and, as Thomas Moore has written, is nourished by "pausing" and
"taking time." In such moments we can become aware of the presence of God
with us and glimpse the surprising epiphanies all around us in the ordinariness
of our life.

The early Celtic Christians made every moment an occasion of prayer. "I
kindle my fire this morning in the presence of the holy angels of heaven," a
cook might say, or "Each meal beneath my roof will be mixed together in the
name of God the Son who gave them growth." It is as we take time for God
and our souls that we learn to see that all life is an occasion of grace. Then
praise becomes our most important seasoning as we prepare to serve others
from the riches of God's grace.

Teach us to care and not to care.
Teach us to sit still
Our peace in His will.
THOMAS STEARNS ELIOT (1888-1965)

THE REVEREND HENRY N. PARSLEY, JR., RECTOR

CAN-OPENER BRUNSWICK STEW

Yield: 6 to 8 servings
Janie Sellers

1 (20-ounce) can Brunswick
   stew
1 can chicken gumbo soup
1 (12-ounce) can spicy
   vegetable juice
2 (6-ounce) cans premium
   chunk white-meat chicken
1 (11-ounce) can shoepeg
   corn or 1/2 box frozen
1/2 box frozen lima beans
   Salt and pepper to taste
1/2 stick butter (optional)
1 bay leaf (optional)
1 teaspoon sugar (optional)
   Worcestershire sauce
   to taste (optional)
   Lemon juice to taste
   (optional)
   Tabasco sauce to taste
   (optional)
1-2 cups thinly sliced onions
   (optional)

† Combine all ingredients and simmer on low heat until hot.

CREAM OF CARROT SOUP

Yield: 6 servings
Jane Bruce

2 cups sliced onions
5 cups coarsely chopped
   carrots
2 tablespoons butter, melted
1/2 cup raw white rice
8 cups chicken broth, divided
   Salt and pepper to taste
1/2 cup sour cream for garnish

† Sauté onions and carrots in butter until tender for 7-8 minutes.
† Add rice and 4 cups chicken broth. Cover and simmer until rice is tender, 20 to 25 minutes.
† Add remaining broth and season with salt and pepper. Cool and purée in food processor.
† Serve chilled or hot. Garnish with sour cream.

AMISH CHICKEN CORN SOUP

Yield: 4 to 6 servings
Pat Pollard

1   (2¹/2-pound) chicken or 3
     large chicken breast halves
8-10 cups water
1   cup diced celery
4   cups white or yellow corn
1   cup flour
1   egg
2   hard-cooked eggs, diced
     (optional)

† In soup pot, cook chicken in water.
  Remove meat and cut into bite-size
  pieces. Save broth.
† Add celery and corn to broth and simmer
  30 minutes.
† In small bowl, combine flour and egg.
  Blend into broth. Add chicken pieces.

Soup freezes well.

BREAD AND CHEESE SOUP

Yield: 6 to 8 servings
Zoe Wood

6   onions, thinly sliced
3   cloves garlic, minced
1   large bunch broccoli,
     chopped
2   tablespoons oil
4   teaspoons salt
1/2 teaspoon pepper
2   quarts boiling water
1/2 pound whole grain bread,
     divided
2   cups grated Swiss cheese,
     divided
1¹/2 cups grated Parmesan
     cheese

† Preheat oven to 375°.
† Sauté onion, garlic and broccoli in oil
  until onion is golden. Season with salt
  and pepper. Add water, cover and
  cook until tender.
† Line 4-quart casserole with half of bread.
  Combine cheeses. Sprinkle 1¹/2 cups
  cheese on bread. Repeat bread layer.
  Pour soup over bread and sprinkle with
  remaining cheese. Brown in oven 5 to
  15 minutes.

BLACK BEAN VEGETABLE CHILI

Yield: 10 servings
Harrold Vaughn

1/2 cup olive oil
2-3 small cucumbers, cut in
   3/4-inch chunks
2   zucchini, cut into
   3/4-inch chunks
1   eggplant, cut into
   3/4-inch chunks
2   onions, chopped
1   bell pepper, chopped
4   cloves garlic, minced
8   tomatoes, chopped
1   (15-ounce) can tomatoes,
   undrained
11/2 cups corn kernels
1/4 cup lemon juice
1   cup parsley, chopped
1/4-1/2 cup basil, chopped
11/2-3 tablespoons chili powder
1/2-1 tablespoon oregano
1/2 teaspoon salt
1/2 teaspoon black pepper
1/2 teaspoon red pepper
1/2-1 teaspoon cumin
1/4-1/2 cup dill, chopped
1/2-1 tablespoons kosher salt
2   cups cooked black beans

† Heat olive oil and sauté vegetables for 10 minutes. Add seasonings and cook on low heat for 30 to 45 minutes.
† Add beans and cook an additional 15 minutes.
† Use sour cream, grated Monterey jack cheese and chopped green onions for garnish.

For less spicy chili, use less seasonings and serve over rice.

33

CHICKEN CHILI

Yield: 6 to 8 servings
Elisabeth Benfield

6   boneless, skinless chicken
    breast halves
1   cup chopped onion
1   medium bell pepper,
    chopped
2   cloves garlic, minced
2   tablespoons vegetable oil
2   (14 1/2-ounce) cans
    stewed tomatoes
1   (15 1/2-ounce) can
    pinto beans, drained
2/3-3/4 cup picante sauce
1   teaspoon chili powder
1   teaspoon ground cumin
1/2 teaspoon salt
2   cups grated cheddar
    cheese
1   (10-ounce) bag tortilla chips

† Cut chicken into 1-inch pieces. Cook
  chicken, onion, green pepper and garlic
  in oil until chicken loses its pink color.
† Add remaining ingredients, except
  cheese and tortilla chips. Simmer 20
  minutes uncovered.
† Ladle into bowls and top with cheese.
  Serve with tortilla chips.

CHICKEN CHOWDER

Yield: 8 servings
Nan Allison

1   stick butter
2   cups grated carrots
1/2 cup chopped onion
1/2 cup flour
3   cups chicken broth
4   cups milk
2   cups cooked chicken,
    cubed
1   cup corn
1   teaspoon Worcestershire
    sauce
2   cups grated cheddar cheese
1   teaspoon salt
1/2 teaspoon pepper
2   tablespoons white wine
    (optional)

† Melt butter in Dutch oven. Sauté carrots
  and onions until tender.
† Blend in flour. Add broth and milk. Cook
  until thick and smooth, stirring frequently.
† Add remaining ingredients and stir until
  cheese is melted.

34

CURRIED CRAB SOUP

Yield: 4 to 6 servings
Carolyn Coleman

1/2 stick butter
1/2 cup finely chopped onion
1   clove garlic, minced
1/2 cup peeled finely diced
     apple
1   teaspoon curry powder
3   tablespoons flour
1/2 cup peeled chopped ripe
     tomato
3   cups chicken broth
     Salt and freshly ground
     pepper to taste
1/2 pound crabmeat,
     picked over
1/2 cup heavy cream
     Tabasco sauce to taste
     Chopped parsley
     for garnish

† Sauté onion in butter. When wilted, add garlic and apple. Blend in curry powder and flour.
† Whisk in tomato and chicken broth. When thickened and smooth, add salt, pepper and crabmeat. Simmer 10 minutes.
† Add cream and bring to boil. Add tabasco. Serve hot with parsley garnish.

SEAFOOD CHOWDER

Yield: 10 to 12 servings
Patty Adams

3   cups mixed seafood
     (shrimp, crab and/or
     scallops)
1/2 stick butter, melted
1   small onion, minced
1   can cream of shrimp soup
1   can cream of potato soup
1   can cream of mushroom
     soup
1   can tomato bisque soup
5   ounces sherry
1   quart half-and-half
     Fresh dill or parsley
     for garnish

† Sauté seafood in butter until tender, slightly undercooked.
† Combine remaining ingredients, except dill or parsley, in large pot. Heat on low heat until hot, but do not boil.
† Garnish with dill or parsley.

FRUIT SOUP

Yield: 6 to 8 servings
Dot Heaslip

4 tablespoons tapioca
21/2 cups water, divided
2-3 tablespoons sugar
1 (6-ounce) can frozen
   juice
2 cups sliced strawberries
3-4 sliced bananas
1 cup sliced seedless grapes
3-4 fresh peaches, sliced

† Cook tapioca in 1 cup water and sugar until thick and clear. Stir in orange juice to melt.
† Add remaining water and pour over sliced fruit. Chill.

HAM, SAUSAGE AND CHICKEN GUMBO

Yield: 12 cups
Ann Cramer

11/2 pounds ham
11/2 pounds smoked sausage
6 chicken thighs
1/4 cup plus 2 tablespoons
   vegetable oil
1/4 cup all-purpose flour
1 large onion, chopped
4 cloves garlic, minced
1/2 green bell pepper, chopped
2 quarts water
1/2 teaspoon crushed red
   pepper
1/2 teaspoon dried whole thyme
1/4 teaspoon black pepper
1/2 cup chopped green
   onion tops
   Filé powder (optional)
   Hot cooked rice

† Cut ham and sausage into one-half inch cubes.
† Heat oil in large Dutch oven and brown each meat, one at a time, removing to drain on paper towels.
† Add flour to remaining oil and cook over medium heat, stirring constantly, until roux is caramel-colored (10 to 15 minutes).
† Add onion, garlic, and bell pepper to roux, stirring frequently, until tender.
† Add water, meats, red pepper, thyme, and black pepper. Bring to a boil. Reduce heat and simmer uncovered 11/2 to 2 hours.
† Cool and skim off fat.
† Remove chicken from bones and return to pot.
† Bring gumbo to boil and add green onion tops and filé, if desired.
† Cook additional 10 minutes and serve over rice.

GAZPACHO

Yield: 8 to 10 servings
Ann Carmichael

1   (46-ounce) can tomato juice
1   tablespoon parsley
3/4 cup chopped cucumbers
2   tomatoes, coarsely chopped
3/4 cup chopped green onion
1/2 cup chopped sweet onion
1   clove garlic, crushed
2   tablespoons white wine
    vinegar
1   tablespoon olive oil
1/2 teaspoon Worcestershire
    sauce
3   drops Tabasco sauce
1/2 teaspoon salt
1/4 teaspoon freshly ground
    pepper
    Finely chopped cucumber,
    bell pepper and onion
    for garnish

† Combine ingredients in large metal bowl
and chill.
† Garnish with cucumber, bell pepper and
onion.

AUNT GRACE'S CREAM OF CURRIED PEA SOUP

Yield: 4 to 5 servings
Frances deWitt

1   cup shelled fresh peas
    or frozen
1   medium onion, sliced
1   small carrot, sliced
1   stalk celery with leaves,
    chopped
1   medium potato, sliced
1   teaspoon curry powder
1   teaspoon salt
2   cups chicken broth, divided
1   cup cream
    Whipped cream, yogurt
    or sprig of parsley
    for garnish

† Place vegetables, seasonings, and 1 cup
of broth in saucepan. Boil, then simmer
15 minutes.
† Blend mixture in food processor. Add
remaining broth and cream. Chill.
† Serve in cold soup bowls and top
with garnish.

CHILLED SQUASH SOUP

Yield: 4 to 6 servings
Henrietta Palmer

1   pound yellow squash, sliced
1   medium onion, chopped
2   chicken bouillon cubes
1   cup water
    Salt and pepper to taste
1   (8-ounce) carton sour
    cream or cottage cheese
    Chopped dill for garnish

† Simmer squash, onions and bouillon
  cubes in water until tender.
† Purée squash and liquid in food
  processor. Add salt and pepper to taste.
  Fold in sour cream and chill overnight.
† Garnish with dill.

ITALIAN BEAN SOUP

Yield: 4 to 6 servings
Anna Stanley

2   tablespoons olive oil
2   large cloves garlic, minced
1   large onion, chopped
2   medium stalks celery,
    chopped
2   medium peeled carrots,
    chopped
1   medium zucchini, chopped
1   cup peeled cubed
    red potatoes
2   cups chopped plum
    tomatoes
2   cups cooked cannellini
    beans, drained
6   cups chicken broth
1   tablespoon tomato paste
4-5 large basil leaves, chopped
1/4 cup minced parsley
1   small dried chili,
    finely minced
    Salt and pepper to taste

† Heat oil in large pot and sauté garlic
  and onion until tender.
† Add celery, carrots, and zucchini and
  sauté several minutes.
† Stir in other ingredients and simmer
  partially covered 30 to 40 minutes.

HAMBURGER VEGETABLE SOUP

Yield: 10 to 12 servings
Ann Carmichael

1 pound ground chuck
1 (28-ounce) can whole
   tomatoes, undrained
2 medium onions, chopped
3 large potatoes, diced
3 carrots, sliced
1 7-ounce can corn,
   undrained
1 8-ounce can green
   beans, drained
3 beef bouillon cubes
2 teaspoons salt
4 whole peppercorns
3 cups water
1 can tomato soup
   Oregano to taste
1 bay leaf

† Brown and drain ground chuck.
† Chop tomatoes.
† Combine all ingredients.
† Simmer 1 hour.

TACO BEEF SOUP

Yield: 6 or 8 servings
Charlotte Smith

1   pound ground beef
1/2 cup chopped onion
2   (16-ounce) cans stewed
     tomatoes
2   (8-ounce) cans tomato
     sauce
1   (16-ounce) can kidney
     beans (optional)
1   (11/4-ounce) package
     taco seasoning mix
3   cups water
     Grated cheddar cheese
     Sour cream

† Brown beef and onion in large pot.
  Drain off fat.
† Add remaining ingredients, except
  cheese and sour cream. Simmer covered
  20 to 30 minutes.
† Pour soup in bowls and garnish with
  cheese and sour cream.

In Order To Serve

BAVARIAN GOULASH SOUP

Yield: 5 servings
Gail Carr

2-3 pounds boneless chuck, cubed
3/4 cup water
3/4 cup vinegar
4 tablespoons olive oil
3 onions, chopped
3 cloves garlic, minced
6 cups water
4 tablespoons paprika
12 allspice berries
2 (6-ounce) cans tomato paste
1 tablespoon salt
1 teaspoon coriander
1/2 teaspoon caraway seeds
1/4 teaspoon pepper

† Marinate meat in water and vinegar several hours. Drain and pat dry.
† In Dutch oven, sauté onions and garlic in oil. Add meat and brown.
† Add remaining ingredients. Cook covered on low heat for 2 hours. Remove lid and continue cooking the soup, breaking up the meat, until it thickens.

Carrots and potatoes may be added for a stew.

SPLIT PEA SOUP

Yield: 21/2-3 quarts
Kassie Minor

1 (16-ounce) package dried green split peas
4 quarts water, divided
1 ham hock
1 large yellow onion
2 whole cloves
1-2 carrots, chopped
Salt and pepper to taste
Liquid smoke (optional)

† Pick over and rinse peas. Put in a large pot with 2 quarts water. Bring to a boil and simmer 2 minutes. Remove from heat and let sit 1 hour.
† Rinse and drain peas. Return to pot with 2 quarts of water. Put cloves in onion and add to peas along with remaining ingredients. Simmer until peas are very soft.
† Remove ham hock and pull off meat. Remove cloves from onion. Put peas, carrots and onion through food mill. May be chopped in small batches in food processor. Add shredded ham and liquid smoke.

This is a thick soup that freezes well.

40

POTATO SOUP - A LIGHTER VERSION

Yield: 4 servings
Elizabeth Jones

5   small to medium potatoes
1   carrot
1   medium white or yellow onion
1 1/2 cups water
1/4 teaspoon salt
1/2 stick light margarine
1   cup milk (can use 1/2%)
1/4-1/2 cup grated sharp
     cheddar cheese
     Freshly grated black pepper
     Grated cheddar cheese,
     chopped scallions and/or
     bacon bits for garnish

† Peel and dice potatoes, carrot and onion.
  Simmer in water 20 to 30 minutes
  until tender.
† Lightly mash. Add salt, margarine,
  milk and cheese. Blend well, adding
  pepper to taste.
† Garnish before serving.

VEGETABLE LENTIL SOUP

Yield: 3 to 4 servings
Mimi Rees

2   tablespoons olive oil, divided
1   medium-size yellow squash,
     cut into 1/2-inch cubes
1   medium onion, chopped
1   clove garlic, chopped
1/4 teaspoon curry powder
1/2 cup lentils, picked over
     and rinsed
3   cups water
1 1/2 cups chicken broth
1   cup packed escarole
     or spinach, chopped
2   plum tomatoes, peeled
     and chopped
1/4 cup chopped fresh
     parsley leaves
1   teaspoon red wine
     vinegar
     Salt to taste
     Freshly ground black
     pepper to taste

† Sauté squash in 1 tablespoon oil until
  golden. Remove.
† Add remaining oil to saucepan and sauté
  onion until tender. Stir in garlic and curry
  powder. Cook one minute.
† Add lentils, water and broth. Simmer 20
  minutes or until lentils are tender.
† Stir in squash and remaining ingredients,
  except salt and pepper, and simmer 3
  minutes. Season with salt and pepper.

41

TACO CHICKEN SOUP

Yield: 10 to 12 servings
Clarissa Chandler

1   pound boneless chicken
    breasts
5-6 cups chicken broth
1   onion, chopped
1   bell pepper, chopped
1   clove garlic, minced
1   (15-ounce) can diced
    tomatoes
1   (10-ounce) can diced
    tomatoes
    and green chilies
1   (15-ounce) can pinto
    beans, drained
1   (15-ounce) can
    creamed corn
1-11/2 (11/4-ounce) packages
    taco seasoning
1/2 teaspoon cumin
1   (1.6-ounce) package dry
    ranch dressing mix
1   (141/2-ounce) bag
    tortilla chips

† In soup pot, cook chicken in broth with
  onion, pepper and garlic until chicken
  is tender. Remove chicken and when
  cool cut into pieces. Return to broth.
† Add tomatoes and remaining ingredients,
  except tortilla chips. Simmer 20 minutes.
† To serve, place chips in bowl and ladle soup
  over chips.

Especially good cooked one day ahead and reheated.

MARINATED ASPARAGUS AND HEARTS OF PALM

Yield: 6 servings
Ann Perry

1   pound fresh asparagus, cooked
1   (14-ounce) can hearts of palm, drained, cut in bite-size pieces
3/4 cup vegetable or olive oil
1/2 cup apple cider vinegar
11/2 teaspoons salt
1   teaspoon pepper

† Place asparagus and heart of palm in large ziplock bag.
† Combine remaining ingredients and pour over vegetables. Marinate overnight.

MT'S MEXICAN BEAN SALAD

Yield: 10 servings
Civil McGowan
Camille Salisbury

2   (15-ounce) cans black beans, drained and rinsed
1   (16-ounce) can white corn, drained
1   (16-ounce) can yellow corn, drained
1/2 red bell pepper, diced
1/2 bell pepper, diced
1/2 bunch green onions, chopped
1/2 bunch cilantro, chopped in food processor
1   lemon
2   large tomatoes, peeled, seeded and diced, or unpeeled Romas or cherry
2-3 tablespoons red wine vinegar
    Tabasco to taste
    Olive oil to taste
    Pepper to taste

† Toss mixture as ingredients are added.
† Refrigerate 24 hours before adding more seasonings. Will keep indefinitely.

Flavors intensify in 24 hours.

43

In Order To Serve

BLACK BEAN SALAD

Yield: 4 to 6 servings
Sally Serenius

2 (16-ounce) cans black
    beans, drained
1 yellow bell pepper, seeded
    and diced
1 red bell pepper, seeded
    and diced
1/2 cup chopped red onion
    Salt and pepper to taste

DRESSING:
1 teaspoon cumin
1/2 cup dry white wine
4 tablespoons extra virgin
    olive oil

† Combine salad ingredients.

† Whisk cumin and vinegar together. Add olive oil and pour over bean mixture and refrigerate. Remove from refrigerator one hour before serving.

MARINATED BLACK-EYED PEA SALAD

Yield: 10 servings
Robin Riggins

1 cup chopped onion
3 cups frozen black-eyed peas
3 cups frozen white corn
2 1/4 cups water
1/2 teaspoon pepper, divided
1 (10.5-ounce) can
    chicken broth
2 tablespoons white wine
    vinegar
1 tablespoon olive oil
1 tablespoon lemon juice
1 teaspoon honey
1/2 teaspoon salt
1/2 teaspoon dried dill
1/2 teaspoon dried thyme
2 cloves garlic, crushed
1 cup cherry tomatoes,
    halved
1/3 cup sliced scallions

† Coat large saucepan with cooking spray and sauté onions until soft. Add peas, corn, water, 1/4 teaspoon pepper and broth. Bring to a boil. Cover and reduce heat. Simmer 30 minutes. Drain.

† Combine vinegar, 1/4 teaspoon pepper and next seven ingredients in large bowl. Add peas, tomatoes, and scallions. Cover and marinate in refrigerator 8 hours.

BROCCOLI SALAD

Yield: 6 servings
Kate Buckfelder

1   head of broccoli, chopped
1   cup green grape halves
1   cup seedless red grape
    halves
1/2 pound cooked bacon,
    chopped
1/4 cup chopped purple onion

† Combine all ingredients in large bowl.

DRESSING:
1   cup mayonnaise
1/2 cup sugar
1   tablespoon vinegar

† Mix all ingredients and pour over broccoli.

Elisabeth Baynard Benfield's variation: Use 1/2 cup raisins and 1/2 cup pecans instead of grapes.

BROCCOLI-CAULIFLOWER SALAD

Yield: 6 to 8 servings
Bette Hudson

1   head broccoli, separated
    into flowerets
1   medium cauliflower,
    separated into flowerets
1   cup cherry tomatoes,
    halved
1   small red onion, sliced top
    to bottom
1   (8-ounce) can sliced water
    chestnuts, drained

† Combine salad ingredients.

DRESSING:
1   cup mayonnaise
2   teaspoons mustard
2   teaspoons cider vinegar
2   tablespoons sugar
    Dash of Worcestershire
    sauce

† Blend dressing ingredients with whisk. Pour over salad. Chill.

If preparing ahead, add tomatoes just before serving.

BLUE CHEESE AND SPINACH SALAD

Yield: 8 servings
Marsha Rich

1	(10-ounce) package fresh spinach
1	medium-size red onion, thinly sliced
1	medium zucchini, thinly sliced
2	(8-ounce) cans mandarin oranges, drained
1/3	pound blue or gorgonzola cheese, crumbled

† Clean and tear spinach into bite-size pieces.
† Layer remaining ingredients.

DRESSING:

1	(0.6-ounce) package Italian salad dressing
1/4	cup balsamic vinegar
2	tablespoons water
1/2	cup olive or vegetable oil

† Combine all ingredients and serve with salad.

CAESAR SALAD

Yield: 4 to 6 servings
Hope Parrott

1	head Romaine lettuce
	Croutons for garnish
	Parmesan cheese for garnish

† Wash and dry lettuce. Tear into bite-size pieces.

DRESSING:

2	cloves garlic, minced
1	teaspoon salt
3	tablespoons plus 1/3 cup olive oil, divided
1	teaspoon capers
1	ounce fresh Parmesan cheese
	Juice of 1 lemon
1	tablespoon Worcestershire sauce
1	teaspoon Dijon mustard

† Mash garlic and salt with spoon in bottom of wooden salad bowl. Add 3 tablespoons olive oil and capers. Mash to consistency of paste.
† Blend in olive oil and remaining dressing ingredients.
† Add lettuce, croutons and Parmesan cheese. Toss.

CUCUMBER MINT SALAD

Yield: 6 to 8 servings
Marsha Rich

3   large peeled cucumbers,
     halved and sliced
1/2 cup chopped fresh mint or
     1/4 cup dried
     Zest of 1 orange

† Combine cucumbers with mint and
  orange rind.

     DRESSING:
1/2 cup olive oil
1/2-1 cup red wine or
     balsamic vinegar
1/4 cup sugar

† Whisk oil, vinegar and sugar. Pour over
  cucumbers. Cover and refrigerate 4 hours
  before serving.

FRUIT AND SPINACH SALAD

Yield: 4 to 6 servings
Meredith Forshaw

1   pound spinach
4   small heads Belgian
     endive
4   small kiwi fruit
1   small cantaloupe

† Wash and drain spinach. Cut each
  endive lengthwise into quarters.
† Cut kiwi into 1/2-inch slices. Cut
  cantaloupe into chunks. Arrange
  salad ingredients on plates.

     DRESSING:
1   large red onion,
     thinly sliced
3/4 teaspoon salt
1/8 teaspoon pepper
1   tablespoon olive or
     vegetable oil
1/2 cup orange juice
2   tablespoons white
     wine vinegar
1/4 pound feta cheese,
     crumbled
2   ounces Jarlsberg or
     Swiss cheese, 1/2-inch
     cubes

† In saucepan, sauté onion in oil with salt
  and pepper until golden. Remove from
  heat and stir in orange juice and vinegar.
† Spoon warm dressing over salad and
  sprinkle with cheeses.

47

ELEGANT FRUIT SALAD WITH ORANGE JUICE DRIZZLE

Yield: 8 to 10 servings
Susan Fitch

1   pint strawberries, halved
1   cup blueberries
2   (11-ounce) cans mandarin
    oranges, drained
1   (20-ounce) can pineapple
    chunks, drained
1   (16-ounce) can pears,
    drained and chopped
1   (16-ounce) can sliced
    peaches, drained
2   bananas, sliced
    Mint leaves for garnish
1   cup orange juice
3   tablespoons white wine
1/4 cup ginger ale
1/2-1 teaspoons sugar
1-2 teaspoons lemon juice

† Combine fruits in glass bowl.
† To make drizzle, blend orange juice, wine, ginger ale, sugar, and lemon juice.
† Serve with fruit.

STRAWBERRIES IN VINEGAR

Yield: 2 to 3 servings
Nan Wilson

1   pint strawberries
2   tablespoons balsamic vinegar
2   tablespoons sugar

† Wash and stem strawberries.
† Combine berries with vinegar and sugar and refrigerate before serving.

GREEK STYLE SALAD

Yield: 4 servings
Gail Carr

4   cups torn spinach or other mixed greens
1/2 medium cucumber, halved lengthwise and sliced
1   medium tomato, cut in thin wedges
1   medium onion, chopped
1   ounce feta cheese, crumbled
2   tablespoons sliced black olives

† Toss salad ingredients together in a large salad bowl.

DRESSING:
2   tablespoons lemon juice
2   tablespoons olive oil
1   teaspoon honey
1   clover garlic, minced
1   tablespoon snipped parsley

† Combine dressing ingredients and mix well.
† Pour over salad and toss. Sprinkle with parsley.

Marsha Rich's variation: Add 16-ounce jar marinated artichoke hearts, chopped and drained.

COMPANY GREEN SALAD WITH DIJON VINAIGRETTE DRESSING

Yield: 8 servings
Ben Hutto

2	medium heads romaine lettuce
1	large red bell pepper
1	medium red onion
1	(11-ounce) can mandarin oranges or grapefruit sections, halved and drained
4	ounces feta or blue cheese, crumbled

† Tear lettuce into bite-size pieces.
† Cut pepper into strips. Cut onion into rings.
† Toss in large bowl with fruit and cheese.

DRESSING:
1/2 cup olive oil
1/4 cup red or white vinegar
Pinch of salt
Pinch of sugar
1 teaspoon Dijon mustard
1 tablespoon mixed fresh herbs or 1 teaspoon dried (basil, oregano, finely chopped parsley)

† Shake all ingredients in jar. Pour over salad before serving.

SCALDED LETTUCE

Yield: 6 servings
Christ Church Cooks I

1 medium head lettuce
6 slices crisp bacon, drippings reserved
3 hard-cooked eggs

† Shred lettuce. Crumble bacon and eggs over lettuce.

DRESSING:
Reserved bacon drippings
3/4 cup vinegar
5 tablespoons sugar
1/2 teaspoon celery seed

† In bacon drippings, add vinegar, sugar and celery seed.
† Immediately before serving, bring dressing to a boil and simmer 1 to 2 minutes. Pour hot dressing over lettuce.

MAKE-AHEAD HEARTY SALAD

Yield: 12 to 16 servings
Betsy Locke

3   cups torn spinach,
    well drained
1/2-1 teaspoon salt
1/2   teaspoon freshly
    ground pepper
1/2   teaspoon sugar
1/2   cup chopped celery
1/4   cup chopped bell pepper
2   tablespoons chopped green
    onion or 1/2 red onion,
    thinly sliced
1   (8-ounce) can sliced water
    chestnuts, rinsed and
    drained
3/4   cup grated Swiss cheese
4   hard-cooked eggs, sliced
1/2   pound bacon, crisply
    cooked and crumbled
3   cups torn Boston or
    leaf lettuce
1   package frozen tiny green
    peas, thawed, rinsed
    and drained
1-1 1/4 cups mayonnaise
3/4   cup grated Romano or
    Parmesan cheese
    Chopped parsley for
    garnish

† In large glass salad bowl, layer ingredients
  in order listed. Sprinkle spinach layer
  with salt, pepper and sugar.
† Continue layering through green peas.
  Spread mayonnaise over top layer to
  cover well and seal to edge of bowl.
† Sprinkle parmesan cheese and parsley
  on top. Cover with plastic wrap and
  refrigerate at least 8 hours. Do not stir.

LIMA BEAN SALAD

Yield: 6 to 8 servings
Robin Riggins

2   (16-ounce) cans lima
    beans, rinsed
2   ripe tomatoes, chopped
1/2   cup chopped celery
    Salt and pepper to taste
1/4   cup mayonnaise
6   slices cooked bacon,
    crumbled

† Combine beans, tomatoes and celery.
† Salt and pepper to taste. Blend in
  mayonnaise and sprinkle bacon on top.
  Chill.

MARINATED MUSHROOM SALAD

Yield: 6 servings
Liz Medearis

1/2 pound sliced fresh mushrooms
2   cups sliced or coarsely
     chopped tomatoes
1   cup thinly sliced onions

MARINADE:
1/2 cup vegetable oil
1/4 cup red wine vinegar
1/3 cup chopped fresh parsley
     or 2 tablespoons dried
1   teaspoon salt
1   teaspoon sugar
1/2 teaspoon garlic powder
1/4 teaspoon pepper

† Combine salad ingredients.

† Blend marinade ingredients and pour over
  mushrooms. Refrigerate at least one hour.
  Serve over lettuce.

ORZO SALAD

Yield: 4 servings
Susan Daisley

1   cup uncooked orzo
1   cup water
1/2 ounce sun-dried tomatoes
1   cup crumbled feta cheese
1/4 cup chopped red onion
1/4 cup chopped bell pepper
1/4 cup chopped red bell pepper
1/4 cup chopped yellow
     bell pepper
2   tablespoons chopped
     fresh parsley
2   tablespoons chopped
     green olives
2   tablespoons chopped
     black olives
1/4 teaspoon freshly ground
     black pepper
2   tablespoons red wine
     vinegar
1   tablespoon balsamic
     vinegar
1 1/2 tablespoons olive oil

† Cook orzo according to directions.
  Drain and set aside.
† Bring water to boil and add tomatoes,
  cooking 2 minutes or until tender. Drain
  and chop tomatoes.
† Combine orzo, tomatoes and remaining
  ingredients in large bowl.

PASTA SALAD WITH SUN-DRIED TOMATOES AND PESTO

Yield: 8 to 12 servings
Beth Bowen

PESTO:
1   large bunch basil
1/4 cup olive oil
4   cloves garlic, minced
4   tablespoons parmesan
    cheese

† Purée all ingredients in blender.

SALAD:
1-2 cups sun-dried tomatoes,
    softened and sliced
1   cup sliced black olives
1   cup marinated artichoke
    hearts, drained and chopped
2-3 tablespoons olive oil
2-3 tablespoons red wine vinegar
1   tablespoon crushed red
    pepper flakes
2   tablespoons basil pesto
2   ounces feta cheese,
    crumbled
1   (12-ounce) box curly
    pasta, cooked, drained
    and cooled

† Combine tomatoes, olives and artichoke
hearts in large bowl. Add olive oil,
vinegar, and pepper flakes, stirring
to coat.
† Blend in pesto. Add feta cheese and
pasta, mixing well. Cover and chill.
Will keep 5 to 6 days.

Leftover pesto can be frozen in ice cube trays and cubes stored in freezer bag for later use.

TABBOULEH

Yield: 31/2-4 cups
DeeDee Dalrymple

1/2-3/4 cup bulghur wheat
2   bunches scallions, chopped
2   medium-size ripe tomatoes,
  · diced
2   bunches parsley, leaves
    chopped
1/4 cup olive oil
1/4 cup lemon juice
    Salt to taste

† Cover wheat with water to soften.
† Combine vegetables.
† Drain wheat and squeeze out water.
    Add to vegetables.
† Blend olive oil and lemon juice and
    combine with salad. Serve with lettuce
    leaves.

ELEGANT SUMMER PASTA SALAD

Yield: 8 to 10 servings
Virginia Bullock

1   (1-pound) package
    pinwheel pasta
3/4-1 pound fresh asparagus
1   pound shrimp
    Juice of 1 large lemon
1   (3-ounce) bottle capers
    with liquid
2-3 tablespoons light olive oil
1   teaspoon dill
    Salt and pepper to taste
16-20 leaves Bibb lettuce
    Tomato wedges
    for garnish

† Cook pasta according to directions.
  Rinse and drain.
† Steam asparagus and cut into 1-inch
  pieces.
† Cook, peel and devein shrimp.
† Combine pasta, asparagus and shrimp
  with remaining ingredients.
† Serve on Bibb lettuce and garnish with
  tomatoes.

CREAMY POTATO SALAD

Yield: 6 servings
Peggy Horne

6   medium-size red potatoes
    (about 2 pounds)
1/4 cup chopped green onions
1   (2-ounce) jar diced pimiento,
    drained (optional)

DRESSING:
1/2 cup reduced calorie
    mayonnaise
1/2 cup light sour cream
2   tablespoons prepared
    mustard
1   tablespoon sugar
1/2 teaspoon celery seed
1/2 teaspoon salt
1   tablespoon white
    wine vinegar
1/4 teaspoon pepper
1/8 teaspoon garlic powder

† Cook potatoes until tender. Cool, peel
  and cut into 1/2-inch cubes. Combine
  potatoes, green onion and pimientos
  in large bowl.

† Mix mayonnaise and remaining
  ingredients. Add to potatoes and chill.

RED POTATO SALAD

Yield: 4 to 6 servings
Nikki Morris

6-8 medium-size red potatoes, boiled and quartered
2 green onions, chopped
2-3 stalks celery, chopped
1/8 teaspoon celery seed
1/4 teaspoon ground pepper
1/4-1/2 cup sliced squash or zucchini (optional)
1/4 cup chopped bell or red bell pepper (optional)
1/4 cup broccoli in small pieces (optional)
1 (8-ounce) bottle ranch salad dressing

† Combine all ingredients, except dressing, while potatoes are still warm.
† Pour enough dressing over salad to coat potatoes. Refrigerate until cool.

HEARTY SUMMER "SALWICH" BUFFET

Yield: Varies with number of guests
Rosemary VanDuyn

Bakery-quality sliced white bread, crustless
Boston or curly lettuce leaves, separated
Well-seasoned egg salad (curry powder, herbs, olives)
Fresh tomatoes, sliced
Baby shrimp
Favorite salad dressing

† Let guests create their own "salwich" combining lettuce, bread, egg salad, tomato, shrimp, and salad dressing!

LO-CAL CURRIED RICE SALAD

Yield: 4 to 6 servings
Lisa Hirsch

1 (6.2-ounce) box fast cooking long grain and wild rice
1/4 cup chopped onion
1/2 cup sliced celery
1 cup green grape halves
1/2 cup water chestnuts, sliced
1/2 cup chopped cashews or slivered almonds
1/2 cup cup nonfat mayonnaise
1-2 teaspoons curry powder

† Cook rice according to directions and cool.
† Combine rice with next five ingredients.
† Blend mayonnaise and curry powder. Toss with rice and refrigerate.

CRUNCHY ROMAINE TOSS

Yield: 10 to 12 servings
Susan Hamilton

4 tablespoons unsalted butter, melted
1 (3-ounce) package ramen noodles with flavor packet, uncooked and coarsely broken
1 cup pecans or walnuts, chopped
1 head broccoli, chopped
1 head romaine lettuce, torn in pieces
4 green onions, chopped

† Sauté noodles and pecans in butter until browned.
† Combine noodles with broccoli, lettuce and onions.

SWEET AND SOUR DRESSING:
1 cup vegetable oil
1 cup sugar
1/2 cup wine vinegar
1 tablespoon soy sauce

† Blend all ingredients in blender until sugar dissolves. Pour over salad before serving.

MIXED VEGETABLE SLAW

Yield: 2 to 3 servings
Jeanne Trexler

2	red bell peppers
1	large cucumber
2	medium carrots
4	radishes, thinly sliced
1/2	cup fresh snow peas

† Seed peppers and cucumber and cut into long thin strips.
† Peel carrots and cut into long thin strips.
† Combine all vegetables in large bowl.

DRESSING:

1/4	cup vinegar
2	tablespoons vegetable oil
1	teaspoon sugar
1/2	teaspoon salt
	Freshly ground pepper

† Mix all ingredients and pour over vegetables. Chill before serving.

ORIENTAL SLAW

Yield: 8 to 10 servings
Meredith Forshaw

1	large head napa cabbage, chopped
1	bunch green onions, chopped
2	tablespoons margarine
1	(3.75 ounce) package sunflower kernels
1/2	cup sliced almonds
1	(3-ounce) package beef flavored ramen noodles without flavor packet, broken into pieces

† Place cabbage and onions in large bowl.
† Sauté sunflower kernels, almonds and noodles in margarine until lightly browned. Sprinkle on top of cabbage.

DRESSING:

1/2	cup oil
1/4	cup vinegar
1/3	cup sugar
1	teaspoon soy sauce
1	teaspoon dry mustard
	Flavor packet from noodles

† Combine all ingredients and toss with cabbage.

MARGARET'S SOUTH CAROLINA SLAW

Yield: 15 servings
Libba Eleazer

1   large cabbage, chopped
4   medium onions, chopped
1 1/2 tablespoons celery seed
1   tablespoon mustard seed
1   (2-ounce) jar chopped
    pimiento, drained
1   cup sliced celery

DRESSING:
2   cups sugar
2   cups vinegar
1   tablespoon turmeric
1   tablespoon salt

† Mix salad ingredients and place in large bowl.

† Bring all ingredients to a boil and pour over cabbage. Refrigerate overnight.

VEGETABLE SALAD

Yield: 8 servings
Fran Stroud

1   (11-ounce) can white
    shoepeg corn
2   (15-ounce) cans small
    green peas
2   cups frenched green beans
1   (15.25-ounce) can lima beans
1   (2-ounce) jar chopped
    pimiento
1   cup chopped celery
1   medium bell pepper, chopped
1/2 cup sugar
3/4 cup white vinegar
3/4 cup vegetable oil

† Drain all cans of vegetables and combine with celery and bell pepper.
† Blend sugar, vinegar, and oil. Pour over vegetables.
† Refrigerate several hours or overnight.

58

ASPARAGUS SALAD

Yield: 12 to 16 servings
Christ Church Cooks I

3   (1/4-ounce) envelopes
     unflavored gelatin
2   cups water, divided
1   cup sugar
1   teaspoon salt
1/2 cup vinegar
1/2 cup lemon juice
2   (15-ounce) cans asparagus
     spears, cut into thirds,
     reserve liquid
1/2 cup chopped celery
1/4 cup chopped onion
1   (2-ounce) jar chopped
     pimiento

† Dissolve gelatin in 1 cup water.
† Combine 1 cup water, sugar, salt and
vinegar and bring to a boil. Blend
gelatin into hot mixture. Cool.
† Add lemon juice, 1 cup asparagus liquid
(add water if necessary). Refrigerate
until syrupy.
† Add vegetables and pour into mold.

Do not use chopped asparagus. It is stringy. May add sliced water chestnuts and
1/2 cup toasted almonds.

FROZEN FRUIT SALAD

Yield: 12 to 18 servings
Sara Boyd

2   cups low-fat sour cream
3/4 cup sugar
1   teaspoon lemon zest
2   tablespoons fresh lemon
     juice
1/8 teaspoon salt
1   (1-pound 4-ounce) can
     crushed pineapple,
     well drained
1   (1-pound) can fruit
     cocktail, well drained
1/2 cup chopped pecans
3   tablespoons maraschino
     cherries, chopped
2-3 medium bananas, diced

† Combine all ingredients and pour into
paper-lined muffin tins and freeze.

Judy Van Namen and Jane Neal Bobbitt's variation: Omit fruit cocktail and lemon zest.

APRICOT JELLO SALAD

Yield: 24 (2-inch) squares
Ruth Conger

2 (3-ounce) packages apricot jello
1 (16-ounce) can crushed pineapple
2 cups cold buttermilk
1 (8-ounce) container frozen whipped topping
1 (11-ounce) can mandarin oranges, drained
1/2 cup coarsely chopped pecans

† Bring jello and pineapple to a boil.
† Add buttermilk. Fold in whipped topping and stir until blended.
† Add oranges and pecans. Pour into lightly greased 9x13-inch dish and chill until set.

Orange jello may be used instead of apricot.

BLUEBERRY SALAD

Yield: 12 large servings
or 20 small servings
Julie Sanniota

3 (3-ounce) boxes blueberry or grape jello
21/2 cups boiling water
1 (21-ounce) blueberry pie filling
1 (12-ounce) can crushed pineapple

† Dissolve jello in boiling water. Add pineapple and pie filling. Pour into 9x13-inch pan and let set overnight in refrigerator.

TOPPING:
2 teaspoons vanilla
1 (8-ounce) package cream cheese
1 cup sour cream
1/2 cup sugar
1 (16-ounce) container frozen whipped topping
1/2 cup chopped pecans for garnish

† Combine topping ingredients, except nuts. Spread over jello and sprinkle with nuts.

60

APRICOT MOUSSE

Yield: 6 to 8 servings
Tat Hicks

1   (3-ounce) package apricot
    or peach jello
1   cup boiling water
1   cup sour cream, regular
    or nonfat
1   (8-ounce) can crushed
    pineapple, undrained

† Dissolve jello into boiling water. Add
  remaining ingredients and pour into 8x8-
  inch dish. Refrigerate until set.

CRANBERRY SALAD

Yield: 12 servings
Mary Vernon Rogers

2   (3-ounce) packages
    raspberry jello
2   cups boiling water, divided
1   (1-pound) can whole berry
    cranberry sauce
1/2 cup chopped pecans
1/2-1 cup sour cream

† Dissolve both packages of jello in one
  cup of boiling water.
† Dissolve cranberry sauce in one
  cup of boiling water.
† Combine jello, cranberry sauce and nuts.
  Pour half of mixture in greased 9-inch
  ring mold and put in freezer to set.
† When set, spoon sour cream on top and
  cover with remaining jello. Place back
  into refrigerator to firm.

FROZEN DELIGHT

Yield: 6 to 8 servings
Gloria Horne

2   (3-ounce) packages
    cream cheese, softened
3   tablespoons mayonnaise
1   (15 1/4-ounce) can
    pineapple tidbits, drained,
    liquid reserved
2   small bananas, sliced
2   (10-ounce) packages
    frozen sweetened sliced
    strawberries, thawed
1   cup heavy cream,
    whipped

† Blend cream cheese and mayonnaise.
  Add 2 tablespoons pineapple liquid.
† Fold in fruit. Blend in whipped cream
  and pour into 2-quart container or tray.
  Freeze until firm.

61

In Order To Serve

GRANNY MATTHEWS GINGER ALE SALAD

Yield: 6 servings
Mary Matthews Vaughn

1 (3-ounce) package lemon jello
1 cup hot water
1 cup cold ginger ale
1/3 cup chopped pecans
1/2 cup halved seedless grapes
1/2 cup chopped pears
3 tablespoons minced crystallized ginger

† Dissolve jello in hot water. Add ginger ale. Refrigerate until mixture begins to congeal.
† Add remaining ingredients. Chill until set.

DRESSING:
1/3 cup mayonnaise
1/3 cup sour cream
3 tablespoons minced crystallized ginger

† Blend all ingredients and serve with salad.

DIFFERENT PERFECTION SALAD

Yield: 8 to 10 servings
Ann McMillan

2 envelopes unflavored gelatin
1/4 cup cold water
1 1/2 cups boiling water
1/3 cup sugar
1/2 cup cider vinegar
1 teaspoon salt
1 teaspoon curry powder
Dash cayenne pepper
2 green onions, chopped
1 1/2 cups finely chopped cabbage
1 1/4 cups finely chopped celery
1/2 cup grated carrots
1/2 cup chopped bell pepper

† Sprinkle gelatin in cold water. Add boiling water and stir until dissolved.
† Add sugar, vinegar and seasonings. Chill mixture until slightly thickened.
† Add vegetables and pour into 8 cup mold. Chill until firm. Serve with mayonnaise or cole slaw dressing.

CONGEALED TOMATO SALAD

Yield: 6 to 8 servings
Guerry Russell

1   (.25-ounce) envelope
    plain gelatin
1/2 cup water
1   (3-ounce) package
    cream cheese (may use
    low fat)
1/2 cup mayonnaise (may
    use low fat)
1   can tomato soup
1/2 bell pepper, finely chopped
1   small onion, finely chopped
1   stalk celery, finely chopped
1/2 cup pimiento-stuffed olives,
    cut in thirds

† Soak gelatin in water. Slowly heat until
  dissolved. Add cream cheese and beat
  until soft.
† Remove from heat and combine with
  mayonnaise. Blend in soup and remaining
  ingredients.
† Pour into 3 to 4-cup ring mold or 6 to 8
  individual molds. Chill until firm.

CHICKEN WITH A TWIST

Yield: 12 to 15 servings
Kay Simpson

6   ounces rotelle pasta
    (little corkscrews)
3   cups cooked, shredded
    chicken
1/2 cup Italian dressing
1/2 cup mayonnaise
3   tablespoons lemon juice
1   tablespoon mustard
1   onion, chopped
1   cup chopped celery
1   cucumber chopped
    Salt to taste
1   teaspoon pepper

† Cook pasta according to package
  directions.
† Combine chicken, pasta and Italian
  dressing. Set aside.
† Mix mayonnaise, lemon juice and
  mustard. Add remaining ingredients
  and combine with chicken mixture.
  Chill.

CHATTANOOGA CHICKEN SALAD

Yield: 6 servings
Adelaide Ingle

1 (11-ounce) can drained mandarin oranges, liquid reserved
1 cup mayonnaise (1/2 cup may be low-fat)
3 cups cubed cooked chicken
1 cup chopped celery
1 Granny Smith apple, chopped
1/2 cup chopped macadamia nuts
2 teaspoons curry powder
1/2 cup white raisins
1/4 cup crumbled blue cheese
Chopped green onions to taste
Seasoning salt to taste

† Mix one-half of liquid from oranges in mayonnaise.
† Combine all ingredients except blue cheese.
† Sprinkle cheese on top before serving.

CHICKEN AND WILD RICE SALAD

Yield: 6 to 8 servings
Neal Orgain

1 (6-ounce) box wild rice
1/4 teaspoon salt
2 cups boiling water
3 large boneless, skinless chicken breast halves, cooked and cubed
1 large tart apple, cored and chopped
1/3 small red onion, chopped
1/2 large red bell pepper, diced
1/3 cup currants or raisins
1/2 cup diced celery
1/2 cup pecan pieces, toasted
2 tablespoons balsamic vinegar
2 tablespoons olive oil
Salt and pepper to taste

† Add rice to salted, boiling water and cook until tender, about 35 minutes. Drain any remaining water.
† In large bowl, combine rice and remaining ingredients.

May be served cold or warm by heating in microwave on high for 3 minutes.

CREAMY CURRIED CHICKEN SALAD
WITH APPLE AND FUSILLE

Yield: 6 to 8 servings
Civil McGowan

2 cups uncooked fusille pasta
21/2-3 cups cooked chicken,
    cut into pieces
1 cup chopped celery
2 medium-size red apples,
    cored and chopped
1/2 cup raisins
1/2 cup green onion tops in
    1-inch pieces
1/3 cup slivered almonds,
    toasted

† Cook fusille until a la dente. Drain and
   rinse in cold water. Drain again.
† Combine with remaining ingredients.
† Chill.

DRESSING:
1 cup mayonnaise
1/4 cup light cream
2 teaspoons curry powder
11/2 teaspoons salt
1/8 teaspoon cayenne
1 tablespoon lemon juice

† Blend dressing ingredients and pour
   over chicken salad.

LOWFAT TARRAGON CHICKEN SALAD

Yield: 4 servings
Cindy Nicholson

6 boneless, skinless chicken
   breasts
1 lemon
1 tablespoon tarragon
1/4 cup light or nonfat
   mayonnaise
   Salt to taste
1/4 cup toasted sliced almonds

† Cook chicken and chop into small pieces.
   Squeeze lemon over chicken.
† Sprinkle tarragon on chicken. Add
   mayonnaise, salt to taste and almonds.
   Salad should be somewhat dry.

THAI CHICKEN SALAD

Yield: 8 to 10 servings
Ann Linde

4   boneless skinless chicken
     breast halves
3   ounces vermicelli, cooked
     and drained
4   cups torn romaine lettuce
2   cups thinly sliced Chinese
     cabbage
2   medium carrots, grated
1   medium cucumber,
     julienned
1   large red bell pepper,
     julienned
1/2 cup chopped peanuts
     (optional)

† Grill chicken 15 to 20 minutes. Cut into
  strips and combine with 3 tablespoons
  peanut ginger dressing. Cover and
  refrigerate 8 hours.
† Toss vermicelli with 3 tablespoons
  dressing. Cover and refrigerate
  8 hours.
† Combine lettuce with remaining
  ingredients except peanuts. Arrange on
  platter. Top with chicken and vermicelli.
  Sprinkle with peanuts.
† Serve salad with remaining dressing.

DRESSING:
1/2 cup rice vinegar
2   cloves garlic, minced
1/3 cup creamy peanut butter
1/4 cup lime juice
2   tablespoons cider vinegar
1   tablespoon molasses
1   tablespoon hot sauce
2   teaspoons grated ginger
2   teaspoons soy sauce

† Combine all ingredients. Set aside.

SPECIAL CURRIED CHICKEN SALAD

Yield: 6 to 8 servings
Virginia Bullock

4   whole, boneless chicken
     breasts
1   large red apple, diced
1   (3-ounce) bottle peach
1   chutney or other chutney
1/2-1 cup light mayonnaise
1   teaspoon curry powder
     Salt and pepper to taste

† Cook chicken and cut into bite-size
  pieces.
† Combine chicken with remaining
  ingredients and chill.

SHRIMP LaMAZE

Yield: 6 to 8 servings
Julia Lackey

Lettuce leaves
Shredded lettuce
2 pounds shrimp, cooked
  and peeled

† Arrange lettuce leaves on individual plates and top with shredded lettuce. Divide shrimp on plates and cover with dressing.

DRESSING:
1 cup mayonnaise
1 cup chili sauce
1/4 cup sweet pickle relish
1 hard-cooked egg, chopped
1 teaspoon chopped fresh
  chives
1/4 bell pepper, chopped
1 1/2 teaspoons chopped
  pimiento
1 teaspoon Dijon mustard

† Combine dressing ingredients and refrigerate covered, for an hour or more.

SHRIMP SALAD

Yield: 6 servings
Clara Godshall

1 pound grilled shrimp, peeled
1 large cucumber, sliced
2 medium tomatoes, cut in
  wedges
6 cups assorted lettuces,
  torn in bite-size pieces

† Combine ingredients except shrimp.

DRESSING:
1/4 cup olive oil
1/4 cup sugar
2 tablespoons lime juice
2 tablespoons wine vinegar
1 clove garlic, minced
1 shallot, minced
1 1/2 teaspoons chopped
  fresh parsley

† Combine all ingredients and toss with salad.
† Top with grilled shrimp.

ORZO AND SHRIMP SALAD

Yield: 6 servings
Louise Bonner

1 1/2 cups orzo or other
    tiny pasta
1   tablespoon olive or
    vegetable oil
3/4-1 pound raw medium-
    size shrimp
2   cups water
1   teaspoon salt
4   peppercorns
2   whole cloves
5   stalks celery with
    leaves, divided
1/4 cup minced parsley
1   tablespoon rinsed and
    drained capers for
    garnish (optional)

DRESSING:

1/3 cup mayonnaise
1/3 cup olive oil
3   tablespoons white wine
    vinegar
1/2 teaspoon salt
1/4 teaspoon freshly
    ground pepper
1/2 teaspoon dillweed

† Cook pasta according to directions, drain and toss with oil. Chill.

† Add shrimp to water seasoned with salt, peppercorns, cloves and 1 stalk of celery. Simmer until shrimp are pink. Drain, shell and cut into coarse pieces. Chill.

† Chop remaining celery and parsley and set aside.

† Mix dressing ingredients and toss in serving bowl with pasta, shrimp, celery and parsley.

† Garnish with capers.

68

SEACOAST SALAD

Yield: 4 to 6 servings
Edith Benson

1   cup uncooked small
    macaroni shells
1   medium unpeeled
    cucumber, diced
1/4 cup finely chopped red onion
1   teaspoon salt
1/4 teaspoon dill
1/8 teaspoon white pepper
2   tablespoons wine vinegar
2   tablespoons vegetable oil
2/3 cup mayonnaise
1   pound fresh crabmeat,
    flaked

† Cook macaroni according to directions.
  Drain.
† Add remaining ingredients to macaroni
  while hot. Let flavors blend for 30
  minutes before refrigerating.
  Serve cold.

BEST FRENCH DRESSING

Yield: 2 1/2 cups
Jean Keitt
Mary Ranson

1/2 cup sugar
2   teaspoons pepper
2   teaspoons salt
2   teaspoons paprika
1   teaspoon onion flakes
1   teaspoon dry mustard
1/2 cup cider vinegar
1/2 cup chili sauce
1   cup vegetable oil
1   tablespoon Worcestershire
    sauce

† Combine ingredients. After shaking
  well, let set on counter for several days.
  Shake as you remember.
† After 3 days, place in refrigerator. Best
  served at room temperature.

Will keep several weeks in refrigerator.

FRENCH DRESSING

Yield: 1/2 cup
Connie Connelly

1/8 cup lemon juice
1/4 cup olive oil
    Pinch of dry mustard
1/2 teaspoon salt
1 egg, coddled

† Combine first 4 ingredients.
† **To coddle an egg:** Drop raw egg in shell into boiling water. Let stand 2 minutes. Separate and strain yolk into other ingredients. Discard white.
† Whisk and toss with salad.

Add garlic and anchovy paste to taste for Caesar salad.

MUSTARD VINAIGRETTE

Yield: 2/3 cup
Paula Freeman

2 tablespoons spicy brown mustard
2 tablespoons red wine vinegar
6 tablespoons olive oil

† Combine mustard with vinegar.
† Whisking constantly, slowly add olive oil. Vinaigrette will be creamy.

STAFFORD SALAD DRESSING

Yield: 1 1/2 cups
Janie Sellers

1 cup vegetable oil
1/3 cup red wine vinegar
2 cloves garlic, minced
    Several dashes of Worcestershire sauce
    Salt and pepper to taste
1 teaspoon paprika
1 teaspoon dry mustard
2 tablespoons sugar

† Whisk together all ingredients. Store in airtight container at room temperature.

FRESH FRUIT DRESSING

Yield: About 21/2 cups
Sue Head

2 cups sour cream
2 ounces frozen
  whipped topping
4 tablespoons orange juice
2-3 tablespoons lemon juice
1/4 cup powdered sugar
1/2 cup toasted almonds

† Combine all ingredients, except almonds. Beat vigorously. Add almonds.

RUM SAUCE FOR COLD FRUIT

Yield: 11/2 cups
Helen Wall

2/3 cup sugar
1/3 cup water
1 teaspoon lime zest
6 tablespoons lime juice
1/2 cup white rum

† Boil sugar, water and lime zest for 5 minutes.
† Cool and add lime juice and rum.

Notes:

Breads And Beverages

The Gifts Of Service

In Order To Serve

III. The Gifts Of Service

What God gives, and what we take
'Tis a gift for Christ his sake
Be the meal of beans and peas
God be thanked for those, and these.
Have we flesh, or have we fish
all are fragments from his dish.
ROBERT HERRICK (1591-1674)

Diversity is one of the original blessings of creation. God made life to be full of infinite variety and beautiful differentness. Like bread rising, we are all unique and infinitely varied. "Behold, it was very good," Genesis tells us when God looked at everything he had made. Oranges, artichokes, leopards, whales, spaniels, black skin, yellow skin, white skin. "All things counter, original, spare, strange; whatever is fickle, freckled (who knows how?) . . . Praise him."

Nowhere is the diversity of creation more wonderfully celebrated than at table. Our ethnic, racial, and national uniqueness is expressed deliciously in the way we select and prepare the food we serve. By their recipes shall ye know them! The infinite variety of taste, smell, appearance, and feel of food served at tables around the world is a sacrament of the beautiful diversity of the earth and its creatures.

One of the hallmarks of Jesus' ministry was open table fellowship. Everyone was welcome and given a place at table with him, as is still true in every celebration of the Holy Eucharist. May our tables, like the holy table in the church, be places of welcome where the cultural diversity of God's world is celebrated in the variety of foods and guests we serve so that "all may be one."

Each day the first day: each day a life
Each morning we must hold out the
chalice of our being to receive, to
carry, and to give back. It must
be held out empty.
DAG HAMMARSKJÖLD (1905-1961)

THE REVEREND HENRY NUTT PARSLEY, JR., RECTOR

74

HAWAIIAN BANANA NUT BREAD

Yield: 2 loaves
Ellen Lowry

3   cups flour
2   cups sugar
1   teaspoon baking soda
1   teaspoon salt
1   teaspoon ground cinnamon
1   cup chopped nuts
3   eggs, beaten
11/2 cups vegetable oil
2   cups mashed ripe banana
1   (8-ounce) can crushed
    pineapple, drained
2   teaspoons vanilla extract

† Preheat oven to 350°.
† Combine dry ingredients. Stir in nuts.
† Combine remaining ingredients and blend with dry mixture.
† Spoon into greased loaf pans or muffin tins. Bake loaf 65 minutes. Bake muffins 15 to 25 minutes.
† Cool 10 minutes before removing from pan.

Will make 1 dozen muffins or 6 dozen miniature muffins.

SKINNY BANANA BREAD

Yield: one loaf
Laura Roberts

13/4 cups flour
1/4 teaspoon baking soda
2   teaspoons baking powder
1/2 teaspoon salt
1/3 cup orange juice
2/3 cup sugar
    Egg substitute equal to
    2 eggs
1   cup mashed ripe bananas

† Preheat oven to 350°.
† Sift flour, soda, baking powder and salt.
† Combine orange juice with sugar. Add egg substitute, mixing well.
† Add bananas alternately with flour to egg mixture.
† Pour into loaf pan and bake 1 hour.

75

In Order To Serve

OATMEAL BREAD

Yield: two loaves
Kathy Hill

2   cups boiling water
1   cup rolled oats
    (old-fashioned or quick)
1/2 cup molasses or honey
2   tablespoons vegetable
    shortening
2   teaspoons salt
1   packet yeast
1/2 cup lukewarm water
6   cups flour

† Pour boiling water over oats, molasses,
  shortening, and salt in large bowl. Cool
  to lukewarm.
† Dissolve yeast in 1/2 cup lukewarm
  water and add to oat mixture.
† Blend in flour and knead until smooth.
  Place in large greased bowl. Cover and
  let rise 1 hour.
† Divide dough in half, shape loaves and
  place in greased loaf pans. Let rise until
  double in bulk.
† Bake for 1 hour at 350°.

ORANGE BREAD

Yield: one loaf
Carolyn Temple

2   tablespoons shortening
1   cup sugar
    Juice of 2 oranges plus
    water to equal 1 cup
1   teaspoon baking soda
1   tablespoon grated
    orange zest
1   egg, beaten
2   cups flour
1   teaspoon baking powder
1/2 teaspoon salt
1/2 cup chopped pecans
    (optional)

† Preheat oven to 350°.
† Cream shortening and sugar.
† Combine orange juice, soda and zest.
  Set aside.
† Add egg to sugar mixture.
† Sift dry ingredients and add alternately
  with liquid to sugar mixture. Add pecans
  if desired.
† Pour into loaf pan and bake for 50
  minutes.

76

POPPY SEED BREAD

Yield: two (9x5x3-inch) loaves
Betsy Parkhurst

3   cups flour
21/2 cups sugar
11/2 teaspoons baking powder
11/2 teaspoons salt
3   eggs
11/2 cups vegetable oil
11/2 cups milk
11/2 tablespoons poppy seeds
11/2 teaspoons vanilla
11/2 teaspoons almond
      flavoring
11/2 teaspoons butter
      flavoring

† Preheat oven to 350°.
† Combine all ingredients with a mixer.
  Beat 2 minutes and pour into two greased
  and floured loaf pans.
† Bake 1 hour then reduce oven to 325°
  and bake 15 minutes.
† Cool before taking out of pans.

Pat Pollard's variation: Use 1 cup butter instead of vegetable oil and only 11/2
cups sugar. Replace almond and butter flavorings with grated rind of one orange.

PUMPKIN SPICE BREAD

Yield: 2 large loaves
Elizabeth Jones

3   cups sugar
1   cup applesauce
4   eggs, beaten or 1 cup
      imitation eggs
1   (16-ounce) can pumpkin
31/2 cups flour
2   teaspoons baking soda
2   teaspoons salt
1   teaspoon baking powder
1   teaspoon nutmeg
1   teaspoon allspice
1   teaspoon cinnamon
1/2 teaspoon ground cloves
2/3 cup water

† Preheat oven to 350°.
† Cream sugar and applesauce. Add eggs
  and pumpkin.
† Sift dry ingredients together and add
  to pumpkin mixture alternately with
  water.
† Pour into 2 well-greased and floured loaf
  pans.
† Bake for 11/2 hours.
† Let stand 10 minutes before removing
  from pan.

CHEDDAR POTATO BREAD

Yield: 1 round loaf
Anna Stanley

4 tablespoons extra virgin
   olive oil, divided
1 cup evaporated milk,
   room temperature
1/2 cup warm water
   (125° to 130°)
2 packages fast-rising yeast
2 tablespoons sugar
1 tablespoon salt
1/2 teaspoon hot pepper sauce
2 cups grated red potatoes,
   peeled
2 cups grated extra sharp
   cheddar cheese, firmly packed
5 cups (approximately)
   unbleached all-purpose flour
   Corn meal

† Lightly brush large bowl with 1
  tablespoon oil.
† Add milk, water, remaining olive oil,
  yeast, sugar, salt and pepper sauce
  to bowl stirring until yeast dissolves.
† Mix in potatoes and 13/4 cup cheese.
† Gradually add enough flour to form
  a soft dough.
† Knead dough on lightly floured surface
  until smooth and elastic, adding more
  flour if sticky. Cover with a towel and
  let set 15 minutes.
† Oil a 12-inch pizza pan and sprinkle
  generously with corn meal.
† After kneading dough 1 minute, form
  into 6-inch diameter loaf and transfer
  to prepared pan.
† Cover with plastic wrap and a towel
  and place in warm area. Let stand
  until doubled in volume, about 1 to 2 hours.
† Preheat oven to 400°.
† Score an x through top of loaf and
  bake 40 minutes.
† Reduce oven to 375°.
† Sprinkle remaining cheese on bread and
  continue baking 10 minutes or until loaf
  browns, cheese melts, and bread sounds
  hollow when tapped.
† Transfer to rack and cool.

CHEESY ITALIAN BREAD

Yield: 1 loaf
Rosemary VanDuyn

1   loaf Italian bread
    Extra virgin olive oil
    Garlic salt to taste
1/2 cup mayonnaise
1/2-1 cup grated Romano
    or Parmesan cheese

† Preheat oven to 350°.
† Split a loaf of Italian bread lengthwise
  and place on cookie sheet. Brush with
  olive oil and sprinkle with garlic salt.
† Spread with mayonnaise and sprinkle
  with cheese. Cut diagonally into serving
  size pieces and bake 10 to 15 minutes.

Elizabeth Jones' variation: Use 1-2 tablespoons finely grated onion instead of garlic salt and oil.

ONION-CHEESE SUPPER BREAD

Yield: 6 to 8 servings
Connie Linde

1/2 cup chopped onion
1/3 cup plus 1 tablespoon
    vegetable oil, divided
1   egg, beaten
3/4 cup milk
2   cups self-rising flour
1   cup grated sharp cheese,
    divided
1   tablespoon poppy seeds
    (optional)
2   tablespoons butter or
    margarine, melted

† Preheat oven to 400°.
† Sauté onion in 1 tablespoon oil
  until golden.
† Combine egg and milk. Blend in
  flour and remaining oil. Add onions
  and 1/2 cup cheese.
† Spread dough in greased 8-inch round
  pan. Top with remaining cheese and
  poppy seed.
† Drizzle with melted butter and bake
  20 to 25 minutes.

SPINACH BREAD

Yield: 6 to 8 servings
Lynn Armstrong

1   small onion, chopped
1 1/2 sticks margarine, divided
1   package frozen chopped
    spinach, thawed and
    squeezed dry
1   cup grated mozzarella cheese
1   cup grated cheddar cheese
1   pound loaf French bread
    (preferably 2 mini-French
    loaves)
    Parmesan cheese

† Preheat oven to 350°.
† Sauté onion in stick of butter.
  Remove from heat and blend in
  spinach and cheeses.
† Slice bread lengthwise and butter both
  sides lightly. Spread spinach mixture
  on each side of bread. Sprinkle with
  Parmesan cheese.
† Put bread back together and slice into
  1 1/2 to 2-inch pieces crosswise. Wrap
  tightly in foil. Bake 20 minutes.

FOOL-PROOF SPOON BREAD

Yield: 8 servings
Barbara Plumlee

1   teaspoon salt
1   cup white corn meal
1 1/2 teaspoons baking powder
1/2 teaspoon sugar
1   cup boiling water
2   eggs, well beaten
1/2 cup milk
1   tablespoon butter,
    not margarine

† Preheat oven to 400°.
† Sift together dry ingredients. Add boiling water.
† Stir in eggs and milk. Pour into 1 1/2-quart baking dish. Dot with butter.
† Bake 35 minutes.

DELUXE CORNBREAD

Yield: 6 servings
Suzie Lowe
Marie Palmer

2   eggs, beaten
1   cup sour cream
1/2 cup canola oil
1   cup creamed corn
1   cup yellow corn meal
1 1/2 teaspoons salt
1   tablespoon baking powder

† Preheat oven to 325°.
† Combine all ingredients and pour into greased 1 1/2-quart casserole.
† Bake 45 to 50 minutes.

1 cup self-rising corn meal may be substituted for yellow corn meal, salt and baking powder.

LOWFAT APPLE COFFEECAKE

Yield: 16 servings
Sue Hardwick

4   cups chopped Granny
    Smith apples
1/2 cup unsweetened orange
    juice, divided
1 1/2 teaspoons ground
    cinnamon
1/2 cup skim milk
1   stick margarine, softened
1   cup sugar
1   (8-ounce) carton egg
    substitute, thawed
2 1/2 teaspoons vanilla
3   cups sifted cake flour
2   teaspoons baking powder
1/4 teaspoon salt
2   tablespoons brown sugar

† Preheat oven to 350°.
† Combine apples, 1/4 cup orange juice and
  cinnamon. Set aside.
† Combine remaining orange juice and milk.
  Set aside.
† Cream margarine and sugar with electric
  mixer. Add egg substitute and vanilla.
† Combine flour, baking powder and salt.
  Gradually add flour to cream mixture
  alternately with milk mixture.
† Place half of batter in 10-inch square pan
  coated with nonstick cooking spray. Top
  with half of apple mixture. Repeat layers
  and top with brown sugar.
† Bake 1 hour.

OVERNIGHT COFFEE CAKE

Yield: 8 to 10 servings
Jo Griffith

1   (25-ounce) package frozen
    dinner rolls
1 1/2 teaspoons cinnamon
1/2 cup sugar
1 1/2 cups chopped pecans
1/2 cup brown sugar
1   (3.5-ounce) package
    butterscotch or vanilla
    pudding, not instant
1 1/4 sticks butter

† Grease 12-cup Bundt pan. Layer frozen
  rolls in pan. Combine cinnamon and sugar.
  Sprinkle over rolls.
† Place a layer each of pecans, brown sugar
  and dry pudding mix over rolls. Slice butter
  and place around rolls. Cover with a
  cloth and place in "off" oven overnight.
† Remove cake and preheat oven to 350°
  in morning.
† Bake for 35 to 40 minutes.
† Remove from oven and invert pan. Allow
  to set about 5 minutes.

BLUEBERRY BUCKLE

Yield: one cake
Kate Buckfelder

COFFEECAKE:
1	stick butter or margarine
3/4	cup sugar
1	egg
2	cups flour
2	teaspoons baking powder
1/2	teaspoon salt
1/2	cup milk
1 1/2-2 cups blueberries	

† Preheat oven to 350°.
† Cream butter and sugar and add egg.
  Blend in flour, baking powder, salt and milk.
† Fold in blueberries and spread in greased
  9x13-inch baking dish.

TOPPING:
2/3	cup sugar
2	tablespoons flour
1	teaspoon cinnamon
1/2	stick butter or margarine

† Combine sugar, flour and cinnamon and
  sprinkle on blueberries. Dot with butter
  and bake 30 minutes.

CINNAMON-LACED SWIRL COFFEE CAKE

Yield: one cake
Louise Bonner
Jane Bruce
Muriel Williams

1/2	cup chopped pecans
2	tablespoons sugar
1	teaspoon ground cinnamon
2	sticks butter or margarine, softened
2	cups sugar
2	eggs
2	cups sifted cake flour
1	teaspoon baking powder
1/8	teaspoon salt
1	teaspoon vanilla extract
1	(8-ounce) carton sour cream

† Preheat oven to 350°.
† Combine pecans, 2 tablespoons sugar
  and cinnamon. Set aside.
† Cream butter in mixer and add sugar,
  beating well at medium speed. Add
  eggs one at a time, beating after each
  addition.
† Combine flour, baking powder and salt.
  Add to creamed mixture, mixing until
  blended. Stir in vanilla. Fold sour cream
  into batter.
† Pour half of batter into greased and floured
  10-inch Bundt or tube pan. Sprinkle half of
  pecan mixture over batter. Repeat procedure.
† Bake 55 to 60 minutes or until toothpick
  inserted in center comes out clean. Cool
  in pan 10 minutes. Remove cake and cool
  on wire rack.

GLAZED COFFEE CAKE

Yield: 20 servings
Barbara Finn

BREAD:

3/4 cup brown sugar
1/2 cup granulated sugar
1 teaspoon cinnamon
3/4 cup chopped pecans
1 stick butter, melted
2 (10-count) cans of flaky biscuits, separated

† Preheat oven to 350°.
† Combine sugars, cinnamon and pecans.
† Dip biscuits separately in butter and then in brown sugar mixture. Stand them in upright position in lightly greased 10-inch tube pan. Do not pack tightly. (Two loaf pans may also be used).
† Bake 30 to 35 minutes.
† Cool 1 to 2 minutes and turn out on serving plate.

GLAZE:

1 cup powdered sugar, sifted
2 tablespoons milk
1 tablespoons butter, melted
1/2 teaspoon vanilla

† Combine glaze ingredients until smooth. Pour over warm coffee cake.

CINNAMON BLINTZES

Yield: 8 dozen
Della Rising
Deborah McCann

2 (1-pound 8-ounce) loaves white or whole wheat bread
2 (8-ounce) packages cream cheese, softened
2 egg yolks
1/2 cup sugar
1 cup margarine
1 cup brown or white sugar
2-3 teaspoons cinnamon

† Preheat oven to 350°.
† Trim crust from bread and roll thin.
† Combine cream cheese, eggs, and sugar, and spread thinly on bread slices. Roll up.
† Melt margarine.
† Mix brown sugar and cinnamon.
† Dip rolls first in margarine then in sugar mixture, placing close together. Freeze 5 minutes.
† Remove and slice each roll in half. Refreeze in bags until ready to use.
† Bake for 15 to 20 minutes.

APPLESAUCE MUFFINS

Yield: 3 dozen
Marcia Gilbert

2	sticks margarine, softened
2	cups sugar
2	eggs
1	teaspoon vanilla
4	cups flour
1	teaspoon ground cloves
2	teaspoons allspice
3	teaspoons cinnamon
1	(1-pound) jar applesauce
2	teaspoons baking soda

† Preheat oven to 400°.
† Cream margarine, sugar, eggs and vanilla.
† Sift flour, cloves, allspice and cinnamon. Add to creamed mixture.
† Combine applesauce and soda and add to mixture.
† Bake in greased muffin tins for 20 minutes.

Batter will keep in refrigerator for weeks.

BLUEBERRY MUFFINS

Yield: 1 dozen
Susan Plott

1	cup blueberries
3/4	cup sugar, divided
2	cups flour
1/4	teaspoon salt
3/4	teaspoon baking soda
1	egg, beaten
1	cup buttermilk
1/4	cup vegetable oil

† Preheat oven to 400°.
† Combine blueberries and 1/2 cup sugar and set aside.
† Sift flour, salt, soda and remaining sugar. Combine remaining ingredients and add to dry ingredients. Stir just until mixed.
† Add blueberries and fill greased muffin cups 2/3 full. Bake 20 minutes.

Cranberries can also be used.

SOUR CREAM MUFFINS

Yield: 24 mini muffins
Patty Adams

2	cups self-rising flour
1 1/2	sticks butter, melted
1	(8-ounce) carton sour cream

† Preheat oven to 350°.
† Combine all ingredients and spoon into small, ungreased muffin tins. Bake 30 minutes.

May be frozen.
Jane Dowd's variation: Add 1-2 cups grated cheddar cheese.

MORNING GLORY MUFFINS

Yield: 18 to 20
Judy Van Namen

2	cups flour
1	cup sugar
2	teaspoons baking soda
2	teaspoons cinnamon
1/2	teaspoon salt
1	apple, cored and shredded
2	carrots, shredded
1/2	cup raisins
1/2	cup coconut
1/2	cup chopped pecans
3	eggs, beaten
1	cup vegetable oil
2	teaspoons vanilla

† Preheat oven to 350°.
† Sift dry ingredients and add apples, carrots, raisins, coconut and nuts, mixing well.
† Add remaining ingredients and pour into greased muffin pans.
† Bake for 25 minutes.
† Let stand 5 minutes before removing from pans.

ENGLISH MUFFIN LOAF

Yield: 2 loaves
Lynne Ford

51/2-6	cups flour
2	(1/4-ounce) packages active dry yeast
1	tablespoon sugar
2	teaspoons salt
1/4	teaspoon baking soda
2	cups milk
1/2	cup water
	Corn meal for dusting loaves (optional)

† Combine 3 cups flour, yeast, sugar, salt and soda.
† Heat milk and water until very warm (120° - 130°F). Add to flour mixture. Beat well.
† Stir in enough flour to make stiff batter. Spoon in 2 loaf pans that have been greased and sprinkled with corn meal.
† Cover and let rise in warm place for 45 minutes.
† Preheat oven to 400°.
† Bake 25 minutes.
† Remove from pans immediately.

FRENCH BREAKFAST PUFFS

Yield: 1 dozen
Gail Carr

8 tablespoons vegetable shortening, divided
1 cup sugar, divided
1 egg
1 1/2 cups all-purpose flour
1 1/2 teaspoons baking powder
1/2 teaspoon salt
1/2 teaspoon nutmeg
1/2 cup milk
3 tablespoons butter, melted
1 teaspoon cinnamon

† Preheat oven to 350°.
† Mix 5 tablespoons shortening, 1/2 cup sugar, and egg.
† Sift together flour, baking powder, salt and nutmeg.
† Alternating with milk, add dry ingredients to egg mixture.
† Fill greased muffin tins two-thirds full of batter and bake 20 to 25 minutes.
† Mix butter and 3 tablespoons shortening.
† Mix 1/2 cup sugar and cinnamon.
† Immediately roll puffs in melted butter mixture and then in sugar mixture.

Will freeze well.

MARSHMALLOW CRESCENT PUFFS

Yield: 16
Judy Gaines

1/4 cup sugar
1 teaspoon cinnamon
2 (8-ounce) cans crescent dinner rolls
16 large marshmallows
1/2 stick margarine, melted

† Preheat oven to 375°.
† Combine sugar and cinnamon. Separate dough into 16 triangles.
† Dip marshmallows into margarine and sugar mixture. Place on triangle. Wrap and squeeze edges to seal. Dip in margarine and place seam side down in muffin tin.
† Bake 10 to 15 minutes or until browned.

GLAZE:
1/2 cup powdered sugar
1/2 teaspoon vanilla
2-3 teaspoons milk
1/4 cup chopped nuts (optional)

† Blend powdered sugar, vanilla and milk. Drizzle on warm puffs. Sprinkle with nuts.

May be made ahead and refrigerated for 2 to 3 hours before baking.

YEAST ROLLS

Yield: 80 to 90
Anne Tomlinson

1   cup vegetable shortening
3/4 cup sugar
2   teaspoons salt
1   cup boiling water
2   (1/4-ounce) packages
    dry yeast
1   cup warm water
2   eggs, beaten
6   cups sifted flour
    Butter

† Combine shortening, sugar and salt. Pour boiling water over mixture and stir until melted. Set aside.
† Dissolve yeast in warm water. Let rise.
† Add eggs and yeast to shortening mixture, mixing well. Slowly add flour. Cover and let rise until double in bulk, about 2 hours.
† Knead and roll out dough on floured surface. Shape into "pocketbook" rolls (see note).
† Preheat oven to 375°.
† Bake 15 to 20 minutes or until brown.
† May be made into loaf.

Pocketbook rolls are made by putting a tiny piece of butter on each roll before folding over.

KERAH'S TEA SCONES

Yield: 8
Jean Spratt

1/2 cup milk
3   tea bags
1   egg, slightly beaten
2   cups flour
2   teaspoons baking powder
1/2 cup sugar
1/4 teaspoon salt
1/2 stick cold butter,
    cut into pieces

† In small pan bring milk to boiling point. Add tea bags. Cover and brew 5 minutes (off burner). Remove tea bags and cool Beat egg in this mixture. Set aside.
† Preheat oven to 400°.
† In food processor, combine flour, baking powder, sugar and salt. Add butter and process for 25 seconds. Gradually add tea mixture to processor. Mix until just combined.
† Turn onto cookie sheet that has been sprayed with cooking spray and floured. Pat into 8-inch circle. Lightly cut into 8 wedges (do not separate).
† Bake 20 to 25 minutes until golden brown.
† Cool on wire rack.

BEACH DRINK

Yield: 1 serving
Mary Gregory

Sweetened Kool-Aid mix
Water

† Pour a little sweetened Kool-Aid mix into a blender with lots of ice.
† Add a little water and blend on high. Adjust taste by adding more Kool-Aid mix or water.

This is really just like a Slurpee but can easily be made at home for your kids!

BLOODY MARYS

Yield: Six (10-ounce) drinks
Meredith Forshaw

1   (46-ounce) can spicy vegetable juice
1/2 cup ketchup or cocktail sauce
1   teaspoon prepared horseradish
2   tablespoons Worcestershire sauce
1/2 teaspoon Tabasco sauce
1/2 teaspoon celery salt
3   tablespoons lemon juice
    Dash of salt
    Dash of pepper
12 ounces of vodka
    Stalks of celery for garnish

† Blend all ingredients and pour over ice cubes.
† Add celery for garnish.

Will keep in refrigerator two weeks.

HOT CIDER

Yield: 1 gallon
Celia Marshall

1   gallon unsweetened apple juice
8   whole cloves
1   large cinnamon stick
1/8 teaspoon nutmeg
3   tablespoons lemon juice
1/4 cup brown sugar

† Combine all ingredients in large pot over low heat.

HOT RUM CIDER

Yield: 12 servings
Judy Gaines

81/2 cups apple cider
2   teaspoons pumpkin
    pie spice
2-3 cups rum, to taste
12 cinnamon sticks
12 whole cloves
12 lime slices (optional)

† In large saucepan, bring cider and pumpkin
  spice to boil. Remove from heat and
  add rum.
† Ladle into mugs and add cinnamon stick
  and whole clove. Serve at once.

DELLA ROBBIA PUNCH

Yield: 30 (6-ounce) servings
Jane Bolt

2   cups sugar
3   cups water, divided
2   apples
3   bananas
1   (24-ounce) can
    unsweetened pineapple juice
2   (6-ounce) cans frozen
    orange juice
1   (6-ounce) can frozen
    lemonade
1   orange, thinly sliced
1   lemon, thinly sliced
3   (28-ounce) bottles ginger ale

† Bring sugar and 11/2 cups water to boil.
  Stir and let cool.
† Peel only one apple. Core and quarter both.
  Cut bananas. Blend apples, bananas
  and remaining water in blender.
† Combine mixture with other ingredients,
  except ginger ale.
† If desired, freeze a portion of punch
  mixture in a mold. Slices of orange or
  lemon may be added to mold before freezing
  or float dices in punch and add remaining
  chilled punch and ginger ale.

KAHLÚA

Yield: 1/2 gallon
Elisabeth Benfield

21/2 cups water, divided
33/4 cups sugar
4   tablespoons freeze-dried
    coffee or 5 tablespoons
    instant
1   tablespoon glycerin
4   teaspoons vanilla extract
1   fifth vodka

† In a 2-quart pan, bring 2 cups water and
  sugar to a boil. Lower heat and simmer
  10 minutes.
† Bring remaining water to a boil and add
  instant coffee. Add to sugar mixture.
  Stir and cool to room temperature.
† Add glycerin and vanilla extract.
† Pour into half-gallon jug and add fifth of
  vodka. Put top on jug. Store in cool dark
  place for 2 to 4 weeks. Pour into
  decorative bottles.

89

GINGER-ALMOND TEA

Yield: 12 cups
Ann Linde

1   cup boiling water
5   regular-size tea bags
1 1/2 cups sugar
4   cups water
3/4 cup lemon juice
1   tablespoon vanilla extract
1   teaspoon almond extract
1   (1-liter) bottle ginger ale, chilled

† Pour boiling water over tea bags. Cover and steep 5 minutes.
† Remove tea bags, squeezing gently. Stir in sugar, water, lemon juice, vanilla and almond extracts. Chill.
† Stir in ginger ale just before serving.
† Serve tea over ice.

LEMONADE ICE TEA

Yield: 1 gallon
Fred Rees
Margaret Williams

2 1/2 quarts water
3/4 cup sugar
4   family size tea bags
4-5 mint leaves (optional)
1   (12-ounce) can frozen lemonade, thawed

† Bring water to boil. Add sugar, tea bags and mint leaves. Steep 5 minutes.
† Remove tea bags. Add lemonade and enough water to mixture to make 1 gallon.

In winter, for hot tea, add 8 cloves.

ORANGE DELIGHT

Yield: 8 to 10 servings
Mary Jenrette

1   (6-ounce) can frozen orange juice
1/2 cup sugar
Dash of vanilla extract
1   cup water
1   cup milk
1   tray of ice

† Combine ingredients in blender. Serve immediately.

RUSSIAN TEA

Yield: 1 1/4 cups
Lynne Ford

1/2 cup regular Tang
3 tablespoons presweetened lemonade Kool-aid
1/2 cup unsweetened instant tea
1/2 teaspoon ground cloves
1 teaspoon cinnamon
1/4 cup sugar

† Combine all ingredients.
† Add 2 to 3 heaping teaspoons with 6 to 8 ounces hot water.

SUNSETS

Yield: 1 serving
Mary Gregory

Cranberry juice or red Kool-Aid
Orange juice
Splash of soda water or Sprite
Cherry for garnish

† Pour one serving of cranberry juice or Kool-Aid and orange juice over ice in a glass. Add splash of soda water or Sprite and garnish with cherry for a special treat.

Nice for children while adults are having summer drinks. Kids like the way it looks like a summer sunset!

TAILGATE PUNCH

Yield: 3 quarts
Mary Jenrette

1 quart vodka
1 pint orange juice
1 pint grapefruit juice
1 pint cranberry juice
1 pint mai tai cocktail mix

† Combine ingredients in a gallon jug. Pour over ice.

EASY PARTY PUNCH

Yield: 65 (4-ounce) cups
Mary Jenrette

4-5 (28-ounce) bottles ginger ale
1 fifth bourbon
1 fifth cold duck or sparkling Burgundy
Frozen ring of ginger ale, cherries and cherry juice to float in punch.

† Combine all ingredients in large bowl.

91

WASSAIL

Yield: 20 cups
Charlotte Ferebee

2 (48-ounce) bottles
 apple juice
1 (46-ounce) bottle
 cranberry juice
4 or 5 whole cloves
10 whole allspice
1 stick cinnamon

† Combine juices.
† Place spices in teaball or tie in cheesecloth.
† Simmer all ingredients over a medium heat
 for 20 minutes.
† Serve warm.

Will keep several days in the refrigerator.

GOLDEN WASSAIL

Yield: 21/2 quarts
Rosemary VanDuyn

1 quart unsweetened
 pineapple juice
1 quart apple cider
1 (12-ounce) can apricot
 nectar
1 cup orange juice
2 sticks cinnamon
1 teaspoon whole cloves
1/4 teaspoon whole
 cardamom seeds

† Combine all ingredients in a large saucepan
 and bring to a boil. Simmer for 15 minutes
 and then strain. Serve hot with cinnamon
 sticks or orange slices.

WHISKEY SOURS

Yield: 10 (6-ounce) servings
Lisa Tomlinson

2 (6-ounce) cans frozen
 lemonade
12 ounces bourbon
2 (12-ounce) cans beer
12 ounces water

† Combine all ingredients. Serve over ice.

Vegetables And Side Dishes

Teaching Children To Serve

In Order To Serve
IV. Teaching Children To Serve

God is great and God is good
and we thank him for our food.
By his hand we all are fed.
Give us, Lord, our daily bread.
[TRADITIONAL GRACE]

One of the most memorable meals of my life was in England years ago with distant cousins of my mother's family. One by one their children helped serve the meal. Each rose from his seat at table and served one course and at the end they cleared the table together and brought coffee. It seemed to me that this was the solution to all our difficulty about our children grousing over eating different foods. My English cousins enjoyed the meal because they had an active part in it, much the same as children enjoy worship far more when they are singing or acolyting than when they are sitting in the pew.

There is little the "me generation" of our time needs to learn more than the wisdom of service. Serving others is not a chore or an imposition, but a sacred privilege. When this is learned at a young age, it carries throughout our life. Our homes are not meant to be fortresses from the world but havens of hospitality for others. Our jobs and professions are not meant only for profit or self-aggrandizement but for serving others and for the common good. Serving guests at table is a model for all of life.

When Jesus said, "Let the greatest among you become as the youngest," he was inviting all of us to discover the child within who loves to serve. As Michael Quoist has written so beautifully, God says:

"It is I, your God, the Eternal, risen from the Dead,
coming to bring back to life the child in you...
I am ready to give you again the beautiful face
of a child, the beautiful eyes of a child
For I love children, and I want everyone to be like them."

THE REVEREND HENRY NUTT PARSLEY, JR., RECTOR

EAST INDIAN CURRIED APPLES

Yield: 8 to 10 servings
Judy Gaines

1/2 cup sugar
1 tablespoon curry powder
2 tablespoons finely chopped onion
3/4 teaspoon salt
  Juice of 1 lemon
1 cup water
15 tart cooking apples, peeled and quartered

† Preheat oven to 350°.
† Combine all ingredients, except apples, in a saucepan and bring to a boil.
† Place apples in a buttered 2-quart casserole. pour hot syrup over apples and bake 30 minutes.
† Raisins, nutmeg or cinnamon may be added.

ARTICHOKE CASSEROLE

Yield: 4 to 6 servings
Christ Church Cooks I

1 (14-ounce) can artichoke hearts, drained and halved
1 (8-ounce) can water chestnuts, sliced
1/2 cup olives, sliced
3 hard-cooked eggs, sliced
1 can mushroom soup
1/2 cup milk
1/2 cup grated sharp cheese
  Bread crumbs for garnish

† Preheat oven to 350°.
† In 1 1/2-quart casserole, layer artichokes, water chestnuts, olives and eggs.
† Combine soup and milk. Pour over casserole. Sprinkle with cheese and bread crumbs.
† Bake 1 hour.

MICROWAVED ASPARAGUS

Yield: 4 or 5 servings
Rosemary VanDuyn

1 pound washed asparagus, trimmed
2 slices fresh ginger
1/4 teaspoon lemon zest
  Vinegar-based salad dressing of your choice
  Freshly ground pepper
  Garnish (optional)

† Place asparagus, ginger and lemon in resealable plastic bag. Close and microwave at medium (50%) power for 3 to 4 minutes.
† Unseal bag and fill with cold water. Drain and pour salad dressing in bag.
† Remove to serving platter.

In Order To Serve

ASPARAGUS CASSEROLE

Yield: 8 to 10 servings
Marcia Gilbert

3 tablespoons butter
3 tablespoons flour
1 cup milk, room temperature
1 1/2 cups grated cheddar cheese
3 (15-ounce) cans asparagus
  spears, drained
1/4-1/2 cup slivered almonds

† Preheat oven to 350°.
† Blend butter and flour over low heat until smooth. Add milk and cheese. Stir until melted.
† Drain asparagus and layer in 2-quart casserole with almonds and cheese sauce, making two layers.
† Bake for 30 minutes.

MEXICAN PIE

Yield: 4-6 servings
Mimi Rees

1 clove garlic, crushed
1 teaspoon olive oil
2 medium zucchini, grated
1/4 teaspoon salt
2 tablespoons chopped
  red pepper
1 package frozen corn
1 (15-ounce) can black
  beans, drained
1/4 teaspoon cumin
1 (16-ounce) jar salsa
1/4 cup chopped cilantro
10 (5-inch) corn or flour tortillas
1 1/2 cups grated cheddar cheese

† Preheat oven to 350°.
† Sauté garlic in olive oil 1 to 2 minutes. Add zucchini and cook 3 to 4 minutes until limp. Add salt, pepper and corn, cooking 1 minute. Blend in black beans, cumin, salsa and cilantro. Remove from heat.
† Coat 9-inch pie pan with nonstick cooking spray.
† Place 4 tortillas around bottom of pie pan. Add 1/3 of bean mixture, topping with 1/3 of cheese.
† Repeat bean and cheese layers two more times using only 3 tortillas on second and third layers.
† Bake 35 to 40 minutes.

Teenagers love this recipe!

MARINATED GREEN BEANS

Yield: 8 servings
Nikki Morris

VEGETABLE:

1 1/2 pounds green beans,
    steamed al dente
1   pound mushrooms, sliced
1   medium-size red onion,
    thinly sliced and in rings
1/2 cup finely chopped celery

† Combine vegetables in bowl.

MARINADE:

1   cup tarragon wine vinegar
1/2 cup olive oil
1/2 cup vegetable oil
1   teaspoon dried whole
    oregano
1   teaspoon dried mustard
1   teaspoon whole basil
1/8 teaspoon pepper
1/8 teaspoon salt

† Combine marinade ingredients in a jar.
  Shake and pour over vegetables.
† Cover and refrigerate.

MEXICAN BEANS AND RICE

Yield: 4 to 6 servings
Cantey Gannaway

2/3 cup uncooked rice
1   (15-ounce) can black
    beans, drained
4   ounces mild salsa
1/2 cup grated cheddar
    cheese
    Chopped green onions
    to taste
    Diced roma tomatoes
    to taste
2   ounces feta cheese,
    diced

† Cook rice according to directions on box.
† Add beans, salsa, and cheese, stirring
  until cheese is melted.
† Top with onions, tomatoes, and feta cheese.

GREEN BEANS GRUYERE

Yield: 16 servings
Liz Lea

VINAIGRETTE:
3/4 cup olive oil
1/4 cup sherry wine vinegar
4 tablespoons Dijon mustard
Chopped Italian parsley
to taste
Salt and freshly ground
pepper to taste

† Combine all ingredients and whisk until creamy. Set aside.

GREEN BEANS:
3 pounds fresh green beans, whole and trimmed
1/2 pound Gruyere cheese, coarsely grated
1/2 pound mushrooms, trimmed and thinly sliced

† Blanch green beans in boiling water for 3 minutes. Drain and cool in ice water for 10 minutes. Drain and chill 1 hour.
† Toss beans with vinaigrette until completely coated. Add Gruyere cheese and mushrooms.
† Chill until ready to serve.

SWISS BEANS

Yield: 4 to 6 servings
Diane Wilkerson

2 packages frozen French-style green beans
2 tablespoons butter or margarine
2 tablespoons flour
1 teaspoon salt
1/4 teaspoon pepper
2 tablespoons grated onion
1/2 teaspoon sugar
1/2 pint sour cream
1/2 pound Swiss cheese, sliced

† Preheat oven to 325°.
† Cook beans according to package directions. Drain well.
† Melt butter in saucepan and blend in flour, salt, pepper, onion, and sugar.
† Add sour cream gradually and stir until thick.
† Fold in beans and pour into 2-quart casserole. Cover with cheese.
† Bake 15 minutes or until cheese is melted.

LES HARICOTS VERT

Yield: 4 to 6 servings
Suzie Lowe

1   pound stringless green beans
    Minced garlic cloves to taste
1/2 stick butter
    Finely chopped parsley
    for garnish

† French green beans (see remarks).
  Remove ends and place in skillet of
  boiling water and simmer 7 minutes.
† Pour off water and shake over heat for
  several minutes. Melt butter and garlic
  with beans. Sprinkle with parsley.

Frenched beans are cut lengthwise into very thin strips.

BROCCOLI CASSEROLE

Yield: 6 to 8 servings
Kathryn Horne

2   packages frozen broccoli
1   can cream of mushroom
    soup
1/2 cup mayonnaise
1   teaspoon curry powder
    Dash of Worcestershire
    sauce
1/2 teaspoon lemon juice
1/2 cup grated cheddar cheese
2   tablespoons margarine,
    melted
1   cup dried bread crumbs

† Preheat oven to 350°.
† Cook broccoli and drain. Arrange in
  8x8-inch casserole.
† Combine soup, mayonnaise, curry
  powder, Worcestershire sauce and
  lemon juice. Pour over broccoli.
† Sprinkle with cheese. Combine
  margarine and bread crumbs and
  spread on top.
† Bake 45 minutes.

99

COPPER CARROT PENNIES

Yield: 8 to 10 servings
Christ Church Cooks I

2 pounds carrots, sliced
1 small bell pepper,
   sliced into rings
1 medium onion, thinly
   sliced
1 can tomato soup
1/2 cup vegetable oil
1 cup sugar
3/4 cup vinegar
1 teaspoon mustard
1 teaspoon Worcestershire
   sauce
   Salt and pepper to taste

† Boil carrots in salted water until tender. Cool.
† Alternate layers of carrots, pepper rings, and onion in bowl.
† Combine remaining ingredients until well blended. Pour over vegetables and refrigerate.

This keeps a long time in the refrigerator and can be served warm.

CURRIED CAULIFLOWER CASSEROLE

Yield: 4 to 6 servings
Betsy Westerberg

1 head cauliflower
1 can cream of chicken soup
1/3 cup mayonnaise
1 teaspoon curry powder
1 cup grated cheddar cheese
1/2 - 3/4 cup bread crumbs
1/4 stick butter

† Preheat oven to 325°.
† Boil cauliflower for 10 minutes. Cut into small pieces and place in 11/2-quart casserole.
† Blend soup, mayonnaise, curry powder and cheese. Pour over cauliflower.
† Sprinkle bread crumbs on top and dot with butter. Bake 40 minutes.

CHILIES RELLENOS

Yield: 8 servings
Judy Van Namen

3 (4-ounce) cans whole
   green chilies
3/4 pound Monterey Jack
   cheese, sliced 1/4-inch
   thick
1 cup flour
21/4 cups milk
11/4 teaspoons salt
3 eggs, slightly beaten

† Preheat oven to 350°.
† Split chilies to open and remove inside seeds.
† Alternate one layer of chilies with one layer of cheese in 11/2-quart casserole.
† Blend flour, milk, and salt with eggs. Pour over chilies and cheese.
† Bake for 50 minutes. Will puff like a soufflé.

CORN FRITTERS

Yield: 6 to 8 servings
Sis Cranz

1/2 cup flour
1/2 teaspoon baking powder
1 (8-ounce) can creamed corn or 1 package frozen creamed corn, thawed.
2 tablespoons milk
1 egg, separated
Oil for frying

† In small bowl, combine flour and baking powder.
† In large bowl, combine corn, milk and egg yolk. Add flour mixture and stir well.
† In small bowl, beat egg white until stiff but not dry. Fold into corn mixture.
† Heat oil in skillet. Drop batter by spoonfuls into oil and fry until golden brown. Drain on paper towels.

AUNT MAMIE'S CORN PUDDING

Yield: 4 to 6 servings
Dede Thompson

2 eggs
2 cups fresh corn kernels (4 to 6 ears)
1 cup milk
2 teaspoons sugar
1 rounded teaspoon butter or margarine
Salt to taste

† Preheat oven to 375°.
† Beat eggs and add remaining ingredients.
† Bake in uncovered 2-quart casserole for 30 minutes.

FRESH CRANBERRY RELISH

Yield: 1 1/2 to 2 cups
Tat Hicks

1 orange, seeded
1 apple, cored
1 cup fresh cranberries
1 cup pecans
Sugar to taste

† Chop individually orange, apple, cranberries and pecans in food processor.
† Combine all together and add sugar to taste.

101

EGGPLANT BRUSCHETTA

Yield: 6 servings
Missy Wooten

3   cloves garlic, minced
1/4   cup shredded fresh spinach
1   (28-ounce) can tomatoes, drained, or 4 ripe tomatoes, chopped
1/4   cup roasted red peppers, chopped
2   medium eggplants, sliced 1/2-inch thick
    Freshly ground pepper to taste
1/2   cup olive oil

† Combine garlic, spinach, tomatoes and pepper. Set aside.

† Slice eggplants into 1/2-inch slices. Salt and let drain 30 minutes. Pat dry.

† Brush both sides of eggplant slices with olive oil. Grill until brown (medium heat, 4 minutes each side).

† Season with pepper. Top with spinach mixture. Sprinkle with cheese and grill until cheese is melted. Serve immediately.

Can broil in oven until lightly brown, 2 minutes on each side.

CURRIED FRUITS

Yield: 8 servings
Mary Redding

1   (16-ounce) can pineapple
1   (16-ounce) can peach halves
1   (16-ounce) can pear halves
1   (16-ounce) can apricots
1   (6-ounce) jar maraschino cherries
51/3 tablespoons butter
3/4   cup brown sugar
2   teaspoons curry powder
2/3   cup slivered almonds, blanched, or 1/2 cup chopped pecans (optional)

† Preheat oven to 325°.

† Drain fruit and arrange in 2-quart casserole.

† Melt butter and combine with brown sugar and curry powder. Pour over fruit. Sprinkle with almonds or pecans before baking if desired.

† Bake for 1 hour.

FRUIT COMPOTE

Yield: 4 servings
Julie Sanniota

1 (1-pound) can sliced pears, drained
2 apples, peeled and sliced
1/2 (1-pound) can whole berry cranberry sauce
1/4 teaspoon ground cinnamon
1/4 teaspoon ground cloves
1/4 teaspoon ground allspice

† Combine all ingredients in 1-quart casserole and microwave 6 to 8 minutes on high.
† Serve hot or cold as side dish.

LINDSAY DANIEL GRITS

Yield: 10 to 12 servings
Lindsay Daniel

1 cup white or yellow grits, cooked
21/4 cups grated sharp cheddar cheese, divided
1/2 stick butter
1/3 pound cooked bacon, crumbled, reserve drippings
1 (1-pound) can tomatoes, drained and chopped
1 onion, chopped
1 bell pepper, chopped
1 clove garlic, minced
Salt and pepper to taste

† Preheat oven to 350°.
† Add 2 cups cheese and butter to hot grits. Stir until melted.
† In bacon drippings, sauté tomatoes, onion, bell pepper, garlic and salt and pepper.
† Combine vegetables and bacon with grits. Sprinkle with remaining cheese.
† Pour into buttered 2-quart casserole and bake 30 minutes.

Freezes well.

GOUDA GRITS

Yield: 6 servings
Judy Gaines

1	cup quick grits
1	stick butter
1	(8-ounce) round gouda cheese
1	(5-ounce) can evaporated milk

† Preheat oven to 350°.
† Cook grits according to directions.
† Blend with remaining ingredients and pour into 1 1/2-quart casserole. Bake 45 to 60 minutes.
† Garnish with paprika.

MUSHROOMS FLORENTINE

Yield: 8 servings
Marsha Rich

2	packages frozen chopped spinach
	Garlic salt to taste
1/4	cup chopped onion
2	tablespoons butter, melted
1	cup grated sharp cheddar cheese, divided
2	(4-ounce) cans mushrooms, drained
	Garlic salt

† Preheat oven to 350°.
† Cook and drain spinach. Place in shallow casserole.
† Sprinkle with salt, onions and butter.
† Layer 1/2 cup of cheese. Layer all of mushrooms.
† Sprinkle with garlic salt and remaining cheese.
† Bake for 20 minutes.

SHERRIED MUSHROOMS

Yield: 4 to 6 servings
Sue Hardwick

1/2	cup sliced green onions
1-1 1/2	pounds whole medium mushrooms
2	tablespoons dry sherry
1	tablespoon Worcestershire sauce
1/2	teaspoon ground pepper

† Spray skillet with cooking spray and sauté onions until tender.
† Slice mushrooms and add with remaining ingredients.
† Cover and cook about 10 minutes.

PORTOBELLO MUSHROOM FAJITAS

Yield: 6 servings
Mimi Rees

3 tablespoons water
3 tablespoons lime juice
1 tablespoon olive or
   vegetable oil
2 large cloves garlic, minced
1/2 teaspoon ground cumin
1/4 teaspoon dried oregano,
   crushed
10 ounces Portobello
   mushrooms, thinly sliced
1 medium-size red, yellow
   or green pepper,
   cut into thin strips
4 green onions, cut into
   1 1/2-inch pieces
6 (7-inch) flour tortillas
   Lime wedges, sour cream,
   and salsa for garnish

† Combine water, lime juice, oil, garlic, cumin and oregano in large zip-top plastic bag.
† Add mushrooms, pepper strips and green onions. Marinate 15 to 30 minutes at room temperature.
† Preheat oven to 350°.
† Wrap tortillas in foil and heat 10 minutes to soften.
† In large skillet, heat undrained vegetables until peppers are tender and most of liquid evaporates, about 5 minutes.
† Spoon mushrooms onto tortillas and roll up.
† Garnish with lime, sour cream and salsa.

FRESH OKRA AND TOMATOES

Yield: 6 servings
Nancy Hemmig

1 clove garlic, minced
1/2 cup chopped onion
1/2 cup chopped bell pepper
1/4 stick butter, melted
2 cups sliced fresh okra
3 cups chopped ripe tomatoes
1/4 teaspoon oregano
1/2 teaspoon salt
1/2 teaspoon pepper

† Sauté garlic, onion, and green pepper in butter until tender.
† Add remaining ingredients and cook 5 minutes.

OKRA CASSEROLE

Yield: 6 to 8 servings
Ann McMillan

2 cups sliced okra
1 small onion, chopped
1/2 cup grated cheddar cheese
2 tablespoons butter, melted
1 1/2 cups buttered bread crumbs, divided
1 egg, beaten
1/2 teaspoon salt
1/2 teaspoon black pepper

† Preheat oven to 350°.
† Combine all ingredients, except 1/2 cup buttered bread crumbs, in 1 1/2-quart greased casserole.
† Top with bread crumbs and bake covered 15 minutes.
† Uncover and continue baking 15 minutes.

PALMES' PINEAPPLE AU GRATIN

Yield: 6 to 8 servings
Jo Ann Earnhardt

2 (1-pound 4-ounce) cans pineapple chunks, drained
3/4-1 cup sugar
6 tablespoons flour
2 cups grated sharp cheddar cheese
1/4-1/2 cup crumbled buttery crackers
1 stick butter, melted

† Preheat oven to 350°.
† Combine pineapple, sugar, flour and cheese in 1 1/2-quart casserole.
† Blend cracker crumbs and butter.
† Sprinkle on pineapple and bake 25 minutes.

VIDALIA ONION AND RICE CASSEROLE

Yield: 6 to 8 servings
Meredith Forshaw

6 large Vidalia onions
1/2 stick butter
2 cups cooked rice
1 cup grated Swiss cheese
  Dash of nutmeg
2/3 cup milk

† Preheat oven to 325°.
† Cut onions into chunks and sauté in butter.
† Combine with rice, cheese and nutmeg in 2-quart casserole. Pour milk over rice.
† Bake for 1 hour.

Betsy Locke's variation: Use 1 1/2 cups grated Swiss cheese and 1 1/2 cups half-and-half.

VIDALIA ONION PIE

Yield: 8 to 10 servings
Sybil Gray

1   unbaked deep-dish pie shell
2   medium Vidalia onions,
     very thinly sliced
1   cup sour cream
1   cup mayonnaise
1/2 cup grated sharp cheddar
     cheese
1/2 cup grated mozzarella cheese
1/2 cup grated Swiss cheese
1/2 teaspoon oregano
1/2 teaspoon basil
     Dash of salt
1/4 cup crumbled buttery
     crackers

† Preheat oven to 350°.
† Place onions in pie crust. Combine all
   ingredients, except crackers, and spread
   over onions.
† Sprinkle crackers on pie and bake 45
   minutes.
† Serve at room temperature.

VIDALIA ONION CASSEROLE

Yield: 8 to 10 servings
Marcia Gilbert
Anita Griffin

4   large Vidalia onions,
     sliced in rings
2   sticks unsalted butter, room
     temperature, divided
6   ounces or 50 buttery
     crackers, crushed
8   ounces cheddar cheese,
     shredded
     Salt to taste
     Paprika to taste
3   large eggs, beaten
1   cup milk

† Preheat oven to 350°.
† Sauté onion rings in 1/4 cup butter.
† Combine remaining butter with crushed
   crackers. Reserve 1/4 cracker mixture
   for topping and spread remaining mixture
   on bottom of greased 9x13-inch casserole.
† Spread sautéed onion rings over that
   layer and sprinkle with cheese, salt, and
   paprika.
† Combine eggs and milk and pour over the
   layers. Top with reserved cracker mixture.
† Bake for 35 to 40 minutes.

BLACK-EYED PEA CAKES

Yield: 6 cakes
Sis Cranz

1   (15-ounce) can black-eyed
    peas, drained and rinsed
1   onion, chopped and sautéed
1/2 cup fresh bread crumbs
1   egg, slightly beaten
1/2 teaspoon cayenne pepper
1/2-1 cup cornmeal
2   tablespoons vegetable oil,
    butter or margarine
1   cup medium salsa

† Mash peas and combine with remaining
  ingredients, except oil and salsa.
† Shape into 3-ounce cakes and pan fry
  in oil or butter.
† Top with salsa.

May add one 4.5-ounce can chopped chilies, well drained, to the peas before shaping.
Do not use salsa.

HOPPIN' JOHN

Yield: 4 to 6 servings
Anne Bailey

2   cups dried black-eyed peas
    or other dried field peas
8   cups water
1 1/2 teaspoons salt
1 1/4 cups long-grain white rice
3   slices bacon, cooked crisp
    and drippings reserved
    Salt and pepper to taste

† Soak peas overnight in 8 cups water.
† Add salt to peas and bring to boil. Simmer
  2 hours or until tender.
† Add rice to peas when tender. Cook 10
  minutes and stir in bacon drippings. Lower
  heat, cover, and cook 1 hour.
† Crumble bacon over the Hoppin' John.
† Season with salt and pepper.

GREEN-PEA CASSEROLE

Yield: 10 to 12 servings
Anne Scott

1   (2-pound) package frozen
    green peas
1   (4-ounce) jar pimientos,
    drained
1   pound mushrooms, sliced
1   (1-ounce) package ranch
    dressing mix
1   stick butter, melted

† Preheat oven to 350°.
† Combine all ingredients and put in 4-quart
  casserole.
† Bake uncovered 40 minutes or until bubbly.

108

BREAKFAST POTATO CASSEROLE

Yield: 10 servings
Mary Vernon Rogers

1   (1-pound) bag frozen
    southern-style hash
    brown potatoes
1   can creamy potato soup
1   (16-ounce) carton sour
    cream
2   cups grated cheddar cheese
1/2 stick butter or margarine
1/2 cup sautéed onions
    Salt and pepper to taste

† Preheat oven to 350°.
† Combine all ingredients and pour into
  9 x 13-inch casserole.
† Bake 1 hour.

Freezes well unbaked.

POTATO GRATIN WITH BOURSIN

Yield: 8 servings
Anne Neal

2   cups whipping cream
1   (5-ounce) package Boursin
    cheese with herbs
3   pounds round red potatoes,
    thinly sliced and unpeeled
    Salt and pepper to taste
1 1/2 tablespoons chopped
    fresh parsley for garnish

† Preheat oven to 400°.
† Combine cream and cheese in heavy
  saucepan over medium heat until mixture
  is smooth.
† Arrange half of potatoes in greased
  4-quart casserole. Season with salt and
  pepper. Pour half of cheese mixture
  over potatoes. Layer remaining potatoes
  and cheese. Bake one hour or until top is
  golden and potatoes are tender. Garnish
  with parsley.

OVEN-ROASTED POTATOES

Yield: 6 servings
Robin Riggins

1   (1-ounce) envelope dry
    onion soup mix
1/4-1/3 cup olive oil
2   pounds new potatoes,
    quartered

† Preheat oven to 450°.
† Combine soup and oil in ziplock bag.
  Add potatoes and shake until coated.
† Place potatoes on large baking pan and
  bake for 40 minutes.

*Jo Griffin's variation: Sprinkle potatoes with onion salt and Parmesan cheese
instead of dry onion soup mix.*

POTATO CHEESE CHIPS

Yield: 4 to 6 servings
Anita Griffin

4   medium baking potatoes
2   sticks margarine, melted
1   cup Parmesan cheese
     Salt and pepper to taste
     Dash of paprika

† Preheat oven to 375°.
† Peel potatoes and slice into 1/8-inch rounds.
† Dip slices in butter and then into cheese and place on baking sheet lined with greased foil.
† Sprinkle with salt and pepper and paprika
† Bake 20 minutes.

PARTY POTATOES

Yield: 8 servings
Brenda Hill

8-10 medium potatoes, peeled
1   (8-ounce) package cream cheese, softened
1   (8-ounce) carton sour cream
1/2 cup fresh chives or 1/4 cup dried
     Salt and pepper to taste
     Paprika for garnish
4   tablespoons butter

† Preheat oven to 350°.
† Cut potatoes in cubes and boil until tender.
† Combine cream cheese and sour cream. Blend into hot potatoes until smooth. Add chives and seasonings.
† Pour into greased 2-quart casserole. Dot with butter and paprika.
† Bake 25 minutes.

Clarissa Chandler's variation: Add 6-8 slices cooked, crumbled bacon and garnish with grated cheddar cheese.

GRATIN DAUPHINOIS

Yield: 6 to 8 servings
Clarissa Chandler

13/4 pounds Idaho potatoes, peeled
     Salt and pepper to taste
2   cups scalded whole milk
1   egg
3   tablespoons unsalted butter, divided
11/3-2 cups grated Gruyere cheese (to taste)
     Garlic salt to taste

† Preheat oven to 400°.
† Place thinly sliced potatoes in large bowl. Toss with salt and pepper.
† Combine milk and egg.
† Grease 2-quart casserole with 1 tablespoon butter. Layer half of potatoes in casserole. Sprinkle with half of cheese and garlic salt.
† Add remaining potatoes and cover with milk mixture. Sprinkle remaining cheese and garlic salt. Dot with butter and bake 45 to 50 minutes until well browned.

SWEET POTATO SOUFFLÉ

Yield: 6 to 8 servings
Daisy Hicks

POTATOES:

3	cups mashed sweet potatoes
1	cup sugar
1/2	teaspoon salt
2	eggs, lightly beaten
1	stick margarine, melted
1/2	cup milk
1	teaspoon sherry (optional)

† Preheat oven to 350°.
† Combine ingredients and pour into greased 2-quart casserole.

TOPPING:

1	cup brown sugar
1/3	cup flour
1	cup chopped pecans
1/3	stick margarine, melted

† Combine topping ingredients and sprinkle on potatoes.
† Bake 35 minutes.

SWEET POTATO AND CARROT CRUMBLE

Yield: 8 servings
Marsha Rich

VEGETABLES:

2	(17-ounce) cans sweet potatoes, cut up and drained
2	(16-ounce) cans sliced carrots, drained
1/2	teaspoon pumpkin pie spice
3	tablespoons pure maple syrup

† Preheat oven to 350°.
† Combine potatoes and carrots in greased 2-quart casserole. Drizzle spice and syrup on top.

CRUMBLE:

1/3	cup flour
1/3	cup sugar
1/4	teaspoon salt
1/2	teaspoon pumpkin pie spice
3	tablespoons butter
1/3	cup rolled oats
1/3	cup chopped pecans

† Mix flour, sugar, salt and spice in bowl. Cut in butter with pastry knife. Add oats and pecans. Sprinkle over vegetables
† Bake for 45 minutes.

Wonderful holiday side dish.

CURRIED RICE

Yield: 6 to 8 servings
Sally Hartsock

1   medium onion, chopped
1/2 stick margarine or butter
2   medium carrots, julienne
21/4 cups water
1   cup uncooked rice
1/2 cup raisins
1   tablespoon instant chicken
     bouillon
1/2 teaspoon curry powder
1/4 teaspoon salt
1/4 teaspoon dried thyme
1/4 cup toasted slivered
     almonds for garnish

† Sauté onion in margarine until tender.
† Add remaining ingredients, except
  almonds. Heat to boiling. Cover and
  simmer 20 minutes. Do not lift lid or
  stir.
† Garnish with almonds.

ORANGE RICE

Yield: 4 servings
Paula Freeman

1   cup raw long-grain
     white rice
1   teaspoon salt
1/2 teaspoon thyme
1/4 cup minced onion
1/2 cup raisins
1   medium orange, quartered
     and cut in 1/8-inch thick
     slices
1   (10.5-ounce) can chicken
     broth
6   tablespoons orange juice
1/2 cup dry sherry

† Preheat oven to 350°.
† Combine rice, seasonings, onion, raisins
  and orange dices in a greased 2-quart
  casserole.
† Bring broth, orange juice and sherry to
  a boil in small saucepan.
† Pour boiling liquid over rice mixture. Stir
  once.
† Cover and bake 45 minutes.

OREGANO RICE

Yield: 8 servings
Della Rising

1	bunch green onions, chopped
1	cup raw rice
1/2	stick margarine
1	can beef consommé soup
3/4	cup water
1	teaspoon salt
1/2	teaspoon pepper
1	teaspoon oregano
1	(4-ounce) can sliced mushrooms

† Preheat oven to 350°.
† Sauté onion and rice in margarine over medium heat for 5 minutes. Do not brown.
† Add remaining ingredients and pour into 1 1/2-quart casserole.
† Cover and bake 45 minutes.

ZOE'S RICE CASSEROLE

Yield: 6 to 8 servings
Libba Eleazer

2/3	stick margarine, melted
1	cup long-grain rice
1	can onion soup
1 1/3	cups water
1	(8-ounce) can thinly sliced water chestnuts, drained
1	(4 1/2-ounce) jar button mushrooms, drained
1	cup pecan halves

† Preheat oven to 350°.
† Combine butter and rice. Add soup and water and simmer 2 minutes.
† Pour into 2-quart casserole. Add water chestnuts and mushrooms and bake 45 to 60 minutes.
† Top with pecans and heat last 15 minutes.

SPINACH AND RICE FANTASTIC

Yield: 6 servings
Anne Neal

1 (6-ounce) package long-
   grain and wild rice mix.
2 packages frozen chopped
   spinach, thawed and drained
2 cups grated Monterey
   Jack cheese
1/2 stick butter or margarine,
   melted
1 tablespoon chopped onion
3/4 teaspoon dry mustard
1/2 teaspoon salt

† Preheat oven to 350°.
† Cook rice according to directions.
† Combine rice and remaining ingredients
   and place in greased 2-quart casserole.
† Bake uncovered for 35 to 40 minutes.

SQUASH AND CARROT CASSEROLE

Yield: 8 to 10 servings
Camille Salisbury

1/2 pounds squash, sliced
1 carrot, thinly sliced
1 onion, coarsely chopped
1 (2-ounce) package
   slivered almonds
2 cups dry herb seasoned
   stuffing mix
1/2 stick margarine, melted
1/2 cup sour cream
1 (2-ounce) jar sliced pimientos
1 can cream of chicken soup

† Preheat oven to 350°.
† Cook squash, carrot, and onion until
   crisp tender. Drain and add almonds.
† Combine stuffing mix and margarine.
   Place 1 cup of mix in bottom of 2-quart
   casserole and cover with squash.
† Blend remaining ingredients and pour over
   squash. Top with stuffing mix.
† Bake for 30 to 45 minutes.

MARINATED TOMATOES

Yield: 10 to 12 servings
Cynthia Gass

1/2 cup vegetable or olive oil
1/4 cup cider vinegar
1 teaspoon salt
1/4 teaspoon pepper
1/2 teaspoon dried oregano
1/2 teaspoon dried thyme
6 large ripe tomatoes,
   peeled and sliced

† Combine all ingredients, except tomatoes,
   stirring well.
† Place tomatoes in shallow dish and cover
   with marinade.
† Cover and refrigerate several hours.

114

SQUASH CASSEROLE

Yield: 4 to 6 servings
Susan Fitch

1 small onion, chopped
2 pounds squash, chopped
1/2 cup evaporated milk
1 teaspoon salt
2 tablespoons butter or
  margarine
2 eggs
1-2 teaspoons sugar
2 cups grated cheddar
  cheese
  Pepper to taste
  Fresh bread crumbs

† Preheat oven to 300°.
† Steam onion and squash until tender.
† Drain and mash, and add remaining ingredients except cheese and bread crumbs.
† Pour into greased 8-inch pan and top with cheese and bread crumbs.
† Bake 25 minutes until brown and bubbly.

TOMATO-BASIL PIE

Yield: 6 to 8 servings
Len Efird

1 (15-ounce) box prepared
  pie crusts
4-6 large tomatoes, sliced
  (peeling optional)
  Fresh basil, chopped
  Salt and pepper to taste
  Garlic powder to taste
  (optional)
1 cup mayonnaise
2 cups grated sharp cheddar
  cheese
1/2-3/4 cup Parmesan cheese

† Preheat oven to 350°.
† Line pie plate with bottom crust and place layer of tomatoes, basil, salt and pepper, and garlic powder.
† Combine mayonnaise, cheeses and spread 1/2 over tomato layer.
† Repeat layers and top with crust. Prick and bake 20 to 25 minutes until brown and bubbly.

Ann Perry's variation: Use 3-4 medium onions, sliced, as first layer and use only 2 tablespoons mayonnaise with cheddar cheese, omitting Parmesan cheese.

TOMATO STRATA

Yield: 6 to 8 servings
Meredith Forshaw

7   tablespoons margarine
1   medium bell pepper,
     chopped
1   onion, chopped
1 1/2 teaspoons sugar
1   teaspoon salt
2   teaspoons Italian salad
     dressing
1 1/2 teaspoons oregano
1   (6-ounce) box croutons
5-6 medium-size ripe
     tomatoes, sliced
4   cups grated mozzarella
     cheese

† Preheat oven to 400°.
† Sauté pepper, onion and seasonings in
  margarine until tender.
† Spread croutons in 7x11-inch casserole.
  Spoon 1/2 of onion mixture over croutons.
† Arrange tomato slices on croutons. Sprinkle
  with cheese. Top with remaining onion
  mixture.
† Bake covered 15 minutes.
† Uncover and bake 10 minutes.

WONDERFUL FRESH TOMATO PIE

Yield: 6 to 8 servings
Pat Pollard

1   (9-inch) unbaked pie shell
3-4 medium-size ripe tomatoes,
     sliced
1   sweet onion, thinly sliced
3/4 cup grated cheddar cheese
3   eggs, lightly beaten
     Dash of salt
     Dash of pepper
4   strips bacon, cut in half

† Preheat oven to 350°.
† In pie crust, alternate layers of tomatoes,
  onions and cheese until crust is filled.
† Combine eggs, salt and pepper. Pour
  over tomatoes and top with bacon.
† Bake 35 to 40 minutes or until bacon is
  crisp.

IDA'S VEGETABLE CASSEROLE

Yield: 6 to 8 servings
Guerry Russell

1　(10-ounce) package frozen French-style green beans, thawed
1　(1-pound) can tomatoes
2　stalks celery, in 2-inch strips
3　medium carrots, in 2-inch strips
1　medium onion, thinly sliced
1/2　medium bell pepper, in strips
2　tablespoons tapioca
1　teaspoon salt
2　teaspoons sugar
1　tablespoon butter or margarine

† Preheat oven to 325°.
† Combine all ingredients, except butter, in greased 2-quart casserole.
† Dot with butter and bake covered 1 1/2 hours.

VEGETABLES TOSSED IN OLIVE BUTTER

Yield: 4 to 6 servings
Shaun Fellers

VEGETABLES:
4　small red potatoes, sliced
1　pound fresh asparagus in 2-inch pieces
1　small red bell pepper in 2-inch strips
1　zucchini, sliced
1/2　pound mushrooms, sliced
1　(7 1/2-ounce) jar baby corn

† Steam potatoes on a rack in large covered Dutch oven with water depth of 1 inch for 5 minutes.
† Add asparagus and bell pepper and steam 5 minutes.
† Add zucchini and mushrooms and steam 5 minutes.
† Add corn and steam 1 minute.
† Transfer to bowl and toss with olive butter.

OLIVE BUTTER:
1/3　cup butter, melted
3　tablespoons lemon juice
1/4-1/3 cup sliced ripe olives
1　tablespoon lemon zest

† Combine all ingredients and toss with vegetables.

One (10-ounce) package frozen asparagus may be substituted and added with bell pepper, zucchini, and mushrooms.

Notes:

Pasta, Eggs, And Cheese

Stretching And Sacrificing In Service

In Order To Serve

V. Stretching And Sacrificing In Service

O Jesus, Master Carpenter of Nazareth, who on
the cross, through wood and nails worked
our whole salvation; wield well your tools
in this our workshop; that we who come to you rough-hewn may by your
hands be fashioned to a truer beauty and greater usefulness.

In the cross of Christ we see the God of the universe stretching out his arms of love to all humanity. It is a reminder of the sacrifice which love always requires and includes. Life depends on our offering ourselves for the other, our recognition that we are interdependent and part of a great chain of giving. "Freely you have received, freely give," Paul wrote to the Galatians, reminding us that stewardship is rooted in the call to offer our gifts in humble service, not to keep them for ourselves alone.

If you have seen the wonderful Danish film, *Babette's Feast*, you will remember that it was Babette's gift and sacrifice of her talents as a cook which brought grace to a small community of people. At her feast old wounds were healed, forgiveness discovered, and joy created. It is no accident that Jesus so often compared the Kingdom of God to a banquet. In the gift and sacrifice of the table, we discover the joy of God who gave all that "we might have life and have it abundantly."

We are invited as God's stewards to return a tithe of our worldly goods to God's service. One of the ways we do this is by stretching ourselves out for others, inviting the stranger to our table, sharing our food with the homeless, setting aside a portion of what we prepare for a neighbor who is alone or in need. For "as you did it to one of the least of these . . . you did it to me."

The truly happy person is the one who has learned how to serve.
ALBERT SCHWEITZER (1875-1965), *Letters to a Godson*

THE REVEREND HENRY NUTT PARSLEY, JR., RECTOR

Pasta, Eggs, And Cheese

"MISS NAN'S" MACARONI AND CHEESE

Yield: 12 servings
Eugenia Allderdice

1 cup uncooked elbow
   macaroni
3 eggs, slightly beaten
4 cups grated cheddar
   cheese
1 (8-ounce) can
   evaporated milk
1 teaspoon dry mustard
   Salt and pepper to taste
1/2 stick butter
   Paprika for garnish

† Preheat oven to 350°.
† Cook macaroni according to directions.
† Combine eggs and remaining ingredients, except butter, with macaroni.
† Pour into a 4-quart casserole. Dot with butter and sprinkle with paprika. Bake for 40 minutes.

THREE CHEESE MANICOTTI

Yield: 4 servings
Jane Bruce

2 cups grated mozzarella
   cheese, divided
1 cup ricotta or creamed
   cottage cheese
1/2 cup Parmesan cheese
2 eggs, beaten
1/4 cup snipped parsley
1/2 teaspoon salt
1/8 teaspoon pepper
8 manicotti shells, cooked
   and drained
1 (14-ounce) jar spaghetti
   sauce with herbs

† Preheat oven to 350°.
† Combine 1 cup mozzarella, ricotta and Parmesan cheese. Add eggs, parsley, salt and pepper.
† Stuff manicotti shells with cheese mixture using about 1/4 cup each.
† Pour 1/2 cup spaghetti sauce into 2-quart casserole. Arrange stuffed shells in dish. Pour remaining sauce over top and sprinkle with mozzarella cheese. Bake uncovered 25 to 30 minutes or until bubbly.

EGG NOODLES WITH LEMON AND HERBS *Yield: 4 servings*
Susan Hamilton

1   (8-ounce) package
    wide egg noodles
33/4 teaspoons salt, divided
2   tablespoons butter,
    room temperature
2   tablespoons coarsely
    chopped flat-leaf parsley
2   tablespoons snipped chives
11/2 teaspoons lemon zest
1/8 teaspoon freshly
    ground pepper

† Cook noodles with 3 teaspoons salt
  according to package directions. Drain
  and transfer to a bowl.
† Add remaining ingredients and toss to
  coat noodles.

LINGUINE WITH TOMATOES AND BASIL *Yield: 4 to 6 servings*
Jane Dowd

4   large ripe tomatoes,
    cut into 1/2-inch cubes
1   pound Brie cheese, rind
    removed, torn into pieces
1   cup fresh basil leaves,
    cut into strips
3   cloves garlic, finely minced
1   cup plus 1 tablespoon extra
    virgin olive oil
21/2 teaspoons salt, divided
1/4 teaspoon freshly ground
    pepper
6   quarts water
11/2 pounds linguine

† Combine tomatoes, Brie, basil, garlic,
  1 cup olive oil, 1/2 teaspoon salt and
  pepper in large bowl. Prepare at least
  2 hours before serving and set aside,
  covered, at room temperature.
† Bring water to a boil with 1 tablespoon
  olive oil and remaining salt. Add linguine
  and boil until tender but firm, about 8 to
  10 minutes.
† Drain pasta and toss with tomatoes.
† Serve at once.

FETTUCCINE ALFREDO

Yield: 6 servings
Marsha Rich

1   pound fettuccine noodles
1/2 stick butter
3   tablespoons flour
1   cup half-and-half
1   cup water
1   cup freshly grated
    Parmesan cheese
1/4 teaspoon pepper
1/4 teaspoon garlic powder
1/4 teaspoon salt
1/2 teaspoon nutmeg

† Cook fettuccine according to directions.
† Melt butter in heavy saucepan over medium heat. Whisk in flour and cook for 1 minute.
† Gradually add half-and-half and water, stirring constantly until mixture is thickened. Stir in remaining ingredients.
† Serve over fettuccine.

FETTUCCINE WITH SPINACH-RICOTTA SAUCE

Yield: 4 servings
Anne Neal

3   tablespoons olive oil
1   medium onion, chopped
3   large cloves garlic, minced
1   tablespoon flour
2   cups milk (not lowfat
    or nonfat)
1   package frozen chopped
    spinach, thawed and well
    drained
1   cup ricotta cheese
1/3 cup freshly grated
    Parmesan cheese
10 oil-packed sun-dried
    tomatoes, thinly sliced
3   tablespoons chopped fresh
    basil or 2 teaspoons dried
    Dash of ground nutmeg
    Salt and pepper to taste
1   pound fettuccine, freshly
    cooked
1/3 cup minced green onions
1/3 cup toasted pine nuts
    Freshly grated Parmesan
    for garnish

† Heat oil and sauté onions 4 minutes. Add garlic and cook 1 minute.
† Stir in flour. Gradually whisk in milk and cook until sauce is smooth, stirring constantly.
† Blend in spinach, cheeses, tomatoes, and seasonings. Simmer over low heat about 5 minutes.
† Place pasta on platter. Spoon sauce on top.
† Garnish with green onions, pine nuts and Parmesan before serving.

ORZO WITH PARMESAN AND BASIL

Yield: 6 servings
Anne Neal

2-3 tablespoons unsalted
    butter
1 1/2 cups orzo pasta
3 cups chicken broth
1 1/2 teaspoons dried basil
    or 6 tablespoons fresh,
    thinly sliced
1/2 cup Parmesan cheese
    Salt and freshly ground
    pepper to taste
    Basil sprigs for garnish

† Melt butter and sauté orzo 2 minutes.
† Add broth and dried basil (if using dried) and bring to a boil. Reduce heat, cover and simmer until orzo is tender and liquid is absorbed, about 20 minutes.
† Blend in Parmesan cheese and fresh basil (if using fresh). Season with salt and pepper.

PENNE WITH ROASTED VEGETABLES

Yield: 4 to 6 servings
Julie Minor

1 (1 1/2-pound) eggplant
    Kosher salt
1/2 cup plus 2 tablespoons
    olive oil
2 pounds plum tomatoes,
    seeded and coarsely
    chopped
1 large onion, coarsely
    chopped
2 cloves garlic, minced
2 tablespoons chopped fresh
    marjoram, oregano or basil
    leaves
1 1/2 tablespoons salt, divided
1 pound uncooked penne
2 tablespoons chopped fresh
    parsley leaves
    Freshly grated Pecorino
    Romano cheese for
    garnish

† Trim and discard stem end of eggplant. Cut into 1-inch cubes. Place in colander and sprinkle with salt. Drain eggplant for 30 minutes.
† Preheat oven to 450°.
† Pour oil into large roasting pan. Add vegetables, garlic and marjoram. Season with salt to taste. Spread vegetables in even layer in pan.
† Bake 25 to 30 minutes on top rack until eggplant and onions are browned. Stir occasionally.
† Bring water to boil and add penne. Cook until tender but firm, 7 to 10 minutes.
† Drain and fold into roasted vegetables. Add 2 tablespoons oil and parsley.
† Serve with grated cheese.

PENNE WITH PESTO

Yield: 4 main dish servings
Paula Freeman

1   (16-ounce) package
    penne pasta
2 1/2 teaspoons salt, divided
1-2 teaspoons olive oil
1   medium onion, coarsely
    chopped
1   (10-ounce) package whole
    mushrooms, chopped or
    sliced
1/4 cup water
2   medium tomatoes, diced
1   (7-ounce) container
    refrigerated pesto with basil

† Prepare penne pasta as label directs using
  2 teaspoons salt in the water; drain.
  Return pasta to saucepan and keep warm.
† Heat olive oil in nonstick skillet on medium-
  high. Add onions, mushrooms, and 1/2
  teaspoon salt. Cook until mixture is lightly
  browned. Stir in 1/4 cup water. Reduce
  heat, cover and continue to cook until onion
  is tender, stirring often.
† Stir tomato and pesto into skillet with
  mushroom mixture. Cook until thoroughly
  heated.
† Pour mixture over pasta; toss gently.

Leftovers are tasty as a cold pasta salad!

PESTO

Yield: About 2 cups
Jane Neal Bobbitt

2   cups fresh basil leaves,
    stems removed
1   teaspoon salt
1/2 teaspoon pepper
2   cloves garlic
1/2 cup Parmesan cheese
1-2 teaspoons pine nuts
    (traditional but optional)
1-1 1/2 cups olive oil

† Blend all ingredients in food processor
  until it thickens.

SPINACH-SPAGHETTI CASSEROLE

Yield: 6 to 8 servings
Lynne Ford

2 (10-ounce) boxes frozen
   spinach
1 large onion, chopped
1 tablespoon olive oil
1/2 pound spaghetti, cooked
1 (8-ounce) carton sour cream
1 (8-ounce) carton cottage
   cheese

† Preheat oven to 350°.
† Cook and drain spinach. Sauté onions in
  oil and add to spinach.
† Combine spaghetti with sour cream and
  cottage cheese.
† In an 11/2-quart greased casserole, spread
  spinach-onion mixture. Top with spaghetti.
† Sprinkle with mozzarella cheese and bake
  30 minutes.

Kassie Minor's variation: Use 16 ounces sour cream, omit cottage cheese and add
4 cups shredded cheese (mozzarella, Monterey Jack or Parmesan) and 1/4 pound
sliced mushrooms.

SPAGHETTI

Yield: 6 to 8 servings
Bill Baynard

2 pounds ground venison
   or beef
21/3 tablespoons olive oil
1/2 teaspoon meat tenderizer
   (optional)
21/2 teaspoons garlic salt,
   divided
1 teaspoon pepper
1 Vidalia onion, chopped
1/2 pound fresh mushrooms,
   sliced
2 tablespoons red wine
2 teaspoons garlic powder
2 (6-ounce) cans tomato paste
1 (1-pound) can whole peeled
   tomatoes
2 tablespoons Parmesan
   cheese
11/2-2 pounds angel hair pasta
   Fat-free grated cheddar
   cheese for garnish

† In large skillet, brown venison in 2
  tablespoons oil, tenderizer, 1/2 teaspoon
  garlic salt, and pepper. Drain.
† In saucepan, sauté onions and mushrooms
  in 1 teaspoon olive oil, red wine, 2 teaspoons
  garlic salt and garlic powder. Add to
  venison.
† Add tomato paste, tomatoes and Parmesan
  cheese.
† Simmer 1 hour, covered, adding water as
  needed.
† Serve over angel hair pasta and top with
  cheese.

PASTA PRIMAVERA

Yield: 4 servings
DeeDee Dalrymple

1 1/2 cups broccoli flowerets
1   cup julienned zucchini
6   asparagus spears, tops only
3-4 tablespoons olive oil
1-2 garlic cloves, chopped
1/2 pound mushrooms, sliced
     Red pepper to taste
     Parsley to taste
     Basil to taste
1   cup whipping cream
1   cup butter
1   cup Parmesan cheese,
     divided
8   ounces linguini, cooked

† Blanch vegetables except mushrooms, 3 to 4 minutes each. Drain.
† Heat oil with garlic 2 to 3 minutes. Add mushrooms and sauté until tender. Add vegetables and heat. Season with pepper, parsley and basil.
† Heat whipping cream, butter and 1/2 cup cheese. Combine with linguini and vegetables.
† Sprinkle with remaining Parmesan cheese on top.

SUNFLOWER PASTA

Yield: 6 servings
Marsha Rich

1   large red bell pepper,
     chopped
1   (3 3/4-ounce) package
     sunflower kernels
1/2 cup extra virgin olive oil
1/4 cup parsley, chopped
1   pound small shell pasta
3/4 pound broccoli flowerets
1   small yellow squash, sliced
     Freshly grated pepper
     Freshly grated Parmesan
     cheese

† Sauté red bell pepper, sunflower kernels and parsley in olive oil for 15 to 20 minutes.
† Cook pasta in large pan of boiling, salted water for 10 minutes.
† Cook broccoli and squash in pasta water for 2 minutes. Drain and rinse.
† Put pasta in large bowl and add red bell pepper mixture.
† Serve with fresh pepper and cheese.

TOMATO PASTA PRIMAVERA

Yield: 4 servings
Kathy Suntken

6   large ripe tomatoes
8   fresh basil leaves,
    chopped, or 1/2
    teaspoon dried
3   tablespoons chopped
    fresh parsley
2   cloves garlic, minced
1 1/2 teaspoon salt
    Freshly ground pepper
    to taste
1   tablespoon olive oil
1   pound linguine or angel
    hair pasta
1/3 cup freshly grated
    Parmesan cheese

† Peel and chop tomatoes and place in
   large glass bowl. Add remaining
   ingredients, except pasta and cheese.
   Let stand 1 hour.
† Cook and drain pasta. Toss with tomato
   mixture and add cheese.

CATHERINE'S THREE CHEESE CHICKEN BAKE

Yield: 8 to 10 servings
Shaun Fellers

1/2 cup chopped onion
1/2 cup chopped bell pepper
3   tablespoons margarine
1   can cream of chicken soup
1   (6-ounce) can sliced
    mushrooms, drained
1/2 cup chopped pimiento,
    drained
1/3 cup milk
1/2 teaspoon basil
8   ounces lasagna noodles
1 1/2 cups cottage cheese
2   cups chicken, cooked,
    bite-size
2   cups grated American
    cheese
1/2 cup Parmesan cheese

† Preheat oven to 350°.
† Sauté onion and pepper in margarine.
   Add next five ingredients.
† In 9x13-inch casserole, lay 1/2 of noodles.
   Top with 1/2 each of sauce, cottage cheese,
   chicken and cheeses. Repeat layers,
   reserving American and Parmesan cheeses.
† Bake for 45 minutes. Top with remaining
   cheeses.
† Bake 5 minutes more.

128

LASAGNA

Yield: 6 servings
Beth Barnes

1/2 pound lasagna noodles
1 pound ground beef
1 clove garlic, crushed
1/3 cup finely chopped onion
1 (16-ounce) jar meatless
 spaghetti sauce
1 1/2 teaspoon salt
1/2 teaspoon oregano
1 cup small curd cottage
 cheese
1 egg, beaten
2 cups grated mozzarella
 cheese
 Parmesan cheese

† Preheat oven to 350°.
† Cook noodles according to directions.
† Cook beef, garlic and onion until browned.
 Drain off fat. Add spaghetti sauce, salt,
 pepper and oregano and simmer 15 minutes.
† Combine cottage cheese and egg.
† In greased 9x9-inch casserole, arrange layer
 of noodles, 1/2 of the cottage cheese mixture,
 mozzarella cheese and meat mixture.
† Top with another layer of ingredients.
 Sprinkle top with Parmesan cheese and bake
 50 minutes. Let stand 5 minutes before
 serving.

SPINACH, CARROT AND ZUCCHINI LASAGNA

Yield: 8 to 10 servings
Beth Bowen

3-5 tablespoons olive oil
1 onion, finely chopped
2 cloves garlic, minced
2 cups grated carrots
1 cup cubed zucchini
1 cup cubed red pepper
1 (28-ounce) can tomato sauce
1/2 teaspoon salt
1 1/2 teaspoons Italian seasoning
9 lasagna noodles, cooked and
 cooled
3 pounds ricotta cheese
3 packages frozen chopped
 spinach, thawed and drained
3 cups grated mozzarella
 cheese
1/2 cup Parmesan cheese

If frozen, cook for 1 hour at 375°.

† Preheat oven to 350°.
† Sauté onion, garlic and carrots in oil until
 soft. Add zucchini and pepper, cooking
 until soft.
† Stir in tomato sauce and simmer 10 to 15
 minutes. Cool slightly.
† In 9x13-inch pan, layer half of ingredients
 as follows: noodles, ricotta cheese, spinach,
 tomato sauce, mozzarella cheese. Repeat
 layer and top with Parmesan cheese.
† Bake 45 minutes.

QUICK AND LIGHT LASAGNA

Yield: 6 servings
Gail Carr

1   (26-ounce) jar spaghetti
    sauce
1/2 pound lean ground beef,
    cooked (optional)
1   (15-ounce) container light
    ricotta cheese
3/4 cup Parmesan cheese,
    divided
1   tablespoon minced fresh
    parsley
6   lasagna noodles, uncooked
11/2 cups grated fat-free
    mozzarella cheese, divided

† Preheat oven to 350°.
† Combine spaghetti sauce and meat.
† Combine ricotta cheese, 1/2 cup Parmesan
  cheese, and parsley.
† Pour 1/4 spaghetti sauce mixture in 9x9-
  inch casserole. Place noodles in rows on
  sauce and top with 1/2 the ricotta mixture,
  1/3 of remaining sauce, and 1/2 cup
  mozzarella cheese.
† Repeat layer using half of remaining
  spaghetti sauce. Top with remaining
  spaghetti sauce, 1/2 cup mozzarella cheese,
  and 1/4 cup Parmesan cheese.
† Cover and bake 45 minutes. Uncover and
  bake 15 minutes. Let stand 10 minutes
  before serving.

Paula Freeman's variation: Add 1/2 cup water, add 1/4 cup dry red wine, use 2 cups cottage cheese instead of ricotta, and use 3 cups mozzarella cheese.

MEDORA'S MESS

Yield: Two 2-quart casseroles
Medora Sheehan

21/2 pounds ground beef
    Seasoned salt flavor
    enhancer (optional)
1/4-1/2 teaspoon garlic salt
    Salt and pepper to taste
45 ounces tomato sauce
1   (8-ounce) package cream
    cheese
2   cups sour cream
1   bunch green onions, finely
    chopped
1   (12-ounce) package thin
    egg noodles, cooked
1   cup grated sharp cheddar
    cheese

† Preheat oven to 350°.
† Brown meat. Add seasonings and tomato
  sauce.
† Combine cheese, sour cream, and green
  onions.
† Butter two 2-quart casseroles and layer
  noodles, cheese and meat. Sprinkle with
  grated cheese.
† Bake 50 to 60 minutes.

BAKED SPAGHETTI

Yield: 8 to 10 servings
Marie Fisher

11/2-2 pounds lean ground
    beef or turkey
    Salt and pepper to taste
    Oregano to taste
1 (32-ounce) jar spaghetti
    sauce
1 pound spaghetti, cooked
    al dente
1 (24-ounce) carton low fat
    or fat-free cottage cheese
4 cups grated cheddar
    cheese, divided
    Parmesan cheese

† Preheat oven to 350°.
† Brown meat. Add salt, pepper and oregano.
   Drain and add spaghetti sauce.
† In 4-quart greased casserole, layer pasta,
   cottage cheese, meat sauce and grated
   cheese, making 2 or 3 layers.
† Sprinkle with Parmesan cheese and bake
   30 to 45 minutes until thoroughly heated.

CHICKEN WITH ARTICHOKES AND MUSHROOMS OVER PASTA

Yield: 6 servings
Marsha Rich

4 boneless, skinless chicken
    breast halves
1 can cream of celery soup
1/2 cup milk
1 (1-pound) can quartered
    artichokes, drained
4 ounces sliced mushrooms
1/4-1/2 teaspoon pepper
1 teaspoon basil
1 pound cooked pasta,
    (noodles, fettuccine),
    drained

† Spray a large skillet with nonstick cooking
   spray and cook chicken for 5 minutes each
   side over medium heat. Cover and cook
   5 more minutes.
† Mix soup and milk, and add with remaining
   ingredients to chicken, simmering until
   thickened, about 15 minutes.
† Serve over pasta.

CHICKEN AND PENNE

Yield: 4 servings
Andrea Reeves

1/2 cup extra virgin olive oil
1/4 cup balsamic vinegar
4   tablespoons sugar
2   tablespoons Grey Poupon
     Country Mustard
2   pinches cayenne pepper
3   cloves garlic, crushed
3   tablespoons water
6   boneless chicken breasts
1   pound penne pasta, cooked
     Parmesan cheese

† Combine first seven ingredients for marinade. Marinate chicken 1 to 2 hours. Broil or grill chicken and cut into pieces.
† Heat the marinade to boiling. Add chicken and toss with pasta. Serve with Parmesan cheese.

EASY CHICKEN TETRAZZINI

Yield: 8 to 10 servings
Ann Long

1   (3-4 pound) hen
1   pound spaghetti
2   large onions, chopped
2   medium stalks celery,
     chopped or 2 small bell
     peppers, chopped
1   (2-ounce) jar chopped
     pimientos
2   cans cream of
     mushroom soup
22/3 cups water
1   (41/2-ounce) jar
     mushrooms, drained
11/2 cups grated sharp
     cheese

† Boil chicken until tender. Drain, reserving two cups broth to cook with spaghetti.
† Preheat oven to 350°.
† Cook spaghetti in reserved broth. Drain.
† Bone and chop chicken into bite-size pieces.
† Combine remaining ingredients, except cheese, adding chicken.
† Place spaghetti in greased 9x13-inch casserole.
† Cover with sauce and cheese and bake for 40 minutes.

CRABMEAT AND ANGEL HAIR PASTA

Yield: 4 servings
Billie Nichols

1/4 cup chopped onion
1/4 cup chopped celery
1/4 cup sliced mushrooms
1/2 cup fat-free chicken broth, divided
1/2 can light cream of mushroom soup
1/2 cup nonfat sour cream
1/4 cup sherry (optional)
1/4 cup Parmesan cheese
8 ounces crabmeat
   Salt and pepper to taste
   Paprika to taste
1 pound angel hair pasta

† Preheat oven to 350°.
† Sauté onion, celery, and mushrooms in saucepan sprayed with nonstick cooking spray.
† Add 1/4 cup chicken broth and cook until vegetables are tender. Add remaining broth and soup to vegetables.
† Stir in remaining ingredients, except pasta. Pour into 2-quart casserole and bake 30 minutes.
† Cook pasta according to directions.
† Serve crabmeat over pasta.

HAM (OR CHICKEN) SURPRISE

Yield: 8 to 10 servings
Guerry Russell

8 ounces small or medium egg noodles
11/2 tablespoons vegetable oil
1 cup chopped celery
1 cup chopped green bell pepper
11/2 cups chopped onion
1 teaspoon dill
1 teaspoon thyme
1 teaspoon salt
2 teaspoons sugar
1/4 teaspoon chili powder
1/4 teaspoon pepper
1 (28-ounce) can tomatoes, chopped
3 tablespoons soy sauce
8 ounces sour cream
3 cups ham, or cooked chicken, cubed
   Grated cheddar cheese for garnish (optional)

† Preheat oven to 325°.
† Prepare noodles according to package directions. Drain.
† Sauté celery, green pepper and onion until soft. Sprinkle with seasonings.
† Blend tomatoes, soy sauce and sour cream into vegetables.
† Add ham or chicken and noodles. Pour into greased 9x13-inch casserole and bake 30 minutes.

PENNE CON BRIO

Yield: 8 to 10 servings
Ben Hutto

2   pounds penne rigate pasta, cooked al dente, divided
1   pound hot Italian sausages
2   medium onions, chopped
1   pound lean ground beef
1/2 teaspoon salt
8-10 drops Tabasco sauce
1/2 teaspoon minced garlic
3   pints tomato-based pasta sauce, divided
1   pound ricotta cheese
1   package frozen chopped spinach, thawed
3   cups grated mozzarella cheese

† Preheat oven to 325°.
† Cook pasta according to package directions.
† Cut sausage into small pieces and brown in frying pan. Remove to drain. Brown onions in sausage drippings. Remove to drain.
† Discard sausage drippings and brown ground beef, salt, Tabasco sauce and garlic. Drain.
† In large bowl, combine sausage, onions, beef and 2 pints pasta sauce.
† In 4-quart casserole, put 1/2 of pasta. Spoon meat sauce over pasta.
† Blend ricotta and spinach, spreading over pasta. Spread remaining pasta over ricotta.
† Drizzle remaining pasta sauce over pasta and top with mozzarella cheese. Bake 45 to 60 minutes.

Freezes well.

SHRIMP AND FETA CHEESE

Yield: 3 servings
Cynthia Gass

2   tablespoons olive oil
1   pound raw shrimp, peeled
1/8 teaspoon ground red pepper
2   cloves garlic, finely chopped or pressed
1   (1-pound) can diced tomatoes
1/4 cup dry white wine
3/4 teaspoon dried basil
1/2 teaspoon dried oregano
1/2 teaspoon salt
    Pepper to taste
4   ounces feta cheese, divided
1   (8-ounce) package vermicelli, cooked
    Fresh basil, chopped

† Heat olive oil in skillet, add shrimp and sprinkle with red pepper. Sauté until pink (1 to 2 minutes) and remove from pan.
† Sauté garlic, then tomatoes, wine and seasonings. Simmer uncovered 8 minutes.
† Add 3/4 of the crumbled feta cheese and simmer 2 to 3 minutes. Add shrimp and heat carefully so as not to overcook shrimp.
† Serve over vermicelli and top with remaining feta cheese and fresh basil.

This dish is best served immediately after preparation.

HOLLY'S SCALLOPS WITH PASTA

Yield: 4 servings
Ann Brewster Jones

1 cup minced parsley, divided
2 shallots, minced
1/2 stick butter
1/2 cup white wine
1 pound bay scallops
3/4 cup heavy cream
3/4 cup milk
1 cup grated Romano or Parmesan cheese
Salt and pepper to taste
Nutmeg to taste
1 (12-ounce) package spinach fettuccine, cooked

† Sauté 1/2 cup parsley and shallots in butter. Add wine and reduce liquid by half on low heat.
† Cut large scallops in half lengthwise and stir into wine mixture. Add cream and milk, stirring well. Simmer 5 to 10 minutes.
† Remove from heat and stir in cheese and rest of parsley, salt and pepper and nutmeg to taste.
† Serve over fettuccine.

HERBED SHRIMP AND THREE CHEESE PASTA CASSEROLE

Yield: 12 servings
Susan Hamilton

2 eggs
1 cup evaporated milk
1 cup plain yogurt
8 ounces feta cheese, crumbled
2 cup grated Swiss cheese
1/2 cup chopped fresh parsley
1 teaspoon dried basil
1 teaspoon oregano
4 cloves garlic, minced
1/2 pound angel hair pasta, cooked
1 (16-ounce) jar mild salsa
1 pound medium-size raw shrimp, peeled
2 cups grated mozzarella cheese

† Preheat oven to 350°.
† Spray 2-quart casserole with nonstick cooking spray.
† Blend first nine ingredients.
† Spread half of pasta in casserole. Cover with salsa. Add half of shrimp.
† Spread remaining pasta over shrimp. Pour egg mixture over pasta. Sprinkle with remaining shrimp and top with mozzarella cheese.
† Bake 30 minutes. Remove and let stand 10 minutes.

Use 12 ounces of salsa to make casserole more firm.

SHRIMP AND SUN-DRIED TOMATO PESTO OVER LEMON FETTUCCINE

Yield: 4 to 6 servings
Marsha Rich

1/2 pound fresh egg fettuccine
1/2 pound fresh lemon fettuccine
3-4 cloves garlic, minced
2 teaspoons extra virgin olive oil
1 1/2 pounds peeled medium-size shrimp
1/2 cup dry white wine
1 cup sun-dried tomato pesto
1/4 cup freshly grated Parmesan cheese

† Cook fettuccine according to directions.
† Sauté garlic in olive oil in large skillet over medium heat. Add shrimp and cook, stirring constantly, about 1 minute.
† Add wine and continue cooking until shrimp turns pink. Stir in tomato pesto.
† Serve over fettuccine and sprinkle with cheese.

LITE 'N EASY SHRIMP AND LINGUINI

Yield: 4 servings
Genie Hufham

5 tablespoons olive oil, divided
1 medium onion, thinly sliced
2 cloves garlic, pressed
1 pound raw shrimp, peeled
1/2 cup dry white wine
8 mushrooms, sliced
1 carrot, julienned
1 medium zucchini, halved, in 1/2-inch slices
1 cup frozen peas
6-8 Chinese snow peas
1 tomato, cubed
2 tablespoons cornstarch
1 tablespoon flour
1 cup chicken broth
1/2 cup milk or half-and-half
1 teaspoon basil
Salt and pepper to taste
1 (8-ounce) package linguini, cooked
Parsley flakes and chopped scallion tops for garnish

† In large skillet, heat 2 tablespoons olive oil and sauté onion, garlic and shrimp until shrimp turns pink, stirring constantly. Remove to warming plate.
† In same skillet, heat 2 tablespoons olive oil and sauté vegetables until crunchy tender.
† Combine cornstarch and flour to make paste. Gradually add chicken broth and milk to cornstarch. (Add water if sauce becomes too thick). Add shrimp to thoroughly heat. Stir in spices to taste.
† Toss 1 tablespoon olive oil with hot linguini.
† Top with shrimp and garnish.

BREAKFAST CASSEROLE

Yield: 6 servings
Marsha Rich

3 cups French bread, torn in bite-size pieces
3/4 cup diced ham
2 tablespoons diced red bell pepper
1 tablespoon chopped green onion
1 cup grated sharp cheddar cheese
1 1/3 cups skim milk
4 eggs, slightly beaten
1/2 teaspoon dry mustard
1/4 teaspoon salt
1/4 teaspoon pepper

† Lightly grease 3-quart casserole. Place bread on bottom. Layer ham, pepper, onion and cheese.
† Combine milk, eggs, mustard, salt and pepper. Pour over ham. Cover and refrigerate 8 hours.
† Preheat oven to 350°.
† Bake 35 to 40 minutes.

BRUNCH DISH

Yield: 8 servings
Mary Redding

12 slices Canadian bacon
12 (3/4-ounce) slices Swiss cheese
12 eggs
2 cups cream
1/4-1/2 cup Parmesan cheese

† Preheat oven to 450°.
† Line 9x13-inch casserole with bacon. Add layer of cheese.
† Break eggs over all being careful not to break yolks. Drizzle cream over whites until yolks peek through. Bake 10 minutes.
† Remove and sprinkle with cheese. Return to oven and bake 10 minutes longer. Cut into squares and serve immediately.

BRUNCH IN A DISH

Yield: 8 servings
Sara Lowe

1 pound sausage, hot or regular
1 (1-pound) package frozen hash-brown potatoes, thawed
6 eggs, beaten
1 1/2 cups milk
Salt and pepper to taste
1 cup grated cheddar cheese

† Preheat oven to 350°.
† Brown sausage and drain. Layer sausage and potatoes in lightly greased 9x13-inch casserole.
† Combine eggs, milk, salt and pepper, and pour over layer. Sprinkle with cheese.
† Bake covered 45 minutes, uncover and bake 15 minutes or until set.

CHILI EGG PUFF

Yield: 10 to 12 servings
Sybil Gray

10 eggs
1/2 cup flour
1 teaspoon baking powder
1/2 teaspoon salt
2 cups cottage cheese
4 cups grated Monterey
Jack cheese
1 stick butter, melted
2 (4-ounce) cans diced
green chili peppers

† Preheat oven to 350°.
† Beat eggs until light with mixer. Add
other ingredients, except chili peppers,
stirring until smooth.
† Blend in chilies. Pour into greased 9x13-
inch casserole and bake 35 minutes.

FOOL-PROOF CHEESE SOUFFLÉ

Yield: 6 servings
Christ Church Cooks I

10 slices soft bread
1/3 cup butter, softened
2 cups grated cheese
3 cups milk
4 eggs, beaten
1 1/3 teaspoon salt
1/3 teaspoon dry mustard

† Remove crust from bread and cut each
into 4 triangles. Spread with butter and
place one layer in 2-quart casserole.
Sprinkle with 1 cup cheese.
† Combine milk, eggs, salt and mustard.
Pour half over bread and cheese.
† Layer remaining bread and cheese and
pour remaining liquid over all. Refrigerate
24 hours.
† Preheat oven to 325°.
† Bake 45 minutes.

SALSA EGG PUFFS

Yield: 6 servings
Missy Wooten

1-1 1/4 cups chopped
country ham
1/2 cup grated cheddar, Colby
or Monterey Jack cheese
6 tablespoons mild chunky
salsa
6-8 eggs

† Preheat oven to 350°.
† Spray muffin pans with nonstick cooking
spray.
† Cover each muffin cup bottom with
country ham.
† Sprinkle with cheese. Spoon one tablespoon
salsa over cheese.
† Beat eggs and divide between muffin cups.
† Bake 15 minutes.

QUICHE LORRAINE

Yield: one pie
Christ Church Cooks I

1   (9-inch) pie shell
6   slices crisp bacon, crumbled
1   small onion, thinly sliced
    (optional)
1 1/2 cups grated Swiss cheese
3   eggs, beaten
1 1/4 cups light cream or
    half-and-half
1/2 teaspoon salt
    Pinch of nutmeg
    Pinch of sugar
    Dash of pepper

† Preheat oven to 425°.
† Sprinkle bacon, onions and cheese in pie shell.
† Combine eggs, cream and seasonings. Pour over cheese.
† Bake 15 minutes.
† Reduce heat to 325° and bake 45 minutes.
† Remove and let sit 5 minutes.

SPINACH QUICHE BY DAD

Yield: one pie
Jane Showalter

1   (9-inch) pie shell
1   small onion, chopped
2   tablespoons butter or
    margarine, melted
1   package frozen creamed
    spinach, thawed
2   tablespoons flour
1   teaspoon salt
1/4 teaspoon pepper
2   eggs, beaten
1   cup half-and-half
2   tablespoons Parmesan
    cheese
1/4 cup grated Swiss cheese

† Preheat oven to 400°.
† Bake pie shell for 5 minutes and set aside.
† Sauté onion in butter. Add spinach, cooking 2 minutes. Add flour and salt/pepper.
† Combine eggs, half-and-half, cheese and stir in spinach.
† Pour into pie shell and bake 35 minutes.

Notes:

Meat, Poultry, And Seafood

Service To Those Near And Dear

In Order To Serve

VI. Service To Those Near And Dear

Lord, make the old tolerant
the young sympathetic,
the great humble,
the busy patient.
Make rich people understanding,
strong people gentle,
those who are weak prayerful.
Make the religious lovable,
happy folk thoughtful,
the clever kindly,
the bad good,
the good pleasant.
And, dear Lord, make me what I ought to be.

Ministry, like charity, begins at home. Our homes and families are our first church, where we learn to serve one another and give of ourselves for the common good. Our life at home is a microcosm of our life in the macrocosm of the great world. What Plato called *techne tou biou*, the craft of life, is learned not in school or the office but in the sacred environment of our homes as we learn to listen, to be responsible, and to guard one another's solitude.

The best part of mealtime is often the conversation at table. It is a time to share all of life and listen to our stories. The art of listening is a primary way in which we minister to one another. Listening is a gift we give, offering an open space in which another can share wonder, feelings, concerns, anger, joy with complete acceptance. Listening is unconditional love in action.

Home is where we begin to discover that my life depends on others and other lives on me. Our age is tempted to want to have everything "my way." Family duties and disciplines teach us that it is the common good which matters and freedom is empty without responsibility. Home and table are where we can be fully ourselves and savor not just food but one another.

To maintain a joyful family requires much from both
parents and the children. . Each member of the family
has to become, in a special way, the servant of the others.
POPE JOHN PAUL II (b.1920)

THE REVEREND HENRY NUTT PARSLEY, JR., RECTOR

PARKER'S EASTERN NORTH CAROLINA BARBECUE WITH SAUCE

Yield: 8 generous sandwiches
Sis Cranz

BARBECUE SAUCE:
1   stick butter
1   cup cider vinegar
1   large or 4 small sour
     pickles, minced
1   tablespoon minced or
     grated onion
2   tablespoons Worcestershire
     sauce
1   tablespoon lemon juice
1   tablespoon molasses

† Combine ingredients and heat over low heat until butter melts. Stir frequently. Use as a basting sauce while pork is cooking.

PORK BARBECUE:
1   (3-4 pound) boneless
     pork roast
1   teaspoon cayenne pepper
     or red pepper flakes
1   tablespoon ground black
     pepper
2   teaspoons salt
1/2 cup barbecue sauce
4   slices bacon

† Preheat oven to 250°.
† Rub roast with 1/2 cup barbecue sauce. Combine peppers and salt. Rub on roast.
† Lay bacon strips on roast. Place in covered roasting pan and bake 8 hours. Baste often with sauce.
† When done, cool. Remove bacon and any fat. Chop meat into small pieces. Season with barbecue sauce.

BAKED HAM

Yield: 12 to 15 servings
Becky Parsley

1   (18-20 pound) ham, uncooked
3-4 cloves garlic, sliced
1   (16-ounce) can peach juice or
1   (12-ounce) can Classic Coke
1/2 cup packed light brown sugar
2-3 tablespoons mustard

† Preheat oven to 325°.
† Trim skin and most of fat from ham. Insert garlic pieces in ham.
† Place in roasting pan and cover with foil. Bake 20 minutes per pound, basting with peach juice or coke.
† Blend brown sugar and mustard. Remove ham from oven 30 minutes before it is done and spread with mixture. Return ham to oven and continue baking, uncovered, until browned on top. Let sit 20 to 30 minutes before serving.

HAM LOAF

Yield: 8 servings
Helen Wall

1 1/2 pounds smoked ham
3/4 pound fresh pork
1 can tomato soup
3 eggs, beaten
1 cup soft bread crumbs
1 bell pepper, chopped
1/4 teaspoon salt
1/4 teaspoon paprika

† Preheat oven to 350°.
† Combine all ingredients and place in loaf pan. Bake 60 minutes.

Marie Palmer's variation: Use 1/2 cup milk instead of soup. Baste loaf frequently with mixture of 1/3 cup sugar, 1/3 cup water, 1 cup brown sugar, and 1 teaspoon ground mustard.

CURRIED APRICOT PORK CHOPS

Yield: 4 servings
Lisa Seaton

4 (3/4-inch thick) pork chops
1 egg, beaten
3/4 cup dried bread crumbs
1/4 cup vegetable oil
1 (16-ounce) can apricot halves in light syrup
2 tablespoons brown sugar
1/2 teaspoon curry powder
1 tablespoon butter

† Preheat oven to 350°.
† Dip pork chops in egg and dredge in bread crumbs. Brown chops in hot oil and place in 2-quart casserole.
† Drain apricots and combine juice with brown sugar and curry powder in small saucepan, heating until sugar is dissolved. Pour over chops.
† Place apricots around chops and dot with butter. Bake for 25 minutes or until tender.

PORK CHOPS ST. JOHN

Yield: 4 servings
Jane Dowd

4 lean pork chops
3 tablespoons Madeira
1/3 cup sour cream
Salt and pepper to taste

† Brown chops in skillet over high heat. Cook until tender, turning often. Remove from pan. Pour off excess fat.
† Add wine and sour cream, blending well. Return chops to pan, season and simmer 5 to 10 minutes.

PORK CHOP CASSEROLE

Yield: 4 servings
Sue Head

3/4 cup rice
4 lean center-cut pork chops
1 onion, sliced
1 tomato, sliced
1 bell pepper, sliced into rings
1 can beef bouillon

† Preheat oven to 375°.
† Place rice in bottom of 2-quart casserole.
† Trim fat from pork chops. Brown in skillet and arrange on top of rice.
† Place onion, tomato, and pepper ring on top of each chop.
† Pour can of bouillon over chops. Cover and bake 1 hour. Add water if needed.

CREOLE GINGER PORK CUBES

Yield: 8 to 10 servings
Chef Ed Steedman, Marais

SAUCE:
1/3 cup grated horseradish
1/3 cup lime juice
1/3 cup mayonnaise
1/2 cup plain yogurt
 Salt and white pepper
 to taste

† Blend horseradish, lime juice, mayonnaise, yogurt, salt and pepper in blender or food processor for 1 minute. Chill overnight.

PORK:
1 1/2 pounds lean boneless pork, cut into 1-inch cubes
3 tablespoons soy sauce
1 clove garlic, crushed
1/2 teaspoon freshly ground pepper
1/2 teaspoon sugar
1 teaspoon minced gingerroot
1 tablespoon peanut oil

† Mix pork with soy sauce, garlic, pepper, sugar, gingerroot and peanut oil. Cover and marinate for 2 to 4 hours, turning meat frequently.
† Preheat oven to 325°.
† Spread pork in single layer on baking sheet and bake for 1 hour, turning several times.
† Serve with sauce.

SHANGHAI PORK MARINADE

Yield: 2 cups
Elizabeth Jones

1   cup orange marmalade
1/2 cup water
1/2 cup soy sauce
1   clove garlic, minced
1   teaspoon ground ginger
    Dash of hot pepper sauce

† Blend all ingredients.
† Marinate pork chops in sauce at least 6 hours, turning every 2 hours.

PORK PAPRIKASH

Yield: 4 to 6 servings
Lisa Seaton

1/4 cup unsalted butter
2   tablespoons vegetable oil
1   (1-pound) pork tenderloin, in bite-size pieces
1   medium-size red bell pepper, in 1/4-inch strips
1   medium onion, finely chopped
1/2 pound wide egg noodles
2   tablespoons hot or sweet paprika
2   teaspoons caraway seeds
1/2 cup dry white wine
2   tablespoons lemon juice
1   cup sour cream
1   tablespoon tomato paste
    Salt and white pepper to taste

† Melt butter and oil in large skillet over medium heat. Add pork, bell pepper and onion. Cook until pork is browned and vegetables are tender.
† Cook noodles in boiling salted water.
† Add paprika and caraway seeds to pork and cook 1 minute. Add wine and lemon juice, bringing to a boil. Reduce heat and simmer 5 minutes.
† Blend in sour cream and tomato paste. Reduce heat and simmer 2 to 3 minutes.
† Adjust seasonings, serve over noodles.

146

PORK LOIN ROAST WITH BBQ SAUCE

Yield: 8 to 10 servings
Anne Neal

1/2 teaspoon salt
1/2 teaspoon garlic salt
21/2 teaspoons chili powder, divided
1   (4-pound) pork loin roast, boned and rolled or tied
1   cup apple jelly
1   cup ketchup
2   tablespoons vinegar

† Preheat oven to 350°.
† Combine salt, garlic salt and 1/2 teaspoon chili powder and rub into roast.
† Bake for 30 minutes per pound or until temperature reaches 155° to 160°.
† 30 minutes before roast is done, combine jelly, ketchup, vinegar and remaining chili powder. Boil for 2 minutes and baste roast. Serve with remaining sauce.

POLYNESIAN PORK

Yield: 4 to 6 servings
Nan Allison

1   (11/2-pound) pork tenderloin
     Salt and pepper to taste
     Rosemary to taste
1/4 cup soy sauce
1/4 cup ketchup
1/8 cup honey
1   clove garlic, crushed

† Preheat oven to 350°.
† Place meat on rack in shallow pan and sprinkle with seasonings.
† Combine remaining ingredients and baste pork frequently. Bake 30 to 45 minutes or until tender.

GRILLED PORK TENDERLOINS

Yield: 12 to 16 servings
Anne Neal

1/2 cup teriyaki sauce
1/2 cup soy sauce
3   tablespoons brown sugar
2   green onions, chopped
1   clove garlic, pressed
1   tablespoon sesame seeds
1/2 teaspoon ground ginger
1/2 teaspoon pepper
1   tablespoon vegetable oil
41/2 pounds pork tenderloins

† Combine all ingredients, except pork, in shallow dish. Add pork and marinate covered and refrigerated 2 to 4 hours.
† Cook tenderloins, covered with grill lid, over medium hot coals (350° to 400°) 20 minutes, turning once.

EASY RED BEANS AND RICE

Yield: 8 servings
Robin Riggins

6   ounces smoked sausage,
     sliced
1   cup chopped onion
3/4 cup chopped bell pepper
1   clove garlic, minced
3   (16-ounce) cans red beans,
     drained
1   (14 1/2-ounce) can stewed
     tomatoes, undrained and
     chopped
1 1/2 cups water
1   (6-ounce) can tomato paste
1/4 teaspoon dried oregano
1/4 teaspoon dried thyme
4   cups cooked long-grain rice

† Coat Dutch oven with nonstick cooking
  spray and heat over medium heat. Add
  sausage, onion, bell pepper and garlic.
  Sauté until tender.
† Stir in beans and remaining ingredients,
  except rice. Bring to a boil. Cover,
  reduce heat and simmer 20 minutes.
† Serve over rice.

RED BEANS OVER RICE

Yield: 16 servings
Suzie Lowe

1   ham hock
2   (1-pound) packages red
     kidney beans
     Salt and pepper to taste
2   bay leaves
1   (14 1/2-ounce) can beef
     broth or bouillon
2   large onions, chopped
5   stalks celery, chopped
1/4 cup bacon drippings
1   tablespoon flour
1   bell pepper, chopped
1   (4-ounce) can tomato purée
1   tablespoon prepared
     horseradish
1   teaspoon thyme
1   teaspoon sage
1   teaspoon cumin
2   (14-ounce) packages Polish
     sausage, sliced
     cooked rice

† Place ham hock and washed beans in
  large pot and cover with water. Season
  with salt and pepper, bay leaves and beef
  broth. Cook on low heat for 5 hours,
  stirring frequently.
† Sauté onions and celery in bacon drippings
  until limp. Stir in remaining ingredients
  except sausage. Add to beans, cooking
  another hour until thick.
† Add sausage for last 30 minutes of cooking.
† Serve over rice.

148

PIZZA BREAD

Yield: 4 to 6 servings
Beth Barnes
Margaretta Leary

1   (1-pound) loaf frozen bread
    dough
    Egg wash (egg beaten with
    small amount of water)
    Oregano or other herb
    to taste
1   pound meat (pepperoni,
    salami, sausage)
1   pound cheese (mozzarella,
    provolone, cheddar), sliced
    or cubed

† Thaw bread and let rise according to
  package directions. Roll into large circle
  on floured surface, approximately 16
  inches in diameter. Brush surface lightly
  with egg wash. Sprinkle with oregano.
† Preheat oven to 350°.
† Slice or cube meat. If using sausage, brown
  and crumble. Spread meat and cheeses
  over entire surface leaving one-inch border.
† Carefully roll up jelly roll fashion. Stretch
  and seal edges. Brush outside with egg
  wash. Bake until bread is done, about 30
  minutes. It will sound hollow when
  thumped.

PEPPERONI SPINACH PIE

Yield: 6 to 8 servings
Jackie Plott

1   package frozen chopped
    spinach, thawed and drained
2   cups ricotta cheese
1/2 cup grated Swiss cheese
1/2 cup Parmesan cheese
1/2 pound mushrooms, chopped
1/4 pound pepperoni, thinly sliced
1/4 cup chopped onion
2   teaspoons mustard
1/2 teaspoon oregano
1/4 teaspoon salt
    Pepper to taste
1   egg, beaten
1   (9-inch) unbaked 2-crust pie
    shell, not deep dish

SAUCE:
1   (15-ounce) can tomato sauce
1/2 teaspoon garlic salt
    Pepper to taste
1   tablespoon Italian seasoning

† Preheat oven to 425°.
† Blend all ingredients, except egg, mixing
  well.
† Stir in egg. Pour into pie crust and cover
  with other crust.
† Seal and bake 25 minutes.

† Combine ingredients and heat. Serve
  with pie.

BEEF TENDERLOIN

Yield: 6 to 8 servings
Anne Tomlinson

1 (4-6 pound) beef tenderloin
Vinegar
Salt and Pepper

† Preheat oven to 500°.
† Rub fillet with small amount of vinegar to prevent splattering. Salt and pepper to taste.
† Put fillet in shallow roasting pan and cook 7 minutes.
† Without opening door, reduce heat to 350° and cook 25 minutes for rare roast. Let stand 15 minutes.

BEEF TENDERLOIN WITH RED WINE SAUCE

Yield: 4 servings
Chef John Alston, Alston's

4 (4-6 ounces) beef tenderloin steaks
Salt and pepper to taste
1 tablespoon oil
3 tablespoons shallots or onions, minced
1/2 cup dry red wine
4 tablespoons butter
2 tablespoons fresh chives or parsley, finely chopped

† Season beef with salt and pepper.
† Heat oil in pan and sauté steaks on medium heat until desired doneness. Remove from pan and keep warm.
† Pour off excess oil. Add shallots and cook slowly 1 to 3 minutes.
† Pour wine into the pan and bring to a boil. Deglaze by rapidly scraping the solids from the bottom of the pan and reducing liquid by one-half.
† Turn off heat, beat in butter a little at a time until incorporated. Add salt, pepper and parsley.

GRILLED LONDON BROIL

Yield: 6 to 8 servings
Sue Head

1 (2-3 pound) London Broil
Uncle Rich's Beef Marinade
or Grainy Mustard Marinade
or Lindy's London Broil
Marinade

See page 155 for marinade recipes.

† Prepare desired marinade as directed.
† Cover steak with marinade and refrigerate for at least 8 hours, turning steak often. Allow to stand at room temperature in marinade for 30 minutes before cooking.
† Remove steak from marinade and grill over medium coals (350°-400°) for 8 to 10 minutes on each side or until desired degree of doneness, basting occasionally with marinade.
† Remove from grill and let stand 5 to 10 minutes. Slice thinly across the grain.

150

STUFFED LONDON BROIL

Yield: 8 to 10 servings
Trudy Gilbert

1	(2 to 3-inch thick) London broil
1/4	pound fresh mushrooms, sliced
1	tablespoon butter, melted
2	tablespoons crumbled blue cheese
1	clove garlic, crushed
1/2-1	teaspoon cracked black pepper

† Cut pocket lengthwise into London broil.
† Sauté mushrooms in butter. Blend in remaining ingredients. Stir until melted and thickened.
† Spoon into steak and close with a skewer.
† Broil or grill 7 to 10 minutes until desired doneness.

Meat may be marinated before grilling.

HERBED POT ROAST

Yield: 6 to 8 servings
Sue Hardwick

1	(4 1/2-pound) lean boneless rump roast
1/2	cup burgundy or other dry wine
1/2	cup tomato sauce
1/4	cup apple cider vinegar or red wine vinegar
1	tablespoon mustard
1	teaspoon dried thyme
1/4	teaspoon dried oregano
1/4	teaspoon dried rosemary
2	shallots, minced
1	bay leaf

† Place roast in large zip-lock bag.
† Combine remaining ingredients and add to bag. Marinate 6 to 8 hours.
† Transfer to Dutch oven and bake at 350° for 2 1/2 to 3 hours, basting often.

Carrots and potatoes may be added 1 1/2 hours before roast is done.

BEN'S BEEF OR LAMB STEW

Yield: 8 to 10 servings
Ben Hutto

5 tablespoons flour, divided
1 teaspoon minced garlic
1 tablespoon Worcestershire
  sauce
  Freshly ground black pepper
  to taste
  Hot pepper sauce
3 pounds lean stew beef, cut
  into bite-size pieces
1 large baking potato
2 medium onions
1 pound carrots
2 medium zucchini
  Salt
1/2 pound mushrooms, sliced
1 (101/2-ounce) can beef
  broth
1 cup red or white wine
8-10 cups cooked rice

† Preheat oven to 350°.
† Sprinkle three tablespoons flour, garlic, Worcestershire sauce, black pepper, and 6 to 10 drops of hot sauce over beef. Work flour into meat and put in large roaster.
† Cut potato, onions, carrots, and zucchini into bite-size chunks and add with salt to meat. Sprinkle mushrooms on top.
† Pour broth and wine over meat and cover. Bake 2 hours.
† Mix two tablespoons flour with 1/4 cup cold water and add to roaster. Cover and cook 1 hour. Serve over hot rice.

Lamb may also be used. For curried stew, add one tablespoon curry powder over meat before baking and another tablespoon curry powder to flour and water before last hour of cooking.

ITALIAN BARLEY STEW

Yield: 6 servings
Elaine Thigpen

11/2 pounds stew beef, cubed
1 (1-pound) can tomatoes
11/2 cups sliced carrots
1 (6-ounce) can tomato paste
1/2 cup sliced celery
1/2 cup pearl barley
1/2 cup water
1/2 cup chopped onion
2 teaspoons seasoned salt
1 teaspoon basil
1/2 teaspoon thyme
1/8 teaspoon pepper
3/4 cup grated Swiss cheese

† Combine all ingredients, except cheese, in crock pot. Simmer 8 hours.
† Last 5 minutes, sprinkle cheese on top.

PAPRIKA BEEF

Yield: 4 servings
Joanna Roberts

1 pound lean beef, cubed
1/2 cup flour
1/4 teaspoon salt
1/8 teaspoon pepper
1/2 pound mushrooms, sliced
1 (1.1-ounce) envelope onion
   soup mix
2 tablespoons paprika
11/2 cups water
1/2 cup sour cream

† Preheat oven to 350°.
† Shake beef in a bag with flour, salt and pepper. Place in 2-quart casserole with mushrooms and onion soup.
† Sprinkle with paprika and add water. Bake covered for 1 hour.
† Just before serving, add sour cream.
† Serve over noodles or rice.

CHEESEBURGER PIE

Yield: 4 to 6 servings
Anita Griffin

1 pound ground beef
1 small onion, chopped
   (optional)
1 (6-ounce) can tomato paste
1 teaspoon salt
1/2 teaspoon Italian seasoning
1/2 teaspoon pepper
1 (8-ounce) can crescent rolls
1 (8-ounce) package grated
   mozzarella cheese

† Preheat oven to 350°.
† Brown meat and onions. Add remaining ingredients, except rolls and cheese. Simmer 10 minutes.
† Line pie plate with rolls and top with meat mixture and cheese.
† Bake 25 to 30 minutes.

HAMBURGER CORNBREAD PIE

Yield: 6 servings
Kate Buckfelder

1 pound ground beef
1/2 cup chopped onion
3/4 teaspoon salt
2 teaspoons chili powder
1 tablespoon Worcestershire
   sauce
1 (16-ounce) can stewed
   tomatoes
1 (16-ounce) can kidney beans,
   drained
1 (8.5-ounce) package cornbread
   mix

† Preheat oven to 400°.
† Brown beef and onion in skillet. Drain.
† Add salt, chili powder, Worcestershire sauce and tomatoes. Simmer 10 minutes.
† Stir in beans. Pour into greased 9x9-inch baking dish.
† Prepare cornbread according to directions and spread over top of beef.
† Bake 20 minutes.

WOMACK'S MEATLOAF

Yield: 4 loaves
Dot Osher

4   pounds lean ground beef
2   onions, chopped
3   bell peppers, chopped
1   cup Italian-style bread crumbs
1   (18-ounce) jar barbecue sauce, divided
1/4 cup ketchup
3   eggs, lightly beaten
2   (5-ounce) cans evaporated milk
    Salt and pepper to taste

† Preheat oven to 350°.
† Combine meat with all ingredients, reserving 1/2 cup barbecue sauce.
† Form into four loaves and cover with remaining barbecue sauce. Bake 50 to 60 minutes.

MEATLOAF

Yield: 6 servings
Elizabeth Jones

1   pound lean ground beef
1   cup Bloody Mary mix
1/2 cup oatmeal
1/4 cup egg substitute or
    1 egg, beaten
1   small onion, chopped
1   teaspoon salt
1/2 teaspoon pepper
1   tablespoon Worcestershire sauce

† Preheat oven to 350°.
† Combine ingredients and pour into loaf pan. Bake 1 hour.

HENRY BAIN SAUCE

Yield: About 7 cups
Beth Barnes

1   (6-ounce) jar Major Grey's chutney
1/2 (6-ounce) jar pickled walnuts (optional)
1   (14-ounce) bottle ketchup
1   (10-ounce) bottle A-1 steak sauce
1   (10-ounce) bottle Worcestershire sauce
1   (12-ounce) bottle chili sauce
    Tabasco sauce to taste

† Combine ingredients in blender.
† Store in sterilized jars.

154

UNCLE RICH'S BEEF MARINADE

Yield: 1 cup
Robin McCoy

1/2   cup red wine
1/4   cup vegetable oil
1/8   cup soy sauce
1/8   cup Worcestershire
      sauce

† Combine all ingredients.
† Pour over meat and marinate at least
  8 hours.

GRAINY MUSTARD MARINADE

Yield: Approximately 1 2 cup
Sue Head

3   tablespoons country-style
    Dijon mustard
2   tablespoons olive oil
2   tablespoons fresh lemon
    or lime juice
1   tablespoon reduced-sodium
    soy sauce
2   cloves garlic, crushed
1   tablespoon peeled and finely
    chopped fresh ginger or 1
    teaspoon ground ginger
1/2 teaspoon freshly ground
    pepper

† Combine ingredients and beat well to
  blend.
† Pour over meat and marinate at least
  8 hours.

LINDY'S LONDON BROIL MARINADE

Yield: 1 cup
Sue Head

1   cup soy sauce
1   small onion, minced
1   teaspoon lemon-pepper
1/2 teaspoon garlic powder
2   teaspoons ground ginger
3   thin slices lemon

† Combine all ingredients in saucepan and
  bring to a boil.
† Pour over beef and marinate at least
  8 hours.

155

VEAL NORMANDE

Yield: 4 servings
Chef Ed Steedman, Marais

1-2 pounds veal tenderloin
2 tablespoons peanut oil
Salt and white pepper to taste
3 Granny Smith apples, cored and diced
1 small carrot, chopped
1 medium onion, chopped
1 stalk celery, chopped
3 tablespoons Calvados brandy
4 cups apple cider
1/2 teaspoon fresh thyme
1 bay leaf
3/4 cup crème fraîche or heavy cream
2 tablespoons unsalted butter

† Clean veal tenderloins well, removing all tendon. Cut into 4 portions, retaining all scraps.

† Season veal lightly with salt and pepper. In skillet, heat oil on medium high heat and sauté veal and scraps until nicely browned. Remove veal portions.

† Continue cooking veal scraps until well browned. Do not burn. Remove scraps and set aside. Pour off excess oil and discard.

† Reheat skillet to medium heat and add apples, stirring occasionally. Cook 2 minutes and add other vegetables, cooking until lightly browned. Deglaze with Calvados (see Note) and add cider, thyme, bay leaf, a pinch of salt and veal scraps. Simmer approximately 20 to 30 minutes, skimming off any excess fat until liquid is reduced by one-half.

† Add crème fraîche and reduce liquid to consistency of very thin gravy. Strain solids through fine sieve, retaining only liquid. Return liquid and veal portions with any meat juices to pan and simmer 20 minutes or until veal is desired degree of doneness. Remove veal to warm serving plates.

† Reduce cooking liquid until it evenly coats a spoon. Bring to a boil and quickly whisk in butter. Season with salt and pepper. Pour sauce over veal and serve.

To deglaze, add brandy to skillet, stirring and scraping the solidified juices from bottom and sides.

FAVORITE VEAL PARMESAN

Yield: 4 servings
Mary Anne Thomas

1 pound (about 5 pieces) veal scaloppine
3 tablespoons margarine
1/4 cup Parmesan cheese
freshly ground pepper to taste
1/4 cup herb-seasoned stuffing mix
1 egg, beaten
1 teaspoon oregano
1 (14-ounce) jar tomato and basil pasta sauce
4 (1-ounce) slices mozzarella cheese
1 pound angel hair pasta, cooked

† Preheat oven to 400°.
† Melt margarine in baking dish until it begins to brown.
† Combine Parmesan cheese, pepper and stuffing mix. Dip veal in egg, then in cheese-stuffing mix. Coat each piece well.
† Place in dish and bake 15 minutes. Turn and bake 10 minutes or until browned.
† Combine oregano and tomato sauce. Pour over meat. Top with mozzarella cheese and return to oven until cheese begins to brown.
† Serve veal in pasta shaped like a nest.

TIFFANY'S LEG OF LAMB

Yield: 8 servings
Charlotte Ferebee

1 leg of lamb
1 medium onion, quartered
1 clove garlic, slivered
1 stick butter, melted
11/2-2 tablespoons flour
Salt and pepper to taste
1 stalk celery with leaves
Water

† Preheat oven to 325°.
† Rub lamb with onion wedge. Cut slits in top and insert garlic slivers.
† Combine butter, flour, salt and pepper into a paste. (Thicken paste with additional flour if too thin). Cover top of lamb with paste.
† Put in shallow pan with onion, celery and 1/2-inch of water. Baste while cooking.
† Cook 35 minutes per pound.

157

ROAST RACK OF LAMB

Yield: 1 rack of lamb
Chef John Alston, Alston's

1   rack of lamb
    Dijon mustard to taste
2   cups stale bread crumbs
3   cloves garlic, minced
1 1/2 bunches parsley, trimmed
8   sprigs fresh thyme
    Salt and pepper to taste
3   tablespoons olive oil, divided
1   tablespoon butter

† Preheat oven to 450°.
† Blend bread crumbs, garlic, parsley, thyme and salt in food processor until well chopped. Add 1 tablespoon oil and 1 tablespoon butter to bind.
† Season lamb with salt and pepper. Heat 2 tablespoons oil in pan over medium heat. Place rack, fat side down, and brown.
† Turn rack over and place in oven 8 to 10 minutes.
† Remove lamb from oven. Brush with mustard and pack with seasoned bread crumbs. Place in oven for an additional 3 to 5 minutes.

LAMB PATTIES WITH MINTED ONION MARMALADE

Yield: 3 to 4 servings
Janie Sellers

MARMALADE:
3/4 pound onion, very thinly sliced
2   tablespoons unsalted butter
    Salt and pepper to taste
1   tablespoon sugar
2   tablespoons white wine vinegar
1/2 teaspoon minced fresh mint or 1/4 teaspoon dried
1/4 cup water

† Cook onion in butter over medium heat. Add salt and pepper, stirring until onions are softened.
† Add sugar and cook until golden. Simmer with vinegar and mint until most of liquid is evaporated.
† Blend in water and simmer until slightly thickened but still moist. Keep marmalade warm and covered.

PATTIES:
1   pound ground lamb

† Shape lamb into seasoned patties with salt and pepper. Cook covered on grill or in skillet. Turn once after 6 minutes or until preferred doneness.
† Serve with warm marmalade.

AUTUMN CHICKEN

Yield: 4 to 6 servings
June "JR" Roberts

1   (2 1/2-3-pound) fryer, cut up,
    or favorite chicken parts
1/2 cup flour
1/2 teaspoon nutmeg
1   teaspoon seasoned salt
1/2 teaspoon paprika
1   stick butter
1   large onion, thinly sliced
1   bell pepper, thinly sliced
2   cooking apples, cored and
    quartered
2   tablespoons brown sugar
    (optional)
1 1/2 cups apple cider

† Coat chicken in flour to which nutmeg,
  salt and paprika have been added. Sauté
  chicken in butter until browned. Remove
  from pan.
† Sauté onion and pepper strips until tender.
  Return chicken to pan.
† Add apples sprinkled with a little nutmeg
  and brown sugar. Pour apple cider over
  chicken.
† Simmer 30 minutes or until tender.

BBQ CHICKEN

Yield: 4 to 6 servings
Jean Harris

1/2 cup sugar
1/2 cup mustard
1/4 teaspoon red pepper
1/4 teaspoon black pepper
1/4 teaspoon garlic powder
1/4 teaspoon paprika
1/4 teaspoon salt
1   tablespoon chili powder
3/4 cup vinegar
3/4 cup water
2   cups tomato juice
1   onion, chopped
1   (2 1/2-3 pound) chicken
    cut up or 4-6 chicken
    breasts with ribs.

† Preheat oven to 275°.
† Combine all ingredients and pour over
  chicken.
† Bake 1 1/2 hours or until tender.

DOT'S VERSATILE BAKED CHICKEN

Yield: 6 to 8 servings
Kate Buckfelder

BUTTER MIXTURE I:

3/4 cup butter
1 tablespoon lemon juice

CRUMB MIXTURE I:

1 cup crushed sesame crackers
1 teaspoon garlic salt
1/2 teaspoon pepper

BUTTER MIXTURE II:

1/2 cup butter
2 cloves garlic, minced

CRUMB MIXTURE II:

1/2 cup Italian bread crumbs
1 1/2 cups grated cheddar cheese
1/4 cup Parmesan cheese
1 teaspoon salt
1/2 teaspoon pepper

BUTTER MIXTURE III:

1/2 cup unsalted butter
2 cloves garlic, minced
1 teaspoon Worcestershire
sauce
1 teaspoon dry mustard

CRUMB MIXTURE III:

2 cups bread crumbs
1/2 cup Parmesan cheese
1/3 cup chopped parsley
1 (3-ounce) can onion rings,
crushed

CHICKEN:

8 boned chicken breasts

† Choose desired butter and crumb mixture combination (I, II, or III).
† For butter mixture, melt butter and add remaining ingredients. Set aside.
† For crumb mixture, combine all ingredients. Set aside.
† Preheat oven to 350°.
† Dip chicken in butter mixture and then roll to coat in crumb mixture.
† Place chicken in 2-quart casserole. Drizzle any remaining butter on top and sprinkle with any remaining crumbs.
† Bake 45 to 60 minutes or until tender.

CHICKEN CACCIATORE

Yield: 4 servings
Frances Wilkins

1 (2 1/2-3 1/2-pound) fryer
1/4 cup vegetable oil
1/2 cup chopped green onion
1/2 cup chopped celery
2 cloves garlic, chopped
1 (4-ounce) can button
  mushrooms, drained
1 (14.5-ounce) can whole
  tomatoes, chopped, with liquid
1/2 (6-ounce) can tomato paste
1/2 cup dry sherry
2 teaspoons sugar
  Salt and pepper to taste
3/4 pound spaghetti, cooked

† Skin and brown chicken in oil over medium heat. Remove chicken. Add onion, celery and garlic. Fry slowly 15 minutes. Pour off oil.

† Stir in mushrooms and remaining ingredients, except spaghetti. Return chicken and cook over low heat until chicken is tender.

† Serve over spaghetti.

CHICKEN CALIENTE CRESCENT CASSEROLE

Yield: 6 to 8 servings
Carol Jennings

1 (8-ounce) can quick crescent
  dinner rolls
3 cups corn chips, coarsely
  crushed, divided
1 can cream of chicken soup
1 (5 1/3-ounce) can evaporated
  milk
2 tablespoons flour
1 cup cubed cooked chicken
1/3 cup chopped onion
1 (4-ounce) can chopped green
  chilies, drained
1 (2-ounce) jar chopped
  pimiento, drained
1 1/3 cups grated cheddar or
  Monterey Jack cheese
1/3 cup sliced black olives

† Preheat oven to 350°.

† Unroll dough into two long rectangles. Place in 9x13-inch pan. Press over bottom and 1/2 inch up sides to form crust. Sprinkle with half of the corn chips. Bake 10 to 12 minutes.

† In saucepan, blend soup, milk and flour until smooth.

† Stir in chicken, onion, chilies and pimiento. Cook over medium heat until mixture comes to a boil and thickens. Stir frequently.

† Pour hot chicken into crust. Sprinkle with remaining corn chips and cheese. Arrange olives in diagonal rows over cheese. Bake 14 to 18 minutes until crust is golden brown.

CHICKEN CORDON BLEU

Yield: 16 servings
Fran Stroud

16 boneless chicken breasts
16 slices Swiss cheese
2   (6-ounce) packages
    processed ham
1   can cream of mushroom
    soup
1   (10-ounce) bottle mustard-
    mayonnaise sauce

† Preheat oven to 250°.
† Wrap chicken breast with a slice of cheese,
  a slice of ham and secure with toothpick.
  Place in a 9x13-inch casserole.
† Combine soup and sauce and pour over
  chicken.
† Bake covered for 21/2 hours.

CHICKEN COUNTRY CAPTAIN

Yield: 4 servings
Nancy Ehringhaus

21/2-3 pounds boneless, skinless
     chicken breasts, cubed
2   tablespoons vegetable oil
11/2 teaspoons salt
1/4 teaspoon pepper
1/2 cup chopped onion
1/2 cup chopped bell pepper
1   clove garlic, crushed
11/2 teaspoons curry powder
1   (28-ounce) can whole
     tomatoes
1   tablespoon browning and
     seasoning sauce
2   tablespoons chopped parsley
1/8 teaspoon mace
1/4 cup raisins
1/4 cup slivered almonds

† Brown chicken in oil and sprinkle with
  salt and pepper.
† Remove chicken from pan and add onion,
  pepper, garlic and curry powder. Cook
  over low heat until tender.
† Add chicken and remaining ingredients,
  except almonds. Cook one hour or until
  tender.
† Sprinkle with almonds and serve over rice.

CHICKEN CRÊPES

Yield: 13 to 14 servings
Anne Tomlinson

CRÊPES:

2 eggs
2 egg yolks
2 tablespoons vegetable oil
8 tablespoons flour
3/4 teaspoon salt
1 cup milk

† Beat egg and yolks with oil. Add flour and salt. Blend in milk. Batter should be consistency of medium cream.
† Heat 7-inch nonstick crepe pan on medium high and brush with oil. Put approximately 1/4 cup batter for each crepe in pan.
† Rotate pan to cover. Cook 1 minute. Turn crepe gently and cook 1/2 minute. Can be made ahead and stacked between waxed paper.

FILLING:

1 stick butter
1 cup vermouth, divided
3 1/2 cooked bite-size pieces of chicken
2 cups half-and-half
1 cup heavy cream
2 1/2 tablespoons cornstarch
4 tablespoons milk
1 teaspoon salt
1/2 teaspoon pepper
  Juice of 1 lemon
1 cup packed grated Swiss cheese, divided
  Butter

† Melt butter and add 1/2 cup vermouth and chicken. Remove chicken, draining well and set aside.
† Add remaining vermouth to pot and simmer, reducing liquid by one-third. Blend in half-and-half, heavy cream, cornstarch softened in milk and salt and pepper. Cook until thick.
† Add lemon juice and 1/2 cup cheese. Cook until cheese melts. Stir a few spoons of sauce into chicken. Place a large spoonful of chicken on each crepe.
† Preheat oven to 350°.
† Place rolled crêpes in greased casserole with seam side up. Pour remaining sauce over crepes and sprinkle with remaining cheese. Dot with butter and bake until bubbly and slightly brown.

Crabmeat may be used instead of chicken.

CHICKEN DIJON

Yield: 6 to 8 servings
Cantey Gannaway

3/4 stick margarine
1 clove garlic, minced
2 tablespoons chopped fresh
   parsley
1 1/2 tablespoons soy sauce
8 boneless skinless chicken
   breast halves
2 tablespoons country-style
   Dijon mustard
1/4 cup white wine
1/2 cup toasted slivered almonds

† In skillet, melt margarine, garlic, parsley and soy sauce. Sauté chicken until done. Remove and set aside.
† Add mustard and wine to pan drippings and bring to a boil.
† Pour sauce over chicken and garnish with almonds.

To toast almonds, bake 7 to 10 minutes at 350°, stirring 2 or 3 times during baking. Sauce will separate if prepared ahead.

CHICKEN ENCHILADAS

Yield: 12 to 20 tortillas
Judy Van Namen

3-4 cups cooked chopped chicken
1 1/2 cups grated Monterey Jack
   cheese
1 small onion, finely chopped
12 (8-inch) or 20 (6-inch) tortillas
1 can cream of mushroom soup
1/2 cup medium or hot salsa
   (to taste)
2 cups grated medium cheddar
   cheese

† Preheat oven to 350°.
† Blend chicken, cheese, and onion in a bowl.
† Microwave tortillas until warm and pliable. Fill with chicken and place seam side down in shallow casserole.
† Combine soup, salsa and cheese. Spoon over each enchilada and bake covered for 20 minutes.

164

LEMON HONEY CHICKEN

Yield: 4 servings
Rebecca Farnsworth

1	whole chicken, cut up
1/4	cup oil
1/4	cup honey
1	egg yolk, slightly beaten
2	tablespoons soy sauce
2	tablespoons lemon juice
1	teaspoon paprika
1/4	teaspoon nutmeg

† Preheat oven to 350°.
† Place chicken in a baking dish. Combine remaining ingredients and mix. Pour over chicken.
† Bake uncovered for 1 hour. Turn and baste chicken twice while baking.

NEIMAN MARCUS LEMON CHICKEN

Yield: 4 servings
Sis Cranz

4-6	pieces boneless chicken
1	tablespoon soy sauce
1 1/2	teaspoons salt, divided
3/4	teaspoon pepper, divided
1	clove garlic, crushed
1/4	cup salad oil
1/2	cup lemon juice
2	tablespoons lemon zest
1/2	cup flour
2	teaspoons paprika
	Lemon slices for garnish
	Parsley for garnish

† Combine soy sauce, 1/2 teaspoon salt, 1/2 teaspoon pepper, garlic, oil, lemon juice and lemon zest. Marinate chicken in marinade at least one hour.
† Preheat oven to 350°.
† Combine flour, paprika and remaining salt and pepper in a plastic bag. Remove chicken from marinade and shake in bag.
† Arrange chicken in shallow casserole. Drizzle with 1/2 of marinade and bake 30 minutes uncovered.
† Pour remaining marinade over chicken and bake 20 to 30 minutes until done.
† Garnish with lemon slices and parsley.

LIME CHICKEN

Yield: 6 servings
Celia Marshall

4   (1/2 pound) boneless skinless
     chicken breasts
1/3 cup olive oil
3   medium limes, juice only
4   cloves garlic, minced
1   teaspoon dried dill
1/2 teaspoon salt
1/2 teaspoon pepper
1 1/2 tablespoons chopped
     fresh parsley

† Pound chicken between waxed paper to
  flatten.
† Combine all ingredients, except parsley,
  and pour over chicken to marinate one
  hour.
† Grill or broil chicken and sprinkle with
  parsley.

TASTY LO-CAL CHICKEN

Yield: 6 servings
Paula Freeman

2   pounds skinless chicken parts
1/2 cup lemon juice
1/4 cup water
3   tablespoons soy sauce
1/4 teaspoon ground ginger
1/2 teaspoon garlic salt

† Preheat oven to 350°.
† Place chicken in baking dish that has been
  sprayed with nonstick cooking spray.
† Shake remaining ingredients in jar and pour
  over chicken. Cover with foil and bake
  45 minutes.
† Uncover and bake 20 to 30 minutes.

CHICKEN IN A HUT

Yield: 4 servings
Anita Griffin

2   cups chicken, cooked and
     cut into 3/4-inch cubes
1/2 (8-ounce) package cream
     cheese, softened
2   tablespoons milk
1/4 teaspoon salt
1/8 teaspoon pepper
1   (8-ounce) package crescent
     rolls

† Preheat oven to crescent roll directions.
† Combine all ingredients except rolls and
  set aside.
† Divide rolls into 4 sets of 2 rolls each. Press
  seams together of 2 rolls to form a square.
† Spoon 1/4 of chicken onto middle of square.
  Fold corners up to make a "hut". Place
  seam side down on foil-covered baking sheet
  and bake according to roll directions.

LOWFAT BAKED CHICKEN AND GRAVY

Yield: 4 servings
Susan Plott

1/2 cup flour
1/2 teaspoon salt
1/4 teaspoon pepper
1/4 teaspoon rosemary,
     oregano or thyme
4   skinless chicken breast
     halves, fat removed
1   cup skim milk
1   can fat-free, low-salt
     chicken broth
     Paprika for garnish

† Preheat oven to 300°.
† Combine flour and seasonings in bag along
  with chicken. Shake until chicken is well
  coated.
† Put chicken pieces in casserole sprayed
  with nonfat cooking spray. Arrange in
  one layer nearly covering bottom of pan.
† Combine milk with chicken broth and pour
  around edges of chicken. Add more milk
  if needed to cover the chicken at least
  halfway.
† Cover and bake 1 1/2 hours or until chicken
  is tender and gravy thickens. Baste once
  or twice with liquid from the pan.
† Sprinkle with paprika and serve with rice.

For more flavor, sprinkle additional herbs on top of chicken right before baking.
Recipe can be doubled but there should be only one layer of chicken in the pan.

MARINATED CHICKEN BREASTS

Yield: 6 servings
Janie Sellers
Anne Neal

1/2 cup firmly packed
     brown sugar
1/3 cup olive oil
1/4 cup cider vinegar
3   cloves garlic, crushed
3   tablespoons coarse-grain
     prepared mustard
1 1/2 tablespoons lemon juice
1 1/2 tablespoons lime juice
1 1/2 teaspoons salt
1/4 teaspoon pepper
6   boneless skinless
     chicken breast halves

† Combine all ingredients and marinate
  chicken breasts for 8 hours. Let stand
  at room temperature for 1 hour, then grill.

In Order To Serve

MEXICAN CHICKEN

Yield: 6 servings
Becky Werden

4   cups crushed corn chips
4   chicken breast halves, cooked
1/4 cup milk
1   (8-ounce) package Mexican processed cheese loaf
1   can cream of mushroom soup
1   tablespoon butter

† Preheat oven to 350°.
† Layer corn chips in bottom of 9x13-inch baking dish.
† Chop chicken and layer over chips. May make 2 layers.
† Heat other ingredients, creating a sauce, and pour over chicken and chips.

Freezes well.

MEXICAN CHICKEN SUPREME

Yield: 6 to 8 servings
Genie Hufham

6   boneless, skinless chicken breasts
1   (12-ounce) package Fajita marinade, prepared and divided
1   onion, thinly sliced
1   bell pepper, thinly sliced
3   packages frozen spinach, cooked and squeezed dry
1   cup sour cream
1-11/2 (16-ounce) jars mild salsa or picante sauce
1   cup grated Monterey Jack cheese
    Black olives and/or jalapeño chili peppers for garnish (optional)

† Put aside 1/4 cup marinade.
† Marinate chicken 4-6 hours in remaining marinade. Grill chicken over medium coals for 8 minutes per side or until done. Cut into bite-size pieces.
† Preheat oven to 375°.
† Arrange chicken in 4-quart casserole. Sauté onion and pepper in reserved marinade and spoon over chicken.
† Layer spinach, sour cream, salsa and cheese over chicken and bake for 20 minutes or until bubbly.

168

RUSTIC PORCINI MUSHROOM CHICKEN

Yield: 4 servings
RoseLynn Imbleau

1/2 pound dried porcini mushrooms (do not substitute)
1 (10.5-ounce) can reduced salt chicken broth
1/3 cup extra virgin olive oil
4 chicken breast halves with ribs or 8 chicken thighs
2/3 cup dry white wine
Sea salt and pepper to taste
1 tablespoon butter
1 tablespoon flour
1 cup tomato or marinara sauce

† Rinse mushrooms and cover with chicken broth for 15 minutes.

† Heat oil in large skillet and brown chicken. Drain off any pan drippings over 1 tablespoon and reserve.

† Return chicken to pan and add wine and salt and pepper to taste. Cook to evaporate wine.

† Make a roux using 1/2 to 1 cup of reserved liquid, 1 tablespoon butter and 1 tablespoon flour. Gradually stir until thickened. Add to skillet.

† Blend in tomato sauce, mushrooms and stock. Cover and cook on low 40 minutes. When sauce is ready, it turns a coppery color with a rustic, woodsy taste. Serve with rice.

CHICKEN PAELLA

Yield: 6 servings
Joanne Leland

2-21/2 pounds skinless chicken parts
1 teaspoon salt
1 teaspoon black pepper
1 tablespoon olive oil
1 cup raw rice
1 medium onion, chopped
2 cloves garlic, minced
21/2 cups chicken broth
1 (8-ounce) can stewed tomatoes, undrained and chopped
1/2 teaspoon paprika
1/2 teaspoon dried oregano
1/8 teaspoon ground saffron or pinch of turmeric
1 small red bell pepper, cut in strips
1 small green bell pepper, cut in strips
1/2 cup frozen green peas

† Season chicken with salt and pepper. Heat oil in Dutch oven over medium heat. Add chicken and brown on both sides. Remove and keep warm.

† Add rice, onion and garlic. Cook, stirring until rice is lightly browned and onion is transparent. Add broth, tomatoes, seasonings and chicken pieces. Bring to a boil. Reduce heat, cover and simmer 10 minutes.

† Add pepper strips and peas. Cover and simmer 15 minutes or until rice is tender and liquid absorbed.

CHICKEN POT PIE

Yield: 6 servings
Jeanne Kutrow

1 (2 1/2-pound) broiler-fryer chicken
2 quarts water
2 teaspoons salt, divided
5 1/3 tablespoons butter or margarine
1 cup chopped onion
1 cup chopped celery
1 cup chopped carrots
1-2 medium potatoes, peeled and chopped
1/2 cup frozen green peas, thawed
1/2 cup plus 1 teaspoon flour, divided
2 cups chicken broth
1 cup half-and-half
1/2 teaspoon pepper
1 refrigerated pie crust

† Bring chicken, water and one teaspoon salt to boil in Dutch oven. Cover, reduce heat and simmer 1 hour.
† Remove chicken, reserving two cups broth.
† Skin, bone and chop chicken. Skim fat from broth.
† Preheat oven to 400°.
† Melt butter in skillet. Add onion and next four ingredients. Cook 10 minutes or until carrots are tender. Add flour, stirring until smooth.
† Gradually add reserved broth and half-and-half. Cook over medium heat, stirring constantly until mixture is thickened and bubbly. Stir in chopped chicken and remaining salt and pepper. Pour into lightly greased 11x7-inch casserole.
† Unfold pie crust and press out fold lines. Sprinkle with one teaspoon flour. Roll pastry into 12x8-inch rectangle. Place over filling. Fold edges under and crimp. Cut slits in top.
† Bake 30 minutes or until golden brown.
† Cover edges with foil after 20 minutes to prevent excess browning.

CHICKEN PIQUANT

Yield: 4 to 6 servings
Deborah McCann

1 pound fresh mushrooms, sliced
1 chicken cut up
4 tablespoons water
2 tablespoons cornstarch
3/4 cup white or rosé wine
1/4 cup soy sauce
2 tablespoons olive oil
2 tablespoons brown sugar
1 clove garlic, crushed
1/4 teaspoon oregano
Cooked rice

† Preheat oven to 350°.
† Place sliced mushrooms in 2-quart casserole and top with chicken.
† Blend water and cornstarch and combine with remaining ingredients, except rice. Pour over chicken and bake uncovered for 1 1/2 hours.
† Serve over rice.

VERMONT CHICKEN POT PIE

Yield: 6 to 8 servings
Carolyn Coleman

FILLING:

1	(3-pound) roasting chicken
1	onion, peeled
2	stalks celery
1	bunch parsley
3/4	stick butter, melted
6	tablespoons flour
2	cups defatted chicken broth
1	(16-ounce) package frozen peas and carrots
1	cup fresh or frozen cut green beans (optional)
1/2	cup chopped fresh chives or 1 tablespoon dried
	Salt and pepper to taste

† Combine chicken with onion, celery, and parsley in large pot and cover with water. Bring to a boil, reduce heat and simmer for 45 minutes or until chicken is cooked. Let chicken cool in broth and then remove meat from bones. Remove and discard fat that rises to top of broth. Strain the broth.

† Preheat oven to 450°.

† In large saucepan, melt butter and whisk in the flour to make smooth paste. Whisk in 4-5 cups of broth, stirring until smooth and thick.

† Stir in chicken, vegetables and seasonings.

† Pour into a 4-quart casserole and bake about 30 minutes until bubbling hot.

BISCUIT TOPPING:

2	cups flour
4	teaspoons baking powder
1	teaspoon salt
51/3	tablespoons butter or shortening
3/4	cup milk

† Combine flour, baking powder, and salt in large bowl. Cut in the butter until mixture resembles soft crumbs.

† Stir in milk to make soft dough. Knead several times on lightly floured board. Cut into 2-inch rounds.

† Arrange biscuits on top when chicken is bubbling hot. Bake for additional 15 minutes until biscuits are golden.

CURRIED ORANGE CHICKEN

Yield: 4 to 6 servings
Judy Gaines

3-3 1/2 pounds chicken parts
    (no backs or wings)
1   cup English orange
    marmalade
1   tablespoon curry powder
1   teaspoon salt
1/2 cup water

† Preheat oven to 350°.
† Place chicken pieces in a buttered 4-quart casserole.
† Combine remaining ingredients and spoon over chicken. Bake uncovered at least 45 minutes, basting several times.
† Remove chicken and skim off fat from sauce.
† Serve sauce over chicken with noodles or rice.

POLLO ESTOFADO

Yield: 5 to 6 servings
Janie Sellers

MARINADE:
1/2 cup olive oil
1/2 cup red wine vinegar
4   teaspoons crushed
    oregano leaves
2   teaspoons salt
    Pepper to taste
2   cloves garlic, minced
3-4 bay leaves
1/2 cup golden raisins
1/4 cup sliced pitted
    green olives

† Combine marinade ingredients. Prick chicken with fork and add to marinade. Coat well.
† Cover and refrigerate overnight.

CHICKEN:
5-6 boneless chicken breasts
4   tablespoons light brown
    sugar
3/4 cup dry white wine

† Preheat oven to 350°.
† Place chicken in baking dish and sprinkle with brown sugar. Combine wine with marinade and pour around chicken so as not to disturb brown sugar.
† Bake uncovered 50 minutes, basting often. Remove bay leaves and boil marinade before pouring over chicken.
† Serve with saffron or wild rice.

POULET VIN JÀUNE

Yield: 4 servings
Frances Wilkins

5   tablespoons butter, divided
8   chicken parts, both white and dark
    Salt and pepper to taste
1/2 pound fresh mushrooms, sliced
1   cup Vin Jàune d'Arbois or dry white wine
3/4 cup heavy cream or crème fraîche
3   tablespoons fresh lemon juice or to taste

† Heat 2 1/2 tablespoons butter in skillet and brown chicken over medium heat. Add salt and pepper and remove from pan.
† Heat remaining butter and mushrooms. Cook for 5 minutes. Stir in wine and bring to a boil, stirring constantly.
† Return chicken to pan. Cover and cook on low heat for 30 to 40 minutes or until chicken is tender.
† Remove chicken and keep warm. Skim fat from the sauce.
† Add cream to the mushrooms and liquid. Simmer 5 minutes. Add lemon juice and return chicken to pan.

CONTINENTAL CHICKEN WITH RICE

Yield: 6 servings
Elaine Thigpen

6   boneless chicken breasts
    Salt and pepper to taste
1/2 teaspoon thyme
1/2 teaspoon basil
1/2 cup white wine
1   can cream of chicken soup
1   (4-ounce) can mushrooms, drained
1   cup sour cream
    Diced pimientos (optional)

† Place chicken and spices in crock pot. Combine remaining ingredients, except sour cream, and pour over chicken.
† Cook in crock pot on low 6 to 8 hours or on high for 2 1/2 to 3 1/2 hours. Add sour cream during last 30 minutes.
† Serve on rice.

If cooking in oven, preheat oven to 350°. Cook one hour and add sour cream last 15 minutes.

173

CHICKEN AND RICE CASSEROLE

Yield: 8 servings
Kate Buckfelder
Barbara Simmons

3   cups cooked chicken
1   (6-ounce) package wild
    rice, cooked
1   (2-ounce) jar pimientos
1   small onion, chopped
1   (16-ounce) can French-
    style green beans (optional)
1   can cream of celery soup
1   cup mayonnaise
1   (8-ounce) can sliced water
    chestnuts
1   (2-ounce) package
    slivered almonds (optional)
    Salt and pepper to taste

† Preheat oven to 350°.
† Combine all ingredients in large bowl.
† Pour into lightly greased 3-quart casserole
  and bake for 25 minutes.

WHITE BARBECUE SAUCE FOR CHICKEN

Yield: 12/3 cups
Judy Gaines

3/4 cup mayonnaise
1/3 cup lemon juice
1/3 cup vinegar
1/4 cup sugar
2   teaspoons salt

† Combine all ingredients. Use sauce for
  chicken on the grill as well as in the oven.

SINGAPORE MUSTARD

Yield: 4 or 5 (8-ounce) jars
Sharon Webb

6   ounces dry mustard
1/2   teaspoon black pepper
1/4   teaspoon white pepper
4   ounces cold water
1 1/2 cups cider vinegar
1/2   teaspoon salt
2   cups sugar
1/2   stick butter, melted
3   eggs, well beaten

† In a large saucepan, combine mustard and
  black and white pepper with cold water to
  make a paste.
† Add vinegar, salt and sugar, stirring between
  each addition to paste.
† Add butter and eggs to mixture. Stirring
  constantly, bring mixture just to a boil. Use
  egg beater to smooth mixture.
† Fill sterilized jars with hot mustard. Will
  thicken as it cools.

Do not try to double recipe.

174

ROANOKE CHICKEN

Yield: 4 to 6 servings
Kaky Cassada

6   slices Smithfield ham
6   boneless skinless chicken
    breast halves
    Salt and pepper to taste
3/4 cup all-purpose flour
1   stick butter
1   cup sliced fresh mushrooms
1   cup chopped celery leaves
1/2 cup chicken broth
1   cup sour cream
1   small avocado, sliced

† Preheat oven to 300°.
† Butter a 9x13-inch baking dish and line with ham slices.
† Lightly season chicken with salt and pepper and dredge in flour.
† Melt butter in skillet and sauté chicken until partially cooked. Place over ham.
† Add mushrooms to chicken drippings and cook 3 minutes before placing on chicken.
† Sprinkle celery leaves over all.
† Stir broth into drippings and bring to a boil. Remove from heat and add sour cream. Pour over chicken and cover with foil.
† Bake for 70 minutes. Remove cover and continue baking until sauce has thickened.
† Place avocado on top before serving.

SHERRIED CHICKEN

Yield: 6 servings
Jane Bruce

6   large chicken breast halves
    or 2 (2 1/2-pound) fryers,
    cut up
3/4 cup flour
2-3 teaspoons salt
1/4 teaspoon garlic powder
    (optional)
3-4 tablespoons olive oil or
    vegetable oil
6   tablespoons butter
3/4 cup dry sherry
3   tablespoons soy sauce
3   tablespoons fresh lemon
    juice
1/2 teaspoon ginger

† Preheat oven to 350°.
† Combine flour, salt and garlic powder in plastic bag. Shake chicken in bag and place in hot oil to brown. Arrange in casserole.
† In saucepan, melt butter and remaining ingredients. Bring to a boil and pour over chicken.
† Bake uncovered 60 minutes or until tender. Baste occasionally and turn chicken once during baking.

CHICKEN SOUFFLÉ

Yield: 8 servings
Mabel Barnhardt

8   slices bread, crusts removed
8   cooked chicken breasts,
    cut into pieces
8   (1-ounce) slices sharp
    cheese
6   eggs
31/2 cups whole milk
1/2 cup sherry
    Salt and pepper to taste
3/4 stick butter, melted
2   cups corn flakes

† Arrange bread in greased 9x13-inch
  casserole. Top with chicken and cheese.
† Combine eggs, milk, sherry, salt and pepper.
  Pour over chicken. Refrigerate overnight.
† Preheat oven to 350°.
† Melt butter and add corn flakes. Sprinkle
  over top of casserole. Bake 60 minutes.

SPICY CHICKEN RAGOÛT

Yield: 4 servings
Susan Hamilton

4   large skinless chicken
    breast halves
    Salt and freshly ground
    pepper
2   teaspoons olive oil
13/4 cups chicken broth
1   (14.5-ounce) can plum
    tomatoes, seeded and
    quartered
12 baby carrots
1/2 pound fresh asparagus,
    cut in 11/2-inch pieces
1   (6-ounce) leek, cut in
    1/4-inch slices
1   cup fresh green peas
    Flat-leaf parsley for garnish

† Season chicken with salt and pepper. Heat
  oil in large skillet and brown chicken.
† Add broth and tomatoes. Bring to a boil.
  Cover and simmer 20 minute. Remove
  chicken.
† Add carrots to skillet and cook, covered,
  until almost tender. Add asparagus, leeks
  and peas, cooking until tender.
† Cut chicken into bite-size pieces.
  Return to skillet and cook until heated
  through. Serve over egg noodles
  or rice.

SOUTHERN CREAMY CHICKEN BREASTS
Yield: 8 servings
Jane Showalter

8   boneless, skinless chicken breast halves
8   (4x4-inch) slices Swiss cheese
1   can cream of chicken soup
1/4 cup dry white wine
1   cup herb-seasoned stuffing mix, crushed
1/2 stick butter, melted

† Preheat oven to 350°.
† Arrange chicken in greased 4-quart casserole. Top with cheese slices.
† Combine soup and wine. Pour over chicken and sprinkle with stuffing mix.
† Drizzle with butter and bake 45 to 55 minutes.
† Can add more butter and stuffing mix as needed.

Barbara Finn's variation: Omit the white wine and use mushroom soup instead of chicken soup.

CHICKEN AND WHITE WINE
Yield: 12 servings
Becky Parsley

1/2 cup flour
1 1/2 teaspoons salt, divided
1/2 teaspoon pepper
12 boneless, skinless chicken breasts, cut in bite-size pieces
1/4 cup vegetable oil
1   stick butter or margarine, divided
1   cup chopped onion
1   can golden mushroom soup
1/2 can water
2   cups white wine
1 1/2 tablespoons lemon juice
1   pound mushrooms, halved
1   package frozen green peas or asparagus, cut in 1-inch pieces
3   cups cooked rice

† Combine flour, 1 teaspoon salt and pepper in brown paper bag. Shake chicken in mixture to coat.
† Heat oil in 2 tablespoons butter in large skillet. Sauté chicken until golden. Remove and sauté onion.
† Blend in soup, water, wine, lemon juice and 1/2 teaspoon salt and bring to a boil. Return chicken and simmer 10 minutes on low heat.
† In another skillet, melt 6 tablespoons butter and sauté mushrooms 5 minutes. Stir in peas or asparagus and cook 5 minutes covered. Add mushroom mixture to chicken mixture and heat.
† Serve over rice.

CRAB IMPERIAL

Yield: 8 servings
Arlene LaPointe

1 cup mayonnaise, divided
2 pounds fresh crabmeat
2 eggs, slightly beaten
1 teaspoon salt
1/2 teaspoon white pepper
2 teaspoons dry mustard
2/3 bell pepper, diced
1 (2-ounce) jar pimientos, diced
lemon juice to taste
1/2 teaspoon paprika

† Preheat oven to 350°.
† Combine 2/3 cup mayonnaise with remaining ingredients, except paprika, in 2-quart casserole.
† Spread 1/3 cup mayonnaise and paprika on top and bake 20 to 25 minutes.

LIZZY'S CRAB CASSEROLE

Yield: 4 servings
Cynthia Gass

2 green onions with tops, chopped
1 stick butter, divided
2 cloves garlic (or to taste), pressed
1 single pack of saltines, crushed, divided
1 pound fresh crabmeat
1/4 teaspoon ground cayenne pepper or to taste
Salt and pepper to taste
1 cup half-and-half

† Preheat oven to 350°.
† Sauté onions in 3/4 stick of butter until translucent. Add garlic and sauté 1 minute. (Do not let garlic brown). Remove from heat.
† Add 3/4 of crushed crackers, crabmeat, cayenne pepper and salt and pepper.
† Place in 2-quart buttered casserole. Sprinkle with remaining crackers. Pour half-and-half over casserole and dot with remaining butter. Bake 30 minutes.

May be frozen. Thaw in refrigerator and heat 45 minutes.

CRAB ON ENGLISH MUFFINS

Yield: 4 servings
Anita Griffin

1   (6½-ounce) can lump
    crabmeat
1/4 cup diced celery
2   tablespoons finely diced
    onion
1/2 cup grated sharp cheddar
    cheese
1/4 cup mayonnaise
4   English muffins, split

† Preheat broiler.
† Combine all ingredients except muffins.
† Spread on muffin halves.
† Broil until cheese melts and muffins
  are browned.

WHITE AND WILD SEAFOOD DELIGHT

Yield: 12 to 16 servings
Jean Keitt

2   cups cooked wild rice
1   cup cooked white rice
1   cup flaked crabmeat
1½ cups chopped celery
1   bell pepper, chopped
1   medium onion, chopped
1   (2-ounce) jar diced pimientos
3   cans cream of mushroom
    soup, divided
1   cup cooked shrimp, in
    pieces, divided
1   pound fresh mushrooms
1/4 stick butter

† Preheat oven to 350°.
† Combine first 7 ingredients. Add 1½
  cans soup and 1/2 cup shrimp. Place
  mixture in 4-quart casserole and bake
  90 minutes.
† Sauté mushrooms in butter and add
  remaining 1½ cans soup and shrimp.
† Serve with rice mixture.

CAROLINA CRAB CAKES

Yield: 4 servings
Liz Lea

1   pound lump crabmeat
1   egg, beaten
1/4 cup minced onion
2   teaspoons Worcestershire
    sauce
2   tablespoons mayonnaise
1½ cups crushed saltine
    crackers
1/2 cup butter, melted

† Mix all ingredients, except crackers, with
  crabmeat being careful not to break up
  lumps of crab. Gently shape into cakes.
† Roll in cracker crumbs.
† Sauté in butter until brown.
† Serve immediately.

FROGMORE STEW

Yield: 6 to 8 servings
Margaret Tabb

1   stick butter or margarine
    (optional)
4   teaspoons salt
6-8 tablespoons crab or shrimp
    boil, divided
2   pounds kielbasa sausage,
    cut into 1/2-inch slices
2   large onions, coarsely diced
5   ears corn, in halves
2   pounds medium-size round
    red potatoes, quartered
3   pounds shrimp (shell on)
    Cocktail sauce

† Fill 8-quart pot 1/3 full with water and bring
  to a boil with salt, four tablespoons shrimp
  boil, sausage, onion and potatoes for 4
  minutes.
† Add shrimp and corn and oil for 5 minutes.
  Cover and let sit for 5 minutes with stove
  turned off.
† Place in large bowl and serve with hot
  melted butter and cocktail sauce.

BARBECUED FISH FILLETS

Yield: 4 to 6 servings
Margaretta Leary

1/4 cup chopped onion
2   tablespoons chopped green
    bell pepper
1   clove garlic, chopped
2   tablespoons olive or
    vegetable oil
1   (8-ounce) can tomato
    sauce
2   tablespoons lemon juice
1   tablespoon Worcestershire
    sauce
1   tablespoon sugar
1-2 teaspoons salt
1/4 teaspoon black pepper
2   pounds mild fish fillets
    (flounder, grouper, mahi-
    mahi)

† Cook onion, green pepper and garlic in oil
  until tender. Add remaining ingredients
  and simmer 5 minutes.
† Fish may be marinated in cooled sauce in
  shallow pan 30 minutes before cooking.
† Cook fish on medium heat on grill 5 to 8
  minutes each side, basting often with sauce.

If planning to serve sauce with fish, remove some of sauce before marinating.

STUFFED FLOUNDER FILLETS

Yield: 8 servings
Mary Jenrette

STUFFED FILLETS:

1/2	cup chopped scallions
1	stick butter
6	ounces chopped mushrooms, fresh or canned (if canned, reserve liquid)
1	pound crabmeat
1	cup crumbled saltines
1	teaspoon salt
1/4	teaspoon pepper
1	tablespoon finely chopped parsley
5	pounds flounder fillets

† Preheat oven to 400°.
† Sauté scallions in butter. Add mushrooms, crab, crackers, salt and pepper and parsley. Stir and spread over fillets.
† Roll up and place in baking dish deep enough for the roll ups to be below edge.

SAUCE:

1/4	stick butter
6	tablespoons flour
1/2	teaspoon salt
2/3	cup milk
2/3	cup dry white wine
2	cups grated Swiss cheese
1	teaspoon paprika

† Melt butter, blend in flour and salt. Add milk, or use liquid from mushrooms and enough milk to make 2/3 cup.
† Blend in wine. pour over fish and bake 25 minutes. Sprinkle with cheese and paprika.
† Bake 5 minutes.

BAKED CATFISH

Yield: 4 servings
Elizabeth Ritchie

1/3	cup yellow cornmeal
1/3	cup flour
1/3	cup Parmesan cheese
1	teaspoon paprika
1/2	teaspoon black pepper
1/4	teaspoon salt
1	egg white
2	tablespoons skim milk
4	catfish fillets
	Sesame seeds

† Preheat oven to 375°.
† Combine first 6 ingredients. Set aside.
† Whisk egg white and milk together.
† Dip fillets in milk mixture and then dredge in dry ingredients.
† Place on baking sheet sprayed with nonstick spray. Sprinkle with sesame seeds.
† Spray top of fillets with nonstick spray.
† Bake 30 minutes or until fish flakes easily.

FLOUNDER SIMMERED IN WINE

Yield: 3 to 4 servings
Mary Jenrette

1 1/2 pounds flounder fillets
2   tablespoons butter
1   tablespoon vegetable oil
1/2 cup dry white wine
1   tablespoon Dijon mustard
1   tablespoon lemon juice
2   tablespoons cream or milk

† Wash the fillets and pat dry. Heat butter
and oil in frying pan. Lightly brown fillets.
† Add wine and simmer covered 5 minutes.
† Combine mustard, lemon juice and cream
in a saucepan.
† Pour over fish before serving.

For less spicy sauce, use 1/2 tablespoon Dijon mustard and 1/2 tablespoon prepared mustard.

BROILED SALMON AND GREEN SAUCE

Yield: 4 servings
Sally Hartsock

SALMON:
1 1/2 pounds salmon fillets
1   tablespoon corn oil
1   clove garlic, finely minced
2   shallots, finely minced
2   tablespoons fresh lemon juice
3   dashes cayenne pepper
1/2 teaspoon dried tarragon
    leaves, crushed

† Wash and pat fish dry. Combine
remaining ingredients.
† Place fish in lightly oiled baking dish.
Brush half of herb mixture over fish. Broil
3 inches from heat for 10 minutes.
† Reduce heat to 375°. Spread remaining
mixture on fish and bake 10 minutes.

SAUCE:
2   tablespoons corn oil
2   cloves garlic, finely minced
1   shallot, finely minced
2   tablespoons unbleached flour
1 1/2 cups warm chicken broth
1/2 teaspoon dried tarragon
    leaves, crushed
4   dashes cayenne pepper
1/2-3/4 cup nonfat milk
1/2 cup tightly packed parsley,
    very finely chopped

† Heat oil until hot, add garlic and shallots.
Cook 1 minute.
† Add flour, whisking well. Cook 2 minutes.
Add broth, tarragon and cayenne.
† Add 1/2 cup milk and parsley. Cook 10
minutes on low heat uncovered, whisking
often.
† Pour over fish and serve.

GRILLED NORWEGIAN SALMON WITH FRESH SUMMER RELISH

Yield: 6 servings
Chef John Alston, Alston's

RELISH:

1	onion, chopped
3	cucumbers, chopped
5	tomatoes, chopped
3	red bell peppers, seeded and chopped
2	ounces capers
7	gerkins, chopped
1/2	cup olive oil
3/4	cup sherry vinegar
4	tablespoons Dijon mustard
2	tablespoons fresh parsley, chopped
2	tablespoons fresh basil, chopped
	Kosher salt and black pepper to taste

† Combine onion, cucumbers, tomatoes, red peppers, capers, and gerkins.
† Mix olive oil, vinegar, mustard, parsley, basil, salt and pepper and combine with vegetables to make relish.
† Refrigerate for 6 hours or overnight.

SALMON:

1	whole Norwegian salmon

† Clean, bone and fillet salmon.
† Cook on grill to 130°.
† Place relish over salmon and serve.

GARLIC SHRIMP

Yield: 4 servings
Anita Griffin

2	pounds cooked shrimp, peeled and deveined
1/2	cup butter, softened
1/2	cup seasoned bread crumbs
2	tablespoons sour cream
2	tablespoons chopped parsley
1	clove garlic, chopped
1	teaspoon salt
1/2	teaspoon Worcestershire sauce
2	teaspoons lemon juice
	Pepper to taste

† Preheat oven to 450°.
† Layer shrimp in 1-quart casserole. Combine remaining ingredients and spread over shrimp.
† Bake 10 minutes or until bubbly and browned.

183

BROILED SWORDFISH WITH HERB BUTTER

Yield: 4 servings
Jeanne Trexler

4   (1-inch thick) swordfish
     steaks
1/4 cup olive oil
2   sticks unsalted butter,
     softened, divided
1   clove garlic, minced
2   tablespoons fresh lemon
     juice
1   tablespoon fresh lime juice
1/4 cup chopped fresh herb
     mixture or 2 tablespoons
     dried (watercress, parsley,
     dill, basil, marjoram,
     rosemary)

† In food processor, combine butter, garlic, citrus juices and chopped herbs. Process until well mixed.

† Form herb butter into a roll 2 inches long and 2 inches in diameter. Wrap well in wax paper and place in freezer for 1 hour or refrigerate for several hours.

† Preheat broiler. Place broiler pan 3 to 4 inches from heating element and heat 3 to 5 minutes.

† Wipe swordfish with damp towels. Lightly brush both sides of steaks with oil. Place steaks on broiler pan and broil 4 to 5 minutes. Turn and broil 2 to 3 minutes longer.

† Cut 1 to 2 generous slices herb butter for each steak. Top steaks with butter and broil 1 minute.

TUNA BURGERS

Yield: 4 servings
Sis Cranz

2   tablespoons nonfat
     mayonnaise
2   tablespoons mustard-
     mayonnaise combination
1   egg white
2   (6-ounce) cans tuna in
     water, drained and flaked
1/2 cup dry bread crumbs or
     seafood breader, divided
1/4 cup chopped scallions
4   hamburger buns, split
4   lettuce leaves
4   slices tomato
4   slices sweet onion
     (optional)

† Combine first three ingredients in a medium bowl. Add tuna, 1/4 cup bread crumbs and scallions, blending well.

† Divide into four equal portions, shaping each into a 4-inch patty. Press remaining bread crumbs evenly onto both sides of patties.

† Spray large skillet with cooking spray. Place over medium high heat. When hot, add patties and cook 3 minutes on each side.

† Spread buns with mayonnaise and top with lettuce, tomatoes, and tuna patties.

SHRIMP EN BROCHETTE

Yield: 4 to 6 servings
Sarah Leak

1 pound jumbo shrimp, cleaned and deveined
4-6 slices of bacon
1/4-1/2 stick butter, melted
1/2 cup sour cream
2 tablespoons lemon juice
1/2 teaspoon salt
1/4 teaspoon white pepper

† On skewers, alternate shrimp with bacon that has been cut into squares. Brush with melted butter.
† Broil 4 to 6 minutes 2 to 3 inches from heat. Baste with butter and turn once.
† Heat sour cream and remaining ingredients along with drippings from shrimp over low heat 5 minutes.
† Pour sauce over skewers.

SHRIMP-CRAB CASSEROLE

Yield: 10 to 12 servings
Lois Ann Partridge

2 pounds cooked shrimp, peeled and deveined
1 (6-ounce) can crabmeat, drained
1-11/2 cups diced celery
8 ounces sliced mushrooms
1/4 cup lemon juice
2 tablespoons minced parsley
11/2 cups raw rice, cooked until fluffy
1/4 cup sliced almonds
1/4 cup grated onion
1/2 cup mayonnaise
3/4 cup milk
2 cans cream of shrimp soup
Salt and pepper to taste
Cayenne pepper to taste

† Preheat oven to 350°.
† Place all ingredients in large bowl and blend thoroughly.
† Pour into 4-quart buttered casserole.
† Bake 30 minutes or until bubbly.

In Order To Serve

EASY SHRIMP CREOLE

Yield: 4 to 5 servings
Sara Lowe

1   medium-size red bell pepper,
       seeded and chopped
1   medium green bell pepper,
       seeded and chopped
1/8-1/2 cup minced onion
1/2 clove garlic, minced very fine
2   tablespoons olive oil
2   (141/2-ounce) cans Cajun-
       style stewed tomatoes
       Salt to taste
11/2-2 pounds raw medium-size
       shrimp
       Green onions, finely chopped,
       or Parmesan cheese for
       garnish
       Cooked rice

† Combine all ingredients, except shrimp,
  and cook over low heat until peppers
  and onion are soft.
† Boil shrimp in water for 3 to 5 minutes
  until pink. Cool and remove shells. Add
  to heated sauce.
† Serve over rice with garnishes.

*Elaine Thigpen's variation: Omit bell peppers and stewed tomatoes and use one
15-ounce can Italian tomato sauce and one 15-ounce can skimmed evaporated milk.*

MAKE-AHEAD BUFFET SHRIMP CASSEROLE

Yield: 12 servings
Betsy Locke
Hope Parrott
Jo Griffith

12-15 slices firm white bread,
       crusts removed, divided
3   pounds cooked shrimp,
       peeled, divided
4   cups grated sharp cheddar
       cheese, divided
1   stick butter, melted
6   eggs, beaten
       Salt and pepper to taste
1   teaspoon dry mustard
1   quart milk

† Break bread in small pieces and place
  one-half in greased 9x13-inch casserole,
  covering the bottom. Use more bread
  if necessary.
† Cover bread with one-half of shrimp and
  one-half of cheese.
† Continue with another layer. Pour
  melted butter over layers.
† Beat eggs. Add seasonings and milk.
  Pour over shrimp and cover with foil. Let
  sit at least 3 hours in refrigerator (overnight
  is best).
† Preheat oven to 350°.
† Bake 1 hour. Remove foil and continue
  baking until browned and bubbly.

PEPPERED SHRIMP

Yield: 8 to 10 servings
Margaret Tabb

5   pounds shrimp (shell on)
1   pound butter, melted
    Juice of 4 lemons
1   (16-ounce) bottle Italian
    salad dressing
1   (2-ounce) box ground
    black pepper

† Preheat oven to 350°.
† Place shrimp in 4-quart casserole.
  Combine remaining ingredients and pour
  over shrimp.
† Cover and bake for 30 minutes or until
  shrimp are pink. Stir occasionally.
† May use less pepper.

*Ann Cramer's variation: Instead of Italian dressing, use 1/2 cup Worcestershire sauce,
2 teaspoons hot sauce, 2 teaspoons salt and 4 cloves of garlic, minced.*

SHRIMP FLORENTINE

Yield: 12 servings
Jane Dowd

4   packages frozen chopped
    spinach, thawed and drained
2   pounds medium shrimp,
    cooked and peeled
1   medium onion, chopped
1   stick unsalted butter
1/2 cup flour
3   cups half-and-half
1   cup dry white wine
    Salt and pepper to taste
2   teaspoons paprika
2   cups grated cheddar cheese

† Preheat oven to 325°.
† Spray 9x13-inch casserole with nonstick
  cooking spray. Spread spinach on bottom
  of casserole and layer shrimp on top.
† Sauté onions in butter until soft. Stir in
  flour and gradually blend in half-and-half
  until thickened.
† Slowly stir in wine and seasonings. Pour
  over shrimp and sprinkle with cheese.
† Bake uncovered 30 minutes. Let rest
  several minutes before serving.

SHRIMP ADDIE

Yield: 4 servings
Laura Whedon

6   slices bacon
1   (16-ounce) can whole
    tomatoes
2   large bell peppers, chopped
1   clove garlic, minced
1/2 teaspoon salt
    Pepper to taste
1   pound peeled shrimp

† Cook bacon and crumble.
† Add remaining ingredients, except shrimp,
  to skillet. Cook on low heat 20 to 30
  minutes until slightly thickened.
† Add shrimp and bacon. Cook 4 minutes.
† Serve over rice.

SHRIMP CHEESE GRITS

Yield: 4 servings
Meredith Forshaw

GRITS:
4 cups water
1 cup grits
1 teaspoon salt
2 tablespoons butter
1 cup grated sharp cheese
Nutmeg to taste
Pepper to taste

† Add grits, salt and butter to boiling water. Cook about 10 minutes. Blend in cheese, nutmeg and pepper.

SHRIMP:
1 pound peeled shrimp
1/2 pound sliced mushrooms
1 medium onion, sliced
1 clove garlic
2 tablespoons butter
5-6 slices bacon, cooked and crumbled, reserve drippings
4 teaspoons lemon juice
Tabasco sauce to taste
1 tablespoon chopped parsley
1/4 cup white wine

† Sauté shrimp, mushrooms, onions and garlic in butter and 1 tablespoon bacon drippings until shrimp turn pink. Season with remaining ingredients.
† Divide grits among 4 warm plates or bowls.
† Spoon shrimp over grits.

SOY BARBECUED SHRIMP

Yield: 6 servings
Judith Thomas

SHRIMP:
2 pounds large shrimp, fresh or frozen and thawed

† Leaving tails on, peel and devein shrimp. Arrange in shallow dish.

MARINADE:
2 cloves garlic
1/2 teaspoon salt
1/2 cup olive or vegetable oil
1/4 cup soy sauce
3 tablespoons finely chopped parsley
2 tablespoons finely chopped onion
1/2 teaspoon freshly ground pepper

† Mash garlic in small bowl with salt. Blend in remaining ingredients.
† Pour over shrimp and marinate, covered, in refrigerator 2 to 3 hours.
† Thread shrimp on skewers and grill 2 to 3 minutes on each side. Use marinade to baste.
† Heat marinade to boiling if using as a dip for shrimp.

188

Desserts

The Sweetness Of Service

In Order To Serve

VII. The Sweetness Of Service

Sing, ye faithful, sing with gladness, wake your noblest, sweetest strain,
with the praises of your Savior let his house resound again;
Him let all your music honor, and your songs exalt His reign.
JOHN ELLERTON (1826-1893), Priest, hymn writer and hymnologist [Hymn 492, v.1]

A meal without dessert is like a liturgy without music: it's quite possible to have one, but it's not nearly as enjoyable. And music in the church, like dessert at the table, appeals to persons of every age and every level of sophistication, except for culinary curmudgeons and those on a spiritual diet.

While few people would claim that either church music or dessert is completely nourishing in itself, either can be, at least temporarily, completely satisfying: surely, we've all heard some music and eaten some desserts that were truly spiritual experiences!

Music can, of course, help us to explore the breadth and depth of God Divine and Human. But it's mainly that good *feeling* that most people like about music in church: the roaring organ, the soaring descants of young choristers, the eight-part motet meticulously rehearsed by experienced adult singers which leaves you wondering "how do they do that!"

Is all this spiritual sucrose good for you? Why, yes: if your soul is healthy and regularly exercised, you can have all the church music you want.

But what about guilt? Two of Anglicanism's great gifts to Christianity are a theology which encourages us to reduce our guilt rather than to carry its weight, and a liturgy which has always served up a rich and attractive buffet of good music. So enjoy our music, and your dessert, with gusto—guilt free!

Ye saints, who toil below, adore your heavenly King,
and onward as ye go some joyful anthem sing;
take what He gives
and praise Him still, through good or ill,
who ever lives.
RICHARD BAXTER (1615-1691), Priest, village parson [Hymn 625, v.3]

BENJAMIN HUTTO, ORGANIST/CHOIRMASTER

190

BRIAN'S BIRTHDAY CAKE

Yield: one cake
Kathy Suntken

5   extra large eggs, separated
2   cups sugar, divided
1   stick butter
1   stick margarine
1/2 teaspoon salt
1 1/2 teaspoons vanilla
1   teaspoon baking soda
1   cup buttermilk
2   cups flour
1   cup finely chopped pecans
1   (3 1/2-ounce) can flaked
     coconut

† Preheat oven to 325°.
† Have ingredients at room temperature.
  Beat egg whites until they form soft
  peaks. Slowly add 1/2 cup sugar and
  beat until consistency of meringue. Set
  mixture aside.
† Cream butter, margarine, remaining
  sugar, salt and vanilla. Add egg yolks
  one at a time until consistency of whipped
  cream.
† Stir soda in buttermilk. Beginning and
  ending with flour, alternately add flour with
  buttermilk to butter mixture.
† Fold in egg white mixture, pecans and
  coconut. Pour batter into three 9-inch
  greased and floured cake pans. Bake 40
  minutes. Cool and remove from pans.

FROSTING:
1 1/2 sticks butter, softened
12   ounces cream cheese,
     softened
1 1/2 teaspoons vanilla
1 1/2 (1-pound) boxes
     powdered sugar

† Have ingredients at room temperature.
  Beat ingredients together to whipped
  cream consistency. Frost cake.
  Refrigerate if not eaten that day.

MARILYN'S CRÈME DE MENTHE CAKE

Yield: one cake
Marilyn Collins

1   (19.25-ounce) box white
     cake mix
6   ounces green crème de
     menthe, divided
1   (11.75-ounce) can chocolate
     fudge topping
1   (16-ounce) container frozen
     whipped topping

† Preheat oven to 350°.
† Prepare cake according to cake mix
  directions, adding 3 ounces crème de
  menthe. Bake in greased and floured
  Bundt pan for 35 to 40 minutes. Let
  cool completely.
† Top with can of chocolate fudge topping
  that has been refrigerated for 24 hours.
† Add 3 ounces crème de menthe to frozen
  whipped topping. Spread on cake and
  refrigerate.

CAROLINA APPLE CAKE

Yield: 12 servings
Sue Head

2   cups sugar
11/2 cups canola oil
3   eggs
3   cups flour
1   teaspoon salt
1   teaspoon baking soda
1   teaspoon cinnamon
1   teaspoon vanilla
1   teaspoon lemon flavoring
3   cups chopped peeled apples
1   cup chopped pecans
    (optional)

† Preheat oven to 300°.
† Blend sugar and oil. Beat in eggs.
† Sift dry ingredients. Add to mixture.
† Add vanilla and lemon flavoring. Fold
  in apples and pecans. Batter will be thick.
  Spread in greased 9x13-inch baking pan
  and bake for 80 minutes.

GLAZE:
11/2-2 cups confectioners
    sugar
1/3-1/2 cup fresh lemon juice

† Combine sugar and lemon juice and
  spread on cake while hot.

CRANBERRY CAKE WITH VANILLA SAUCE

Yield: 12 servings
Anne T. Neal

1/2 stick margarine or butter
11/3 cups sugar
22/3 cups flour
4   teaspoons baking powder
1/4 teaspoon salt
11/4 cups milk
4   cups cranberries

† Preheat oven to 350°.
† Cream butter and sugar. Add dry
  ingredients.
† Blend in milk, mixing well. Fold in
  cranberries. Pour in greased 9x13-
  inch pan and bake 45 minutes. Cut
  in squares and serve with vanilla sauce.

SAUCE:
1   stick margarine or butter
1   cup sugar
3/4 cup whipping cream
1   tablespoon cornstarch
1-2 teaspoons vanilla

† Combine all ingredients in saucepan.
  Bring to a boil, cooking until thickened.

CAMMIE'S LAYER CAKE WITH CARAMEL FROSTING

Yield: one cake
Mary Anne Thomas

11/2 sticks butter, softened
11/2 cups sugar
4 extra large eggs, divided, room temperature
2 cups flour
2 teaspoons baking powder
1/2 teaspoon salt
1/2 cup milk
1 teaspoon vanilla
1/4 teaspoon almond flavoring

† Preheat oven to 325°.
† Cream butter and sugar. One at a time, add all eggs but one.
† Sift flour, baking powder and salt. Alternate with milk while adding to creamed mixture. Stir in vanilla and almond flavoring. Add remaining egg, mixing well.
† Pour into 2 greased and floured cake pans. Bake 25 minutes or until toothpick comes out clean. Cool cake thoroughly before frosting.

FROSTING:
2 sticks butter
2 cups packed brown sugar
1/2 cup milk
31/2-4 cups powdered sugar
1 teaspoon vanilla

† Slowly melt butter and add brown sugar. Bring to a boil. Boil 2 minutes and add milk. Bring back to a boil and remove from heat.
† Add sugar and let sit until cool. Beat and add vanilla.

DIRT CAKE

Yield: 14 to 16 servings
Barbara Finn

1/2 stick butter, softened
1 (8-ounce) package cream cheese, softened
1 cup powdered sugar
2 (3.4-ounce) packages instant chocolate pudding
31/2 cups milk
1 (12-ounce) container frozen whipped topping, thawed
1 (20-ounce) package chocolate sandwich cookies, crushed

† In medium bowl, cream butter, cream cheese, and powdered sugar.
† In large bowl, blend pudding and milk. Fold in whipped topping and blend well.
† In large, clear serving bowl, layer: 1/3 cookies, 1/2 pudding mixture, 1/3 cookies, 1/2 pudding, 1/3 cookies on top.
† Store covered in refrigerator.

For fun, assemble cake in clean bucket or flower pot with gummy worms and artificial flowers on top. Serve with a shovel.

CARROT CAKE

Yield: one 3-layer cake
Teresa Pouliot

2 cups flour
2 cups sugar
2 teaspoons cinnamon
1 teaspoon salt
2 teaspoons baking soda
2 teaspoons baking powder
1 cup vegetable oil
4 eggs
3 cups finely shredded carrots
1 1/2 cups chopped pecans or
　　 walnuts

† Preheat oven to 350°.
† Combine first six ingredients. Blend in oil.
† Beat in eggs one at a time. Stir in carrots and nuts.
† Pour into 3 greased 8-inch cake pans. Bake 35 minutes. Cool before frosting.

FROSTING:
1 (16-ounce) box powdered
　 sugar
1 (8-ounce) package cream
　 cheese, softened
1/2 stick butter, softened
1 teaspoon vanilla

† Blend frosting ingredients and spread on cake.

"GLORY BE" CAKE

Yield: one Bundt cake
Paula Freeman

2 (4-ounce) jars prunes
　 with tapioca
2 cups self-rising flour
2 cups sugar
1 teaspoon cinnamon
1 teaspoon nutmeg
1 teaspoon allspice
1 cup vegetable oil
3 eggs
1 cup chopped pecans

† Preheat oven to 350°.
† Combine all ingredients, except nuts, in a large bowl. Beat until well blended. Do not over mix.
† Stir in nuts and pour into greased and floured 10-inch tube pan. Bake 55 to 60 minutes. Cool and invert on plate. Lightly dust with powdered sugar.

CHOCOLATE RUM CAKE

Yield: one Bundt cake
Sis Cranz

1   (18.25-ounce) box devils
    food cake mix
1   (3.4-ounce) package instant
    chocolate pudding mix
1/2 cup sour cream
4   eggs
1   cup vegetable oil
1/2 cup dark rum
1/2 cup strong coffee or 2
    tablespoons instant coffee
    dissolved in 1/2 cup hot
    water)
1   (12-ounce) package semi-
    sweet chocolate chips
1   cup coarsely chopped walnuts

Genie Hufham's variation: Omit nuts.

† Preheat oven to 325°.
† Sift cake mix and pudding mix in large
  bowl.
† Combine sour cream, eggs, oil, rum and
  coffee. Beat on low speed one minute.
† Pour liquid ingredients into dry ingredients
  and beat on high speed 2 minutes. Fold
  in chocolate chips.
† Sprinkle nuts in bottom of greased and
  floured 10-inch Bundt pan. Pour in
  batter and bake 55 minutes. Let cool
  in pan 30 minutes. Remove and cool
  completely. Wrap in foil for 48 hours.

EASY CHOCOLATE CAKE

Yield: one cake
Louise Bonner
Gayle Gilbert

1   stick butter or margarine
1   cup sugar
4   eggs
1   cup self-rising flour
1   (151/2-ounce) can
    chocolate syrup
1   teaspoon vanilla

    ICING:
1   stick butter or margarine,
    melted
1   cup sugar
1/3 cup evaporated milk
3/4-1 cup semi-sweet
    chocolate chips
1   teaspoon vanilla
1   cup chopped pecans (optional)

† Preheat oven to 350°.
† Cream butter and sugar until light and
  creamy. Add eggs one at a time.
† Add flour gradually, mixing well.
† Add syrup and vanilla. Pour into greased
  9x13-inch baking pan and bake for 30
  minutes.

† Melt butter and add sugar and milk. Let
  boil for one minute.
† Add chocolate chips, pecans and vanilla.
  Stir until chocolate is melted and pour
  over warm cake.

CHOCOLATE BROWNIE CAKE

Yield: one cake
Sue Head
Gloria Horne

2   cups sugar
2   cups flour
1/2 cup vegetable shortening
    or 2 sticks margarine
1   cup water
1/2 cup buttermilk
2   (1-ounce) squares
    unsweetened chocolate
1   teaspoon cinnamon
2   eggs
1   teaspoon baking soda
1   teaspoon vanilla

† Preheat oven to 400°.
† Sift together sugar and flour in large bowl. Set aside.
† Melt in saucepan shortening, water, buttermilk, chocolate and cinnamon. Bring to a boil and cook 1 minute. Pour into flour mixture, beating well.
† Beat eggs with baking soda and add vanilla. Blend into cake batter. Pour into greased 9x13-inch pan and bake 20 minutes.

ICING:
1   stick margarine
2   (1-ounce) squares
    unsweetened chocolate
6   tablespoons milk
1   box powdered sugar
1   teaspoon vanilla or rum
1   cup chopped pecans

† In saucepan, bring to slow boil margarine, chocolate, milk. Beat in sugar, vanilla or rum, and pecans. Pour over hot cake.

HERSHEY BAR CAKE

Yield: one cake
Ann Cramer
Anne Neal

1   cup butter or shortening
2   cups sugar
4   eggs
11 ounces Hershey syrup
8   (.58-ounce) Hershey bars,
    melted
21/2 cups flour
1/4 teaspoon salt
1   cup buttermilk
1/2 teaspoon baking soda
1   teaspoon vanilla

† Preheat oven to 325°.
† Cream butter and sugar until fluffy.
† Add eggs one at a time, beating well after each. Add syrup and melted bars, stirring until well mixed.
† Sift flour with salt. Stir soda into buttermilk. Add these alternately to batter.
† Add vanilla and pour into greased Bundt pan.
† Bake for 1 1/2 hours.

CHOCOLATE COCA-COLA CAKE

Yield: 16 servings
Genie Hufham

CAKE:

1/2	cup margarine
1/2	cup vegetable shortening
3	tablespoons unsweetened cocoa
1	cup Coca-Cola Classic
2	cups flour
2	cups sugar
1/2	cup buttermilk
2	eggs
1	teaspoon vanilla
1 1/2	cups miniature marshmallows

† Preheat oven to 350°.
† Bring to a boil first four ingredients.
† Sift flour and sugar in large bowl. Using electric mixer, blend in heated chocolate mixture.
† Stir in buttermilk. Add eggs, vanilla, and marshmallows, beating well. Pour into a greased and floured 9x13-inch pan. Bake 45 minutes.

ICING:

1/2	cup margarine
3	tablespoons unsweetened cocoa
6	tablespoons Coca-Cola Classic
1	box powdered sugar
1	teaspoon vanilla
1	cup chopped pecans

† Begin icing after cake has baked 40 minutes. Bring to boil first three ingredients.
† With electric mixer, pour chocolate mixture into bowl of sugar and beat until smooth.
† Stir in vanilla and pecans. Pour icing over warm cake. Cover with foil to cool.

OLD FASHIONED BUTTERMILK POUND CAKE

Yield: one tube cake
Barbara Finn

1	cup vegetable shortening
3	cups sugar
6	eggs
2 3/4	cups sifted flour
1/2	teaspoon salt
1/4	teaspoon baking soda
1	cup buttermilk
1	teaspoon lemon extract
1	teaspoon vanilla extract (optional)

† Preheat oven to 350°.
† Cream shortening and sugar. Add eggs one at a time, beating well after each addition.
† Sift flour, salt and soda. Add alternately with buttermilk. Add extracts and blend well.
† Pour into greased and floured 10-inch tube pan. Bake for 1 hour 15 minutes or until cake tests done. Let cool before removing from pan.

ETHEL'S CHOCOLATE POUND CAKE WITH CARAMEL ICING

Yield: 1 large tube cake
Dede Thompson

2 sticks butter, softened
1/2 cup vegetable shortening
3 cups sugar
5 eggs
3 cups flour, sifted
4 tablespoons cocoa powder
1/2 teaspoon baking powder
1/2 teaspoon salt
1 cup milk
1 tablespoon vanilla

† Preheat oven to 325°.
† Cream butter, shortening and sugar. Add eggs one at a time.
† Sift flour with dry ingredients.
† Combine milk and vanilla. Add dry ingredients alternately with milk to creamed mixture. Pour into greased and floured tube pan and bake 1 hour and 20 minutes or until done. Cool.

ICING:
1 (1-pound) box light brown sugar
1 stick butter or margarine
1 (5-ounce) can evaporated milk
1/2 teaspoon salt
1/2 teaspoon baking powder
1 teaspoon vanilla

† Bring sugar, butter, milk and salt to boil. Boil to soft ball stage, stirring constantly while it cooks.
† Remove from heat and add baking powder. Beat for 1 minute. Add vanilla and beat until thick enough to spread.

BROWN SUGAR POUND CAKE

Yield: one cake
Ruth Conger

2 sticks butter, softened
1/2 cup vegetable shortening
31/4 cups light brown sugar, packed
5 eggs
31/2 cups sifted all-purpose flour
1/2 teaspoon baking powder
1 cup milk
11/4 teaspoon vanilla

† Preheat oven to 325°.
† Cream butter and shortening until light and fluffy.
† Add sugar one cup at a time.
† Add eggs, one at a time, beating well.
† Sift flour and baking powder together. Add dry ingredients to creamed mixture, alternating with milk.
† Add vanilla and pour batter into well-greased 10-inch tube pan.
† Bake for 11/4 to 11/2 hours or until done when tested.

DARK RUM POUND CAKE

Yield: one Bundt cake
Karen Reid

1 cup chopped pecans
1 (18.25-ounce) box pound cake mix without pudding
1 (3.4-ounce) package vanilla instant pudding
4 eggs
1/2 cup cold water
1/2 cup vegetable oil
1/2 cup dark rum

† Preheat oven to 325°.
† Grease Bundt pan. Spread pecans in bottom of pan.
† Beat remaining cake ingredients until smooth. Pour over pecans. Bake 1 hour.

GLAZE:
1 stick butter
1/4 cup water
1 cup sugar
1/2 cup dark rum

† Bring to a boil butter, water and sugar. Boil 1 minute. Remove from heat and add rum.
† Pour glaze over cake. Refrigerate overnight.

SURPRISE SPICE CAKE

Yield: one Bundt cake
Hannah Thurber

3 cups packed brown sugar
1 pound uncooked mild sausage
1 egg, beaten
3 1/4 cups flour, divided
2 teaspoons baking soda
3 teaspoons baking powder
2 teaspoons cinnamon
1 teaspoon nutmeg
1/4 teaspoon salt
1 cup strong black coffee
2 teaspoons vanilla
1 cup pecan pieces
1/2 cup raisins
1/2 cup chopped dates

† Preheat oven to 350°.
† Combine brown sugar with sausage and egg.
† Sift 3 cups flour with remaining dry ingredients. Add to sausage mixture alternately with coffee and vanilla.
† Dredge pecans, raisins and dates with remaining flour. Blend into cake. Pour into well-greased Bundt pan. Bake 1 1/4 hours.

CHOCOLATE CHIP CUPCAKES

Yield: 20 cupcakes
Christ Church Cooks I

1/2 cup vegetable shortening
6 tablespoons brown sugar
6 tablespoons granulated sugar
1/2 teaspoon vanilla
1 egg
1 1/4 cups flour
1/2 teaspoon baking soda
1/2 teaspoon salt

FILLING:
1/2 cup packed brown sugar
1 egg
Dash of salt
1 (6-ounce) package chocolate chips

† Preheat oven to 350°.
† Beat shortening, sugars, vanilla and egg. Batter will be thick.
† Blend in dry ingredients. Spoon into paper lined muffin tins. Bake 12 minutes. Remove cupcakes.
† Spoon 1 tablespoon filling over each cupcake. Return to oven and bake 15 minutes.

† Combine filling ingredients, except chocolate chips, and heat until thick. Add chocolate chips.

SPICE CUPCAKES

Yield: 30 cupcakes
Christ Church Cooks I

2 cups flour
3 1/2 teaspoons baking powder
1 1/3 cups sugar
1 teaspoon salt
1 teaspoon cinnamon
1/2 teaspoon nutmeg
1/2 teaspoon ground cloves
1/2 cup vegetable shortening
1 cup milk
1 teaspoon vanilla
2 eggs

FROSTING:
1 (1-pound) box powdered sugar
3 rounded tablespoons vegetable shortening
1 egg white
1 teaspoon vanilla
Dash of salt
1/4 cup milk

† Preheat oven to 350°.
† Combine flour, baking powder, sugar, salt and spices.
† Blend in remaining ingredients until smooth.
† Spoon into lined muffin tins 2/3 full. Bake 15 minutes.

† Combine all ingredients except milk. Add milk and beat on high speed until frosting is fluffy.

BOURBON BROWNIES

Yield: 3 dozen
Celia Marshall

BROWNIES:
1 (21-ounce) box brownie mix
1 cup chopped nuts
1/3 cup bourbon

† Preheat oven to 350°.
† Make brownies according to directions and add nuts and bourbon. Pour into a greased and floured jelly roll pan and bake 20 minutes or until done.

TOPPING:
2 cups powdered sugar
1 stick plus 1 1/2 tablespoons butter
1 1/2 tablespoons almond extract
1 (12-ounce) package chocolate chips

† Beat together sugar, 1 stick butter and almond extract. Spread on cooled brownies and chill.
† Melt 1 1/2 tablespoons butter and chocolate chips. Spread on white layer. Let set 1 minute. Cut brownies and chill again.

KATHERINE HEPBURN'S BROWNIES

Yield: 4 dozen
Kassie Minor

1 stick butter
2 (1-ounce) squares unsweetened chocolate
1 cup sugar
2 eggs
1/2 teaspoon vanilla
1/4 cup unbleached flour
1/4 teaspoon salt
1 cup chopped walnuts

† Preheat oven to 325°.
† Melt butter and chocolate on low heat. Remove and stir in sugar.
† Beat in eggs and vanilla. Blend in flour and salt, mixing well. Stir in nuts.
† Spread in greased 9x13-inch pan and bake 15 minutes. Turn pan around and bake 15 minutes longer. Edges will pull away from pan.

IRWIN'S SUPER BROWNIES

Yield: 48 bars
Betsy Locke

1   (14-ounce) package caramels
2/3 cup evaporated milk, divided
1   (18.25-ounce) box German
    chocolate cake mix
1 1/2 sticks butter, softened
1   (6-ounce) package chocolate
    chips
1   cup chopped pecans

† Melt caramels in top of double boiler
  with 1/3 cup milk. Set aside.
† Preheat oven to 350°.
† Combine cake mix with butter and
  remaining 1/3 cup milk. Pour 1/2 batter
  into greased 9x13-inch pan. Bake
  6 minutes.
† Cover baked mixture with chocolate
  chips. Sprinkle pecans on top and
  drizzle with caramel. Dot with
  remaining cake batter. It will be sticky.
† Bake 15 to 18 minutes. Cool, then freeze
  about 30 minutes in order to cut into bars.

KAHLÚA CHOCOLATE WALNUT SQUARES

Yield: 24 squares
Mary Vernon Rogers

1 1/4 cups flour
3/4 teaspoon baking powder
1/2 teaspoon salt
1/2 cup butter or margarine,
    softened
3/4 cup packed brown sugar
1   large egg
1/4 cup plus 1 tablespoon Kahlúa
1   cup chocolate chips
1/3 cup chopped walnuts

† Preheat oven to 350°.
† Sift flour with baking powder and salt.
† Cream butter, sugar and egg. Stir in
  1/4 cup Kahlúa.
† Blend in flour mixture. Fold in chocolate
  chips and walnuts.
† Pour into greased 7x11-inch pan. Bake
  30 minutes. Cool and brush top with 1
  tablespoon Kahlúa.

LAYERED BROWNIES

Yield: 48 squares
Ann Carmichael

BROWNIES:

2	sticks butter or margarine
4	(1-ounce) squares unsweetened chocolate
1	cup flour
2	cups sugar
	Dash of salt
4	eggs
1	teaspoon vanilla

† Preheat oven to 350°.
† Melt butter and chocolate together. Stir in remaining brownie ingredients. Bake in greased 9x13-inch pan for 25 minutes. Cool.

ICING:

1/4	cup butter or margarine, melted
2	cups sifted powdered sugar
2	tablespoons milk
1	teaspoon vanilla

† Combine all ingredients and spread on cooled brownies.

GLAZE:

2	(1-ounce) squares unsweetened chocolate
1	tablespoon butter or margarine

† Melt chocolate and butter and pour over brownies.

BOOTS' CHOCOLATE GRAHAMS

Yield: 10 to 15 servings
Ann Temple

1	(1-pound) box graham crackers
2	sticks butter, melted
1	cup brown sugar
1	(12-ounce) bag milk chocolate chips

† Preheat oven to 350°.
† Place graham crackers on a foil lined cookie sheet with sides touching. They should cover sheet.
† Bring butter and sugar to a boil. Boil 2 minutes. Spread over graham crackers and bake 8 to 10 minutes.
† Remove from oven and sprinkle with chocolate chips. Spread as chips begin to melt. Cool and break into irregularly shaped pieces.

HELLO DOLLYS

Yield: *24 servings*
Beth Thomas

1   stick margarine
11/2 cups graham cracker
    crumbs
1   (12-ounce) package
    chocolate chips
1/2 cup flaked coconut
1   cup chopped pecans
1   (14-ounce) can
    sweetened condensed milk

† Preheat oven to 325°.
† Melt butter in 9x15-inch casserole.
  Sprinkle graham crackers in bottom
  and press into butter.
† Layer chips, coconut, nuts and milk.
  Press nuts into milk and bake 25 to 30
  minutes. Let cool 2 hours before
  cutting.

*1 (6-ounce) package chocolate chips and 1 (6-ounce) package butterscotch
chips may be substituted for the 12-ounce package of chocolate chips.*

CRÈME DE CACAO BALLS

Yield: *4 dozen*
Lynn Armstrong

21/2 cups finely crushed
    chocolate sandwich cookies
1   cup finely chopped pecans
1   cup sifted powdered sugar
1/3 cup crème de cacao
2   tablespoons dark corn syrup
    Additional sifted powdered
    sugar

† Combine all ingredients except additional
  powdered sugar. Shape into 1-inch balls
  and roll in powdered sugar.
† Store in air-tight container in refrigerator.
  Before serving, roll again in powdered
  sugar.

MISSY'S RICH PRALINES

Yield: *3 dozen*
Kate Buckfelder

21/2 cups sugar
1   teaspoon baking soda
1   cup buttermilk
1/4 teaspoon salt
3   tablespoons butter or
    margarine
21/2 cups pecan halves
2/3 cup perfect pecan halves

† In an 8-quart saucepan, combine sugar,
  soda, buttermilk and salt. Cook over
  high heat for 5 minutes or until candy
  thermometer reaches 210°F. Stir
  constantly.
† Add butter and 21/2 cups pecan halves.
  Continue cooking until soft ball stage
  (230°F). Remove from heat.
† After cooling for 1 to 2 minutes, beat with a
  spoon until thick and creamy.
† Drop by tablespoonsful on waxed paper,
  foil or greased cookie sheet. Dot each with
  a perfect pecan half.

BUCKEYES PEANUT BRITTLE DELIGHTS
Yield: 150-200 candies
Marsha Rich

1   (2 1/2-pound) jar creamy
    peanut butter
4   sticks butter, softened
2   pounds powdered sugar
4   (1-ounce) semi-sweet baking
    chocolate squares
2   (12-ounce) packages
    chocolate chips
2   (8-ounce) German chocolate
    bars
1   (4-ounce) square household
    paraffin wax

† Cream peanut butter and butter. Add powdered sugar a little at a time until mixture forms a ball. Roll into small balls and place on a cookie sheet in refrigerator.

† Melt chocolates and paraffin in a double boiler.

† Insert a toothpick into peanut butter balls and dip into the chocolate. Return to cookie sheet and back to refrigerator to harden.

PEANUT BRITTLE
Yield: 1 pound
Camille Salisbury

1   cup sugar
1/2 cup light corn syrup
1   cup roasted, salted
    peanuts
1   teaspoon butter
1   teaspoon vanilla extract
1   teaspoon baking soda

† In 1/2-quart casserole, stir together sugar and syrup. Microwave on high 4 minutes.

† Stir in peanuts and microwave on high 3 to 5 minutes until light brown.

† Blend butter and vanilla into syrup. Microwave on high 1 to 2 minutes. Peanuts will be lightly browned and syrup very hot. Add soda and gently stir until light and foamy.

† Pour mixture onto lightly greased cookie sheet. Let cool 1/2 to 1 hour. When cool, break into small pieces and store in airtight container.

TING-A-LINGS
Yield: 15 servings
Mary Redding

1   (6-ounce) package
    butterscotch chips
1/2 cup salted peanuts
1   (3-ounce) can chow mein
    noodles

† Melt chips in top of double boiler.

† Add peanuts and noodles. Drop by teaspoonfuls on wax paper. Cool.

205

PRETZEL CRUNCHIES

Yield: 2 dozen
Muriel Livingston

1   pound white chocolate
2   cups pretzel twists
    (not sticks)
1   cup peanuts (best),
    pecans or walnuts

† Chop chocolate into small pieces. Melt in top of double boiler. Remove from heat.
† Break pretzels into small pieces and add to chocolate. Add nuts, mixing well.
† Drop on waxed paper in serving size pieces. Chill.

GRAHAM CRACKER COOKIES

Yield: 2 dozen
Caroline Wallace

1   stick margarine
1   stick butter
1 1/2 cups dark brown sugar
    or 1/2 cup granulated sugar
1 1/2 cups chopped pecans
    (optional)
15   cinnamon graham crackers,
    halved

† Preheat oven to 300°.
† Bring margarine, butter and sugar to a boil.
† Add pecans and spread hot mixture on top of graham crackers that have been placed in jelly roll pan.
† Bake 10 minutes and remove immediately from pan.

May be frozen.

DISAPPEARING OATMEAL-RAISIN COOKIES

Yield: 4 dozen
Mary Long

2   sticks butter or margarine,
    softened
1   cup packed brown sugar
1/2 cup granulated sugar
2   eggs
1   teaspoon vanilla
1 1/2 cups flour
1   teaspoon baking soda
1   teaspoon ground cinnamon
1/2 teaspoon salt (optional)
3   cups quick-cooking or old-
    fashioned rolled oats
1   cup raisins

† Preheat oven to 350°.
† Beat margarine and sugars until creamy. Add eggs and vanilla.
† Combine flour, soda, cinnamon and salt. Add to creamed mixture. Stir in oats and raisins.
† Drop by tablespoonsful on greased cookie sheet and bake 10 to 12 minutes. Cool 1 minute on sheet and remove to wire rack. Store in tightly covered container.

NEIMAN MARCUS COOKIES

Yield: 10 dozen
Denise Beasley

2	cups butter, softened
2	cups white sugar
2	cups brown sugar
4	eggs
2	teaspoons vanilla
4	cups flour
5	cups oatmeal, finely ground
1	teaspoon salt
2	teaspoons baking powder
2	teaspoons baking soda
1	(24-ounce) bag chocolate chips
1	(8-ounce) chocolate bar, grated
3	cups chopped nuts

† Preheat oven to 375°.
† Cream together butter and sugars. Add eggs and vanilla.
† Combine flour, oatmeal, salt, baking powder and soda. Mix with creamed mixture.
† Add remaining ingredients. Make golf ball size cookies and place 2 inches apart on ungreased cookie sheet. Bake 6 minutes.

WEDDING COOKIES

Yield: 2 1/2 dozen
Celia Marshall
Mary Redding

1	stick butter
2	tablespoons granulated sugar
1	teaspoon vanilla
1	cup flour
1/2	cup finely chopped pecans
1/2	cup powdered sugar

† Preheat oven to 350°.
† Cream butter, sugar and vanilla.
† Blend flour, then pecans. Roll into tiny balls and place one inch apart on greased cookie sheet. Bake 15 to 18 minutes.
† Carefully remove from sheet and roll immediately in powdered sugar and cool on wire rack. Then roll again in powdered sugar.

Recipe can be doubled.

PAPA D'S CHOCOLATE CHIP COOKIES

Yield: 2 dozen
Ginny Touma

1   stick unsalted butter, softened
1/3 cup granulated sugar
1/3 cup packed dark brown sugar
1   teaspoon vanilla
1   egg, room temperature
1   teaspoon baking powder
1/4 teaspoon salt
2/3 cup chopped walnuts
1   cup flour
4   ounces semi-sweet
     chocolate, in 1/2-inch chunks

† Preheat oven to 375°.
† Cream butter, sugars and vanilla with electric mixer, about 3 minutes.
† Blend in egg, baking powder and salt. Stir in flour, nuts and chocolate.
† Spoon by rounded tablespoons onto cookie sheet. Bake 10 to 12 minutes.

SONJA HENIE COOKIES

Yield: 10 to 12 dozen
Jean Keitt

2   eggs, separated
4   sticks butter, softened
12/3 cups packed brown sugar
41/2 cups flour
11/2 teaspoons vanilla
2   cups finely chopped nuts
4   tablespoons granulated sugar
1   teaspoon cinnamon
1/2 to 1 cup currant jelly

† Preheat oven to 350°.
† Beat egg yolks and combine with butter, brown sugar, flour and vanilla. Roll into small balls.
† Blend together nuts, sugar and cinnamon.
† Dip the balls in unbeaten egg whites and then into cinnamon mixture and place on ungreased cookie sheet.
† Make a small indentation in cookie and fill with currant jelly. Bake 20 minutes.

Red and green currant jelly make this a great Christmas cookie.

208

Desserts

PUMPKIN SPICE BARS

Yield: 3 dozen
Jeanne Kutrow

2 cups flour
1 teaspoon soda
2 teaspoons baking powder
2 cups sugar
2 teaspoons cinnamon
1/2 teaspoon salt
1/2 teaspoon pumpkin pie spice
1 cup chopped nuts
   and/or raisins
4 eggs, beaten
1 cup vegetable oil
1 (16-ounce) can pumpkin

† Preheat oven to 350°.
† Combine dry ingredients. Blend in remaining ingredients, mixing well.
† Pour batter into greased 9x13-inch jelly roll pan and bake 25 to 30 minutes. Cool.

FROSTING:
1 (3-ounce) package cream cheese, softened
6 tablespoons butter or margarine, softened
1 teaspoon vanilla
1 teaspoon milk
2 cups powdered sugar
   Chopped nuts for garnish

† Combine all ingredients and frost bars. Keep refrigerated.

1/2 teaspoon ginger and 1/4 teaspoon cloves may be substituted for pumpkin spice.

FORGOTTEN KISSES

Yield: 2 dozen
Hope Parrott

2 egg whites
2/3 cup sugar
   Pinch of salt
1 (6-ounce) package chocolate chips
3/4 cup chopped nuts (optional)

† Preheat oven to 400°.
† Beat egg whites, sugar and salt until stiff and hold peak. Fold in chocolate chips and nuts.
† Grease cookie sheet. Drop by teaspoonsful on sheet. Place in oven and turn oven off. Leave 6 hours or overnight. Do not open oven.

HARRIET'S CHOCOLATE CHIP MERINGUES

Yield: 24
Amy Thalman

2 cups flour
1 teaspoon baking powder
1/4 teaspoon baking soda
1 cup butter
1/2 cup sugar
1 1/2 cups packed light
    brown sugar, divided
2 eggs, separated
1 teaspoon vanilla extract
1 (12-ounce) package
    chocolate chips

† Preheat oven to 350°.
† Sift flour, baking powder and baking soda. Set aside.
† Cream butter, sugar and 1/2 cup brown sugar. Beat in egg yolks. Gradually add dry ingredients. Stir in vanilla.
† Spread dough onto 9x15-inch baking sheet. Sprinkle with chocolate chips and press into dough.
† Beat egg whites until stiff. Gradually add remaining brown sugar, beating until well mixed. Spread meringue over cookie dough.
† Bake for 25 minutes and cut into squares when cool.

WORLD'S BEST COOKIES

Yield: 8 to 12 dozen
Frances deWitt
Margaretta Leary

1 cup butter, softened
1 cup granulated sugar
1 cup packed brown sugar
1 egg
1 cup vegetable oil
1 cup rolled oats, not instant
1 cup crushed corn flakes
1/2-1 cup shredded coconut or
    chocolate chips
1/2-1 cup chopped pecans
    (optional)
3 1/2 cups sifted flour
1 teaspoon baking soda
1 teaspoon salt
1 teaspoon vanilla extract

† Preheat oven to 325°.
† Cream butter and sugars together until light in color. Add egg and oil.
† Stir in oats, corn flakes, coconut or chocolate chips and nuts.
† Blend in flour, soda, salt and vanilla.
† Roll into balls the size of large olives. Place on ungreased cookie sheet and press flat with a fork. (Helps to dip fork in cold water). Bake 12 minutes.

PEANUT BUTTER COOKIES

Yield: 3 dozen
Kate Buckfelder

1/2 cup butter, softened
1/2 cup peanut butter
1/2 cup sugar
1/2 cup brown sugar
1 egg
1 1/4 cup flour
1/2 teaspoon baking powder
1/2 teaspoon baking soda
1 teaspoon vanilla
  Additional sugar

† Preheat oven to 350°.
† Cream butter, peanut butter and sugars. Add egg and beat well.
† Combine flour, baking powder and soda. Add to creamed mixture. Stir in vanilla.
† Chill dough for 1-2 hours.
† Roll into 1 1/4-inch balls and place 3 inches apart on ungreased cookie sheet. Flatten with fork dipped in sugar.
† Bake for 8-10 minutes. Cool.

LOWFAT BANANA PUDDING

Yield: 10 to 15 servings
Judy Russo

1 (3.4-ounce) box instant vanilla pudding
1 (5-ounce) box instant vanilla pudding
1 (5-ounce) box sugar-free vanilla pudding
5 cups fat free milk
2 (8-ounce) carton light frozen whipped topping, thawed and divided
1/2 cup fat free sour cream
1 (11-ounce) box reduced fat vanilla wafers
3 bananas

† Combine puddings with milk, stirring until it begins to get firm.
† Fold one carton of whipped topping and sour cream into pudding.
† Cover bottom of large glass bowl with wafers. Layer half of banana slices and pudding on top of bananas.
† Place row of wafers around bowl. Repeat layers. Cover top of pudding with whipped topping. Cover with plastic wrap and refrigerate.

CHOCOLATE MOUSSE

Yield: 4 servings
Mabel Barnhardt

6 (1-ounce) squares semi-sweet chocolate
1/2 cup milk
3/4 stick margarine, cut into pieces
8 egg yolks
8 egg whites, stiffly beaten

† In medium saucepan, melt chocolate in milk over low heat. Add margarine.
† When melted, remove from heat and add egg yolks, stirring very fast.
† Fold in egg whites. Spoon into individual serving dishes or serving bowl. Refrigerate covered.

211

BLINTZ TORTE

Yield: 8 servings
Elinor Wiley

1/2	cup butter
13/4	cups sugar, divided
4	eggs, separated
1	teaspoon vanilla
1	cup flour
1/4	teaspoon salt
1	teaspoon baking powder
3	tablespoons milk
2	tablespoons sliced almonds

† Preheat oven to 350°. Grease, flour and line with wax paper two 8-inch pans.
† Cream butter and 3/4 cup sugar. Gradually add egg yolks and vanilla.
† Sift flour, salt and baking powder. Add, alternating with milk, to butter mixture. Spread dough in pans. Will look thin and be hard to spread.
† Beat egg whites until stiff. Add 1 cup sugar and spread half of meringue on top of each pan. Sprinkle with almonds and two tablespoons sugar on each layer.
† Bake for 25 to 30 minutes. Cool in pans and serve with whipped cream between layers.

BROWNIE PUDDING

Yield: 12 servings
Lynne Ford

1/2	cup plus 2 tablespoons cocoa powder
1	cup flour
2	teaspoons baking powder
1/2	teaspoon salt
3/4	cup sugar
1/2	cup milk
1	teaspoon vanilla
2	tablespoons margarine, melted
3/4	cup chopped nuts
3/4	cup brown sugar
13/4	cups hot water

† Preheat oven to 350°.
† Sift 2 tablespoons cocoa powder and dry ingredients. Blend in milk, vanilla and margarine until smooth. Add nuts. Pour into greased 8-inch square or round pan.
† Combine brown sugar and 1/2 cup cocoa powder and sprinkle over batter. Pour hot water over all. Bake 40 to 45 minutes.
† Serve with vanilla ice cream.

Desserts

BREAD PUDDING WITH WHISKEY SAUCE   *Yield: 10 servings*
Meredith Forshaw

PUDDING:

3/4	cup raisins
2	tablespoons dark rum
1	pound French bread, cut in 1-inch cubes
3	cups milk (not low-fat or nonfat)
1	cup half and half
3	eggs, beaten
2	cups sugar
3	tablespoons butter, melted
2	tablespoons vanilla extract
1/2	teaspoon cinnamon

† Preheat oven to 325°.
† Place raisins in small bowl with rum. Let soak 20 minutes.
† Place bread in large bowl with milk and half-and-half. Let soak 5 minutes.
† Whisk eggs with sugar, butter, vanilla and cinnamon. Pour over bread. Add raisins and rum.
† Transfer bread mixture to buttered 9x13-inch casserole and bake until top is golden brown, about one hour. Bread may puff above rim of casserole.

SAUCE:

1	stick butter
1/2	cup brown sugar
1/2	cup granulated sugar
1	egg
3	tablespoons whiskey

† Melt butter with sugars in saucepan over low heat, stirring until sugars dissolve.
† Whisk egg in small bowl. Gradually whisk in some of melted butter mixture. Return mixture to saucepan and whisk until smooth for one minute. Do not boil. Blend in whiskey.
† Place warm bread pudding onto plate.
† Spoon warm sauce over the top.

ENGLISH APPLE PUDDING

Yield: 8 to 10 servings
Helen Wall

5	large apples, peeled, cored and sliced
1/2	cup granulated sugar
1/2	cup brown sugar
1/2	cup flour
1/2	cup butter, melted
1	tablespoon cinnamon

† Preheat oven to 350°.
† Combine apples, sugars and flour and place in 2-quart casserole.
† Blend butter and cinnamon and pour over apples. Bake 45 minutes.

213

AMARETTO CHEESECAKE

Yield: 8 to 12 servings
DeeDee Dalrymple

CRUST:

13	(5x21/2-inch) cinnamon crisp graham crackers
1	stick butter, melted
1/4	cup sugar

† Crush crackers in food processor.
† Combine crumbs with butter and sugar. Place in 9-inch springform pan that has been sprayed with nonstick cooking spray. Place in refrigerator.

FILLING:

4	(8-ounce) packages cream cheese, softened
11/2	cups sugar
11/2	tablespoons fresh lime juice
	Pinch of salt
4	eggs

† Preheat oven to 350°.
† Cream cheese and sugar.
† Add lime juice, salt and eggs one at a time. Pour into crust and bake 45 minutes or until browned. Remove from oven and let stand 10 minutes.

TOPPING:

1	(16-ounce) carton sour cream
1/4	cup sugar
1	teaspoon almond extract

† Combine all ingredients and spread over cake. Cook 10 minutes. Chill in refrigerator 4 to 5 hours before serving.

DONNIE'S CHEESECAKE

Yield: 10 to 12 servings
Susan Fitch

CRUST:

11/4	cups graham cracker crumbs
2	tablespoons margarine, softened
2	tablespoons sugar
1/4	teaspoon cinnamon

† Preheat oven to 375°.
† Combine crust ingredients. Grease bottom of 10-inch springform pan. Pat mixture evenly in bottom of pan.

FILLING:

4	(8-ounce) packages cream cheese, softened
2	cups sugar
2	teaspoons vanilla
1	(16-ounce) carton sour cream
6	eggs

† Blend filling ingredients. Add eggs one at a time. Pour over crust and bake 45 minutes. Turn oven off and leave in oven 1 hour. DO NOT OPEN OVEN. Take out and let sit at room temperature. Store 24 hours in refrigerator before serving.

Cake must be made the day before serving. Heat knife to cut cake easily.

KAHLÚA CHEESECAKE

Yield: 12 to 15 servings
Nancy Hemmig

CRUST:

11/4 cups graham cracker crumbs
1/4 cup sugar
1/4 cup cocoa powder
51/3 tablespoons butter, melted

† Preheat oven to 325°.
† Combine all ingredients and press into bottom of 9-inch springform pan. Bake 5 minutes. Cool.

FILLING:

2 (8-ounce) packages cream cheese, softened
3/4 cup sugar
1/2 cup cocoa powder
2 eggs
1/4 cup strong coffee
1/4 cup Kahlúa
1 teaspoon vanilla

† Beat cream cheese until fluffy. Add sugar, cocoa powder and eggs. Blend in next 3 ingredients, beating well after each addition. Pour over baked crust. Bake 25 minutes.

TOPPING:

1 (8-ounce) carton sour cream
2 tablespoons sugar
1 teaspoon vanilla

† Preheat oven to 425°.
† Combine sour cream, sugar and vanilla. Spread over hot cheesecake and bake 5 to 7 minutes. Let cool to room temperature. Chill 8 hours. Bring to room temperature to serve.

CHOCOLATE ANGEL CAKE DESSERT

Yield: 14 servings
Ann Brewster Jones

1 (12-ounce) package chocolate chips
2 tablespoons sugar
3 eggs, separated
1 pint whipping cream
1 (8-ounce) angel food cake

† Melt chocolate chips with sugar in top of double boiler. Remove from heat.
† Beat egg yolks and stir into chocolate. Cool 5 minutes.
† Beat egg whites until stiff. Whip cream and fold with egg whites into chocolate mixture.
† Break angel food cake into bite-sized pieces. Spread layer of cake in bottom of buttered 9x13-inch pan or 8-inch spring form pan. Cover with layer of chocolate. Layer remaining cake and top with chocolate. Chill overnight.

TWO-WHISKEY CHOCOLATE MOUSSE

Yield: 5 cups
Ann Cramer

1/4 cup boiling water
1 tablespoon dark roast ground coffee
4 (1-ounce) squares unsweetened chocolate
1/4 teaspoon salt
1 1/3 cups heavy cream, divided
2 tablespoons butter
8-10 tablespoons sugar
1 teaspoon vanilla
1 tablespoon bourbon
1 tablespoon dark rum

† Pour water over coffee and let steep 2 minutes. Strain.
† In a double boiler, add coffee water to chocolate, salt, 1/3 cup cream and butter. When melted, remove to cool.
† Whip remaining cup of cream. Add sugar slowly to form soft peaks.
† Fold vanilla, bourbon and rum into whipped cream. Fold into chocolate mixture.
† Spoon into mousse glasses or baked pie shell. Refrigerate.

CHOCOLATE SOUFFLÉ

Yield: 4 to 6 servings
Anne Tomlinson

1/3 cup flour
3/4 cup sugar, divided
1 1/2 cups milk
3 (1-ounce) squares unsweetened chocolate, grated
6 eggs, separated
1/4 teaspoon vanilla
Sweetened whipped cream for garnish

† Grease a 2-quart soufflé dish with butter. Sprinkle with sugar.
† In saucepan, combine flour and 1/4 cup sugar. Using wire whisk, slowly stir in milk until smooth. Cook over medium heat until thick. When boiling, cook 1 minute. Remove from heat.
† Stir chocolate into mixture until melted. Rapidly beat in egg yolks. Cool.
† Beat egg whites until soft peaks form. Sprinkle in remaining sugar slowly.
† Fold egg whites into chocolate mixture and add vanilla. Pour into prepared dish. Sprinkle with sugar. Bake 35 to 40 minutes until knife comes out clean.
† Serve at once with whipped cream.

CHOCOLATE TORTE

Yield: 15 servings
Kim Hattaway

1   stick butter or margarine
1 1/4 cups chopped pecans, divided
1   cup self-rising flour
1   (8-ounce) package cream cheese, softened
1   cup sugar
1   (12-ounce) container frozen whipped topping, thawed, divided
2   (3-ounce) packages instant chocolate pudding, prepared

† Preheat oven to 350°.
† 1st layer: melt butter in 9x13-inch casserole. Combine one cup pecans and flour and mix well with butter, spreading in bottom of pan. Bake 15 minutes. Let cool.
† 2nd layer: Beat cream cheese and sugar. Fold in 1/2 of whipped topping and spread on crust.
† 3rd layer: Spread pudding on 2nd layer.
† 4th layer: Spread remaining whipped topping on 3rd layer and top with pecans. Refrigerate.

Lemon Lush - Use instant lemon pudding in place of chocolate pudding in 3rd layer.

CHOCOLATE TRIFLE

Yield: 16 to 18 servings
Genie Hufham

1   (19.8-ounce) box brownie mix
1   (5.9-ounce) package chocolate fudge pudding, prepared
8   (4-ounce) English toffee bars, frozen and crushed, reserving some for garnish
1/2 cup Kahlúa or other coffee-flavored liqueur
12   ounces whipped cream or frozen whipped topping, thawed

† Prepare brownie mix according to package directions. Cook, cool, and crumble.
† Layer in glass bowl, 1/3 each brownies, pudding, candy, liqueur and whipped cream.
† Repeat two more times. Sprinkle reserved candy on top.

RUSSIAN CREAM WITH RASPBERRY SAUCE

Yield: 8 servings
Patty Adams

CREAM:

1	envelope unflavored gelatin
1/2	cup water
1/2	cup sugar
1	(3-ounce) package cream cheese, softened
1	cup whipping cream
1	(8-ounce) carton sour cream
1	teaspoon vanilla

† In small saucepan, soften gelatin in water. Let stand 1 minute. Add sugar and stir over medium heat until sugar dissolves. Cool.

† Beat cream cheese until fluffy. Gradually add gelatin.

† Pour in whipping cream, sour cream and vanilla. Beat until well blended and pour into 8 individual molds. Chill.

SAUCE:

1	(10-ounce) package frozen raspberries, thawed (reserve some whole ones for garnish)
2	tablespoons orange flavored liqueur
2	tablespoons sugar

† Put ingredients in blender. Pour over each mold before serving. Top with whole raspberries.

BOILED CUSTARD

Yield: 4 servings
Anne Tomlinson

3	eggs
1/2	cup sugar
2	cups scalded milk
1	teaspoon vanilla

† Beat eggs and add sugar. Pour hot milk over eggs.

† Place mixture in double boiler and cook until thickened, using wire whisk.

† Remove from heat and add vanilla. Cool and refrigerate. Custard will thicken in refrigerator.

CREAM PUFFS OR ÈCLAIRS

Yield: 6 large or 12 to 18 small puffs
Anne Tomlinson

SHELLS:
1/2 stick butter
1/2 cup boiling water
1/2 cup flour
1/4 teaspoon salt
2 eggs

† Preheat oven to 450°.
† Add butter to boiling water to melt. Combine flour and salt. Blend into water. Stir until it no longer sticks to pan.
† Remove from heat. Add eggs one at a time. Beat until stiff. Form into oblong or round mounds on greased baking sheet. Bake 10 minutes. Reduce heat to 375° and bake 25 minutes or until brown.

FILLING:
1/3 cup plus 2 tablespoons sugar
1/8 teaspoon salt
2 tablespoons flour
2 egg yolks
1 1/2 cups milk
2 teaspoons vanilla
Powdered sugar or chocolate icing as garnish

† Combine dry ingredients. Slightly beat eggs in milk and slowly add to dry ingredients.
† Slowly bring to a boil, stirring constantly until thick. Boil 1 minute. Remove from heat and add vanilla. Cool completely.
† Cut off top and hollow out cavities of puffs. Spoon in filling. Replace top.
† Sprinkle cream puffs with powdered sugar or ice with favorite chocolate icing.

MAMA'S CHOCOLATE SAUCE

Yield: 1 1/2 to 2 cups
Suzie Lowe

1 cup sugar
3 tablespoons cocoa powder
3 tablespoons flour
1 stick butter
1 (5-ounce) can evaporated milk
1 teaspoon vanilla

† Combine ingredients and boil 1 minute, stirring constantly.
† Store in refrigerator.
† Warm before serving.

MISTY MOUNTAIN GINGERBREAD
WITH LEMON SAUCE

Yield: 12 servings
Jane Bruce

GINGERBREAD:

1	cup molasses
1	cup vegetable shortening
1	cup sugar
1	tablespoon cinnamon
1	tablespoon ginger
1	teaspoon allspice
1	teaspoon cloves
21/2	cups flour
1	teaspoon salt
1	cup buttermilk
2	eggs, beaten
1	teaspoon baking soda
1/4	cup hot water

† Combine molasses, shortening, sugar and spices in a saucepan. Bring to a boil, beating until shortening melts. Remove from heat.

† Combine flour and salt. Beat into boiled mixture. Add buttermilk and eggs.

† Dissolve soda in hot water and stir into batter. Pour into a greased and floured 12x7-inch pan and bake 50 to 60 minutes.

LEMON SAUCE:

1/2	cup sugar
2	tablespoons cornstarch
1	cup water
1/2	stick butter or margarine
2	teaspoons lemon zest
1/4	cup fresh lemon juice
	Dash of salt

† In a small saucepan, combine sugar and cornstarch. Add water, stirring until smooth. Bring to a boil. Reduce heat and simmer, stirring constantly until mixture is thickened and translucent (about 5 minutes).

† Remove from heat and stir in butter, lemon zest, lemon juice and salt. Serve on warm cake.

MY ONLY DESSERT

Yield: 8 to 12 servings
Ben Hutto

8-12 thin slices any unfrosted cake or nut bread (stale preferred)
1/2 gallon premium vanilla or butter pecan ice cream
Bourbon
Chocolate syrup (optional)
Instant coffee

† Place cake in bottom of individual glass dishes and put scoop of ice cream on top.

† Pour small amount of bourbon over ice cream and sprinkle with dusting of instant coffee.

† May drizzle with chocolate syrup or whipped cream before dusting with coffee.

LEMON PUDDING CAKE

Yield: 8 servings
Jean Spratt

3   eggs, separated
1   cup sugar
1   tablespoon flour
1   cup milk
    Zest of 2 lemons
    Juice of 2 lemons
1   tablespoon butter, melted

† Preheat oven to 300°.
† Beat egg yolks. Add sugar and flour. Beat in remaining ingredients except egg whites.
† Beat egg whites until stiff but not dry. Fold into egg yolk mixture.
† Pour into greased 6-cup casserole or individual custard cups. Place in pan of hot water. Bake 45 minutes or until set.
† Invert on dessert dish. It will be like sponge cake with lemon sauce.

LIME MOUSSE TARTS

Yield: 8 servings
Sis Cranz

1   stick butter or margarine
13/4 teaspoons lime zest
1/4 cup lime juice
11/2 cups sugar
     Dash of salt
3   eggs, beaten
3   egg yolks, beaten
2   cups whipping cream, divided
8   (4-inch) baked tart shells
     Lime zest for garnish

† Melt butter in top of double boiler. Stir in lime zest, lime juice, sugar and salt.
† Gradually add eggs and egg yolks. Cook, stirring constantly, until very thick and smooth.
† Remove from heat and cool completely.
† Beat 1 cup whipping cream and fold into lime mixture.
† Spoon into tart shells and freeze at least 6 hours.
† Serve with sweetened whipped cream and lime zest for garnish.

Use 8 to 12 lime cups in place of tart shells. Cut 3/4 inch off top and 1/3 inch off bottom of lime. Juice and clean limes, being careful to preserve their shape. Spoon mousse into cups and garnish.

ICE CREAM CRUNCH

Yield: 12 servings
Jean Keitt

21/2 cups crispy rice cereal
1 (31/2 ounce) can flaked coconut
1 cup coarsely chopped pecans
1 stick butter, melted
3/4 cup brown sugar, firmly packed
1/2 gallon vanilla ice cream
Hot fudge sauce

† Preheat oven to 300°.
† Spread cereal, coconut, pecans and butter in jelly roll pan and bake 15 to 30 minutes. Stir to brown evenly. Blend in brown sugar.
† Press 1/2 mixture in bottom of 9x12-inch casserole and cover with ice cream that has been cut into 1-inch slices. Top with remaining crunch and refreeze.
† Cut into squares and serve with hot fudge sauce.

OREO COOKIE FREEZE

Yield: 8 to 10 servings
Fran Stroud

28 Oreo cookies, crumbled
1/2 stick butter or margarine, melted
1/2 gallon coffee ice cream, softened
1 cup sugar
1 (5-ounce) can evaporated milk
1 teaspoon vanilla
4 (1-ounce) squares semi-sweet baking chocolate
6 tablespoons butter or margarine
1 (16-ounce) container frozen whipped topping, thawed
Chopped nuts (optional)

† Combine cookies and butter and press in bottom of 9x13-inch pan. Spread ice cream on crust and freeze.
† Mix remaining ingredients, except whipped topping and nuts. Cool and pour over ice cream layer. Freeze again.
† Spread whipped topping over chocolate layer and sprinkle with nuts. Refreeze.

PEACH KUCHEN

Yield: 15 servings
Elaine Thigpen

CRUST:

1 1/4 cups flour
1 teaspoon baking powder
1 tablespoon sugar
1 stick butter
1 egg, lightly beaten
1 tablespoon milk

† Preheat oven to 350°.
† Combine first three ingredients. Add butter, cutting in as for piecrust.
† Blend egg and milk and add to flour mixture. Press on sides and bottom of 9x13-inch ungreased pan.

FILLING:

6 peeled peaches, halved or quartered
1 egg, lightly beaten
1 cup sour cream
1 1/2 tablespoons flour
3/4 cup sugar

† Place peaches on crust, cut side up.
† Blend egg, sour cream, flour and sugar. Pour over fruit.

STREUSEL:

3/4 cup sugar
1/4 stick butter
2 tablespoons flour
1/2 teaspoon cinnamon

† Cream sugar and butter. Blend flour and cinnamon. Cover fruit with streusel and bake 45 minutes or until fruit is baked and streusel is browned.

PEACH SUNSHINE PIZZA

Yield: 8 to 10 servings
Carol Jennings

1 (10-ounce) package frozen pizza crust
1 (29-ounce) can sliced peaches, well drained
1/2 cup lowfat sour cream
3/4 teaspoon ground nutmeg
1 teaspoon almond extract
1/3 cup sugar
1 egg
1 cup plain granola
1/4 cup toasted slivered almonds

† Preheat oven to 425°.
† In greased 12-inch pizza pan, press out dough to cover pan. Prick with fork and bake 5 minutes.
† Combine remaining ingredients, except granola and almonds. Spread over baked crust. Top with granola followed by almonds. Bake 15 to 20 minutes.

PEACH COBBLER

Yield: 12 servings
Julia Lackey

FRUIT:
1	stick butter or margarine
4	cups fresh peaches, sliced
1	tablespoon lemon juice
1	cup sugar

† Preheat oven to 375°.
† Melt butter in 3-quart baking dish.
† Mix peach slices, lemon juice and sugar. Spread in dish over butter.

TOPPING:
1	cup flour
1	cup sugar
1	teaspoon baking powder
3/4	cup milk
	Pinch of salt

† Combine ingredients and spread over the fruit. Bake 45 minutes until golden brown.

PEARS BAKED IN CREAM

Yield: 4 servings
Nancy Ehringhaus

2	tablespoons butter, divided
2	tablespoons sugar, divided
2	pears, unpeeled, halved and cored
1/2	cup heavy cream

† Preheat oven to 400°.
† Butter shallow baking dish with 1 tablespoon butter and sprinkle with 1 tablespoon sugar.
† Arrange pears cut side down in dish. Sprinkle with remaining butter and sugar. Bake 10 minutes.
† Pour cream over pears and return to oven for 20 minutes. Serve warm.

PAVLOVA

Yield: 6 servings
Peg Hutchins

4	eggs whites
1	cup plus 2 tablespoons sugar, divided
1	teaspoon vanilla
1	teaspoon vinegar
1	teaspoon cornstarch
1	pint whipping cream, whipped, for garnish
	Fresh fruit to cover

† Preheat oven to 300°.
† Beat egg whites until stiff. Add 1/2 of the sugar and beat again until stiff. Add remaining ingredients and beat well.
† Line cookie sheet with wax paper. Spread mixture in circle on cookie sheet and bake 60 minutes. Turn off oven and leave to cool.
† Cover with whipped cream and fresh fruit.

FRUIT COBBLER

Yield: 6 to 8 servings
Barbara Finn

FRUIT:

2 to 3 cups fresh fruit, cut
    into chunks or slices
1/2 - 3/4 cup sugar (depending
    on sweetness of fruit)

† At least one hour ahead, cover fruit
   with sugar.

COBBLER:

1   stick butter or margarine
1   cup flour
1   cup sugar
1 1/2 teaspoons baking powder
1/8 teaspoon salt
1/2 cup milk
1   egg

† Preheat oven to 375°.
† Melt butter in 2-quart rectangular dish.
† Sift flour, sugar, baking powder and
   salt. Blend in egg and milk.
† Pour batter evenly over butter. Spoon
   sweetened fruit and juice over batter.
   Bake uncovered 30 to 45
   minutes until top is golden brown.

COCONUT-ALMOND DESSERT

Yield: 8 to 10 servings
Lois Ann Partridge

1   (3.4-ounce) package vanilla
    pudding
1   teaspoon almond flavoring
1/2 pint whipping cream,
    whipped stiff
1/2 cup toasted sliced almonds
1   cup toasted coconut
1   angel food cake

† Prepare pudding according to directions.
   Add almond flavoring and chill 2 hours.
† Fold whipped cream, almonds and
   coconut into pudding mixture.
† Slice Angel food cake into layers and
   ice with pudding.
† Chill 4 hours before serving.

CRANBERRY DESSERT

Yield: 4 to 5 cups
Jane Neal Bobbitt

1   pound raw cranberries,
    washed and picked over
1   pound tokay grapes,
    seeded, halved and drained
2   cups sugar
1   pint whipped cream

† Combine cranberries, grapes and sugar.
† Fold in whipped cream and refrigerate.

No-fat sour cream can be substituted to be heart healthy.

QUEEN CHARLOTTE'S TART

Yield: 8 to 12 servings
Eugenia Allderdice

CRUST:

2   pie crusts, unbaked

† Preheat oven to 350°.
† Press 1 pie crust in bottom of 8-inch springform pan. Allow dough to go up sides of pan about 1/2 inch. Prick and bake until slightly golden. Cool.

FILLING:

1   stick butter
3/4 cup sugar
1   egg
1/2 cup plus 1 tablespoon rice flour
1/3 cup sliced almonds
1   teaspoon almond extract
4-6 tablespoons raspberry jam

† Preheat oven to 400°.
† Melt butter and stir in sugar. Cook 1 minute, stirring constantly.
† Add egg, flour, almonds and almond extract.
† Spread jam on baked crust. Top with filling. Cut second crust into strips. Lay across tart for a lattice look. Bake 30 minutes or until well risen and golden brown.

CREAMY BAKED RICE PUDDING

Yield: 4 to 6 servings
Marie Palmer

1   quart milk
1/4 cup sugar
1/4 cup raw white rice
1   tablespoon butter or margarine
1/4 teaspoon salt
1/4 teaspoon nutmeg
1   teaspoon vanilla extract
1/4 cup raisins, light or dark
    Whipped cream, hot fudge sauce, fruit or maple syrup for topping.

† Preheat oven to 325°.
† In greased 11/2 quart casserole, combine all ingredients, except raisins. Bake uncovered 21/2 hours or until rice is done, stirring often.
† Add raisins after 1 hour of baking.
† Serve with any topping.

226

PECAN SOUFFLÉ

Yield: 4 to 6 servings
Michaelle Moon

1/4 cup butter
1/4 cup all-purpose flour
1/2 teaspoon salt
1   cup milk
3   eggs, separated
1/2 cup sugar
1   cup finely chopped pecans
1   teaspoon vanilla
1/2 pint whipping cream
1/2 teaspoon grated lemon rind

† Preheat oven to 350°.
† Melt butter in top of double boiler. Add flour and salt, mixing well.
† Add milk gradually, stirring constantly. Cook until thick.
† Combine well-beaten egg yolks, sugar, pecans and vanilla, blending well.
† Add to cooked butter and flour mixture, stirring until blended.
† Fold stiffly beaten egg whites into mixture.
† Pour into buttered soufflé dish and place in a pan of hot water to the depth of 1 1/2 inches.
† Bake for 45 to 60 minutes until set or until knife blade comes out clean from the soufflé.
† Whip cream, adding lemon rind.
† Serve at once with whipped cream

STRAWBERRY SHORTCAKE

Yield: 4 to 6 servings
Michaelle Moon

BERRIES:
1-1 1/2 quarts fresh strawberries
3/4 cup brown sugar or 1/2 cup white sugar

† Cut berries, saving about a dozen for garnish. Add sugar and let stand in warm place.

SHORTCAKE:
2 1/4 cups flour
4   teaspoons baking powder
1/2 teaspoon salt
     Trace of ground nutmeg
1/3 cup plus 3 tablespoons butter, softened
1   egg, well beaten
1/3 cup milk
1 1/2 pints whipping cream, stiffly beaten

† Preheat oven to 400°.
† Mix dry ingredients and sift twice. Work in 1/3 cup butter with fingertips. Add egg and then milk.
† Turn, without rolling, into well-greased 9-inch round pan and pat into shape.
† Bake for 15 minutes.
† Split warm shortcake into two layers, buttering each cut side with remaining butter. Keep the buttered sides up.
† Place 1/2 strawberry mixture between the cake layers and 1/2 of mixture on top. Top with whole berries and serve with whipped cream.

APPLE PIE

Yield: one pie
Mimi Rees

2   (9-inch) pie crusts
1 1/4 cups sugar
1 1/2 teaspoons cinnamon
4 - 5 apples, peeled and sliced
    Butter

† Preheat oven to 400°.
† Combine sugar and cinnamon. Sprinkle half of mixture on bottom of crust.
† Place apples in crust and sprinkle with remaining sugar.
† Dot with butter. Cover with top crust. Cut vents in top and bake 60 minutes.

To freeze, make pie according to recipe but do not cut vents. Cover with paper plate and wrap for freezing. May be stored 3 to 4 months. To bake, cut vents in top crust and place frozen pie in preheated 400° oven. Allow 10 to 15 minutes extra baking time.

MIXED BERRY PIE

Yield: one pie
Kate Buckfelder

PIE:
4   cups strawberries
2   cups blueberries
1   cup raspberries or cherries
1 1/2 cups sugar
5   tablespoons quick-cook tapioca
1/4   teaspoon cinnamon
1   (9-inch) deep dish pie shell, uncooked

† Preheat oven to 350°.
† Combine all ingredients and pour into pie shell.

TOPPING:
2   cups flour
1   cup packed brown sugar
2   teaspoons cinnamon
1/2   teaspoon salt
1   stick butter or margarine, melted

† Blend topping ingredients to form a crumbly mixture. Sprinkle on top of pie and bake 60 minutes.

CARAMEL PIE

Yield: one pie
Estelle S. Dyer

2   cups brown sugar
2   tablespoons flour
1   stick butter, melted
2   eggs, beaten
1/2 cup milk
1   teaspoon vanilla extract
2-3 drops almond extract
1   deep-dish prepared pie
    crust (8-inch suggested)

† Preheat oven to 350°.
† Cream sugar, flour and butter.
† Add remaining ingredients and pour
  into pie crust. Bake 45 to 60 minutes.
  Cool before serving.

JUANITA'S CHESS PIE

Yield: one pie
Becky and Henry Parsley

1   stick butter
1   cup sugar
3   eggs
1/2 cup whole milk or cream
    Nutmeg to taste
1   (9-inch) baked pie shell

† Preheat oven to 300°.
† Cream butter and sugar.
† Beat in eggs one at a time. Add milk
  and season with nutmeg. Pour into
  baked pie shell. Bake 45 to 60 minutes
  until firm.

CHOCOLATE-AMARETTO MOUSSE PIE

Yield: one pie
Sis Cranz

2   (1.3-ounce) envelopes
    whipped topping mix
2   cups milk, divided
1/2 teaspoon vanilla
2   (41/2-ounce) packages
    chocolate instant pudding
    and pie filling
1/4 cup Amaretto or other
    almond-flavored liqueur
1   (9-inch) baked pastry
    shell, cooled
1   (8-ounce) container frozen
    whipped topping, thawed
    Chocolate shavings for
    garnish

† Prepare topping mix according to
  package directions.
† Add 11/2 cups milk, pudding mix and
  Amaretto. Beat 2 minutes on high
  speed of electric mixer.
† Spoon mixture into pastry shell. Top
  with whipped topping and chocolate
  shavings. Chill for 4 hours.

CHOCOLATE CHESS PIE

Yield: one (9-inch) deep dish
pie or two (8-inch) pies
Mary Vernon Rogers

1 1/2 cups sugar
2 eggs
3 tablespoons cocoa
1/2 stick margarine, melted
1 teaspoon vanilla
1 (5-ounce) can evaporated milk
1 (9-inch) deep dish pie shell or 2 (8-inch), unbaked

† Preheat oven to 325°.
† Combine all ingredients and pour into pie shell. Bake 45 minutes.
† Use whipped cream or ice cream for garnish.

CHOCOLATE NUT PIE

Yield: one pie
Anne Neal

1 cup sugar
1 stick unsalted butter, melted
1/4 cup cornstarch
2 large eggs
1 teaspoon vanilla extract
1 (6-ounce) package chocolate chips
1 cup chopped pecans or walnuts
1 (9-inch) frozen unbaked pie shell

† Preheat oven to 350°.
† Combine first 5 ingredients in large bowl.
† Stir in chocolate chips and nuts. Pour mixture into pie shell. Bake 40 minutes or until filling is golden brown.

HEATH BAR PIE

Yield: one pie
Missy Strickland

1 pint vanilla ice cream, softened
1 cup milk
1 (3-ounce) package instant chocolate pudding
1 graham cracker pie crust
1 (9-ounce) package chocolate covered toffee candy bars
1 (8-ounce) container frozen whipped topping, thawed

† Combine ice cream with milk and add pudding. Beat until mixture thickens.
† Grate 4 toffee candy bars and spread on bottom of (9-inch) pie shell. Pour pudding mixture into shell and refrigerate.
† Spread whipped topping on top and sprinkle with remaining grated toffee bars.

SOUR CREAM LIME PIE

Yield: one pie
Kassie Minor

CRUST:
1   deep dish pie shell, baked

† Prepare baked pie shell.

FILLING:
1   cup sugar
3   tablespoons cornstarch
1/4 cup butter, softened
1/3 cup fresh lime juice
1   tablespoon lime zest
1   cup half and half
1   cup sour cream

† Combine all ingredients, except sour cream, in saucepan. Bring slowly to a boil, stirring constantly. Cook until thickened and smooth. Cool. Fold in sour cream and pour into pie shell.

TOPPING:
1   cup heavy cream
1   tablespoon powdered sugar
1   cup sour cream
    Lime zest for garnish

† Whip cream and fold in sugar and sour cream. Spread on top of pie. Garnish with lime zest.

PEACH CUSTARD PIE

Yield: one pie
Meredith Forshaw

1   deep-dish pie shell
6   cups sliced peaches
1/2 cup sugar
2   eggs
1   tablespoons flour
2   tablespoons lemon juice
1/2 teaspoon vanilla
1/4 stick butter
    Cinnamon

† Preheat oven to 325°.
† Fill pie shell with peaches.
† Combine remaining ingredients, except butter and cinnamon, and pour over peaches.
† Dot pie with butter and sprinkle with cinnamon. Bake one hour until pie sets.

ANN'S KENTUCKY DERBY PIE

Yield: one pie
Betsy Locke

1   (9-inch) unbaked pie shell
2   eggs
1/2 cup packed dark brown sugar
1/2 cup granulated sugar
1/2 cup flour
1   stick butter, melted
3   tablespoons bourbon
1   (6-ounce) package chocolate
    chips, melted
1   cup chopped pecans
1/2 cup heavy cream, whipped
    and sweetened
    Shaved chocolate or chocolate
    sprinkles for garnish

† Preheat oven to 350°.
† Beat eggs until foamy. Gradually add
  sugars and flour, beating until smooth.
† Add melted butter, beating until blended.
  Stir in remaining ingredients, except
  whipped cream, and pour into pie shell.
† Bake 35 minutes. Cool and serve with
  whipped cream and shaved chocolate.

ROCHET BLAIR'S LEMON PIE

Yield: two pies
Christ Church Cooks I

2   prepared (9-inch) pie shells
6   eggs
1 1/2 cups sugar
1   stick margarine, melted
    Juice of 2 lemons

† Preheat oven to 325°.
† Beat eggs and fold in remaining
  ingredients. Pour into pie shells and
  bake 35 minutes.

RAISIN PIE

Yield: one pie
Sue Head

1   (9-inch) pie shell,
    unbaked
1   cup dark or golden raisins
2   eggs, lightly beaten
1/2 cup milk
1   cup sugar
1/8 teaspoon salt
1   teaspoon vanilla
3/4 cup chopped nuts
2   tablespoons butter, melted

† Preheat oven to 450°.
† Soak raisins in very hot water for a
  few minutes. Drain.
† Combine remaining ingredients with
  raisins and pour into pie shell. Bake 10
  minutes.
† Reduce oven to 350° and bake 35
  minutes or until set in center.

CHILLED STRAWBERRY PIE

Yield: one pie
Patty Adams

SHELL:

3	egg whites
1	cup sugar
1	teaspoon vanilla extract
1	cup vanilla wafer crumbs
1	cup chopped pecans

† Preheat oven to 350°.
† Beat egg whites until soft peaks form. Gradually add sugar and vanilla and beat until stiff peaks form.
† Fold in wafer crumbs and pecans. Spread mixture in a buttered 10-inch pie pan. Spread sides slightly higher and bake 30 minutes or until lightly brown. Cool.

FILLING:

1	cup whipping cream
2	tablespoons powdered sugar
2	cups sliced strawberries
	Whole strawberries for garnish

† Beat whipping cream until foamy. Gradually add powdered sugar, beating until soft peaks form.
† Fold in strawberries and spread evenly in pie shell. Garnish with whole strawberries. Chill pie at least 4 hours before serving.

Janie Sellers' variation: Use 1/4 teaspoon baking powder, 1/8 teaspoon salt, 1/8 teaspoon baking soda and 10 crushed saltines instead of vanilla wafer crumbs.

STRAWBERRY PIE

Yield: one pie
Jo Rankin

3	tablespoons cornstarch
3	tablespoons strawberry jello
1/2	cup sugar
1	cup hot water
1	pint fresh strawberries, sliced
1	(9-inch) pie shell, baked

† Bring to boil first four ingredients in saucepan and let cool.
† Add strawberries and pour into pie shell. Let congeal in refrigerator and serve with whipped cream.

TURTLE PIE

Yield: one pie
Connie Linde

1 (9-inch) deep-dish pie shell, baked
12 caramels
1 (14-ounce) can sweetened condensed milk, divided
2 (1-ounce) squares unsweetened chocolate
1/2 stick butter or margarine
2 eggs
2 tablespoons water
1 teaspoon vanilla extract
Dash salt
1/2 cup chopped pecans

† Preheat oven to 325°.
† In small saucepan, over low heat, melt caramels with 1/3 cup condensed milk. Spread evenly on bottom of pie shell.
† In saucepan, over low heat, melt chocolate with butter or margarine.
† In large bowl, beat eggs with remaining milk, water, vanilla, and salt.
† Add chocolate mixture and pour into pie shell. Top with pecans.
† Bake for 35 minutes or until center is set. Cool and top with frozen whipped topping if desired.

ROSE WINE JELLY

Yield: 8 servings
Dede Thompson

2 tablespoons gelatin
1/3 cup lemon juice
3 cups rosé wine
3/4 cup sugar
1 tablespoon grated lemon rind
Whipped cream, sweetened

† In small bowl, sprinkle gelatin over lemon juice to soften.
† Combine wine, sugar and lemon rind in saucepan and simmer 3 to 4 minutes.
† Add gelatin, stirring until dissolved.
† Let cool and pour into 1 quart decorative mold or crystal bowl.
† Chill until set and garnish with whipped cream.

Menus

Meals To Share With Others

In Order To Serve
VIII. Meals To Share With Others

I was hungry and you gave me food,
I was thirsty and you gave me drink,
I was a stranger and you welcomed me.
[JOHN 25:35]

Sharing food and drink in hospitable circumstances is at the heart of the Christian life, both in worship and in secular surroundings.

The ancient Hebrews, of which our Lord was one, were a desert people, who, like other desert peoples of the world then and now, knew the importance of hospitality to strangers: without food and drink, strangers in the desert are condemned to die.

The central act of Christian worship is, of course, a symbolic meal of bread and wine, transferred from the great and historic Passover meal of deliverance which Jesus shared with his friends on the night before he died.

While few of us sit down to a meal famished, dehydrated, or unacquainted with our dining companions, we all need reminding that hunger—physical, emotional and spiritual—is at the core of our being, and that sharing with others is its cure. It is not enough to have food and drink, or even to give it away; the *welcome* is the third, equally important, element.

We have all been strangers before: as newly born, as newcomers in the parish, as newly baptized or confirmed, as suddenly ill and dependent upon others for basic needs, as grieving and without accustomed emotional support.

The menus in this section are designed not only to provide food to the hungry and drink to the thirsty but also welcome to the stranger, through the sacrament of hospitality.

All our meals and all our living make as sacraments of thee,
that by caring, helping, giving, we may true disciples be.
Alleluia! Alleluia! We will serve thee faithfully.
PERCY DEARMER (1867-1936), Priest; social activist; Editor, *The English Hymnal*

BENJAMIN HUTTO, ORGANIST/CHOIRMASTER

Meals To Share With Others
A Baptismal Brunch

The King of love my shepherd is, whose goodness faileth never;
I nothing lack if I am his and he is mine forever.
HENRY WILLIAMS BAKER (1821-1877), Priest; Editor, *Hymns,*
*Ancient and Modern,*1861
Paraphrase of Psalm 23 [Hymn 645,v. 1]

Baptism is a time when a person publicly becomes a member of another family-God's family, specifically those united with God incarnate, Jesus Christ. For parents and godparents of infants and small children being baptized, it is an occasion for remembering that this little person is a gift on loan from God and our primary responsibility is to celebrate and nurture that ultimate relationship of God and child. For older persons being baptized, it is a time to claim one's divine heritage and accept the responsibilities inherent therein. Baptism is a purely graceful occasion when we rejoice in all God has given us- life itself, new life in Jesus Christ, eternal life beyond the present -in other words, abundant life.

THE REVEREND MARTHA H. HEDGPETH, ASSOCIATE RECTOR

After the 8:45 Service:

Curried Fruits – page 102
Brunch in a Dish – page 137
Gouda Grits – page 104
Cheese Biscuits – page 11
Cinnamon–Laced Swirl Coffee Cake – page 82
Carolina Apple Cake – page 192

After the 11:15 Service:

Cheese Dollars – page 12
Polynesian Pork – page 147
Potatoes Gratin with Boursin – page 109
Marinated Asparagus and Hearts of Palm – page 43
Yeast Rolls – page 87
Amaretto Cheesecake – page 214

In Order To Serve
Meal for the New Baby's Family

Our Father, by whose Name
All Fatherhood is known,
Who dost in love proclaim
Each family thine own,
Bless thou all parents, guarding well,
With constant love as sentinel,
The homes in which thy people dwell.
F. BLAND TUCKER (1895-1984), Priest; Editor, *The Hymnal 1940* [Hymn 504, v.1]

The arrival of a new child in a home is marked with great joy and thankfulness. Yet an infant requires around-the-clock care and pampering. How glorious to turn the tables and pamper the family with a gift of a fully prepared meal to renew the parents' spirits and make siblings feel special and important. In serving, we are channels of God's blessing in the family, "guarding well" their energy to love and know love in the larger family of God.

THE REVEREND LISA G. SAUNDERS, ASSISTING PRIEST

Meals To Share With Others
Dinner for the Adult Confirmands

Jesus, confirm my heart's desire to work , and speak, and think for thee;
still let me guard the holy fire and stir up the gift in me
CHARLES WESLEY (1707-1788), Priest; author of 9000 hymns and poems [Hymn 704, v.3]

Confirmation, Rite 13, First Communion for Children, Adult Catechumenate: it's all more complicated now than in "the old days," when children age 12-14 knelt before the Bishop to receive the Laying on of Hands, and, coincidentally, their ticket up to the Eucharist and out of Sunday School. Like so much in our secular life today, Confirmation in the Episcopal Church offers choices, branch locations and varietals for different age groups.

As progeny of the Apostles, however, we are all, regardless of physical development, spiritual maturity, or ecclesiastical involvement, called to make a commitment to " guard the holy fire" and to "stir up the gift" in ourselves. Eventually, in the historic way of our church, we have the privilege of making humble and public witness in receiving the Laying on of Hands by the Bishop.

But let us also use the several other rites we now have, both before and after this time-honored act, to "confirm our heart's desire." Even a holy fire needs refueling, and spiritual food not stirred may scorch.

BENJAMIN HUTTO, ORGANIST /CHOIRMASTER

Roasted Red Pepper And Garlic Dip – page 16
Linguine with Tomatoes and Basil – page 122
Lime Chicken – page 166
Greek Style Salad – page 49
French Bread
Chocolate Trifle – page 217

In Order To Serve
A Dinner for a Couple to be Married

O gracious God, you consecrate all that is lovely, good and true.
Bless thou who in your presence wait and every day their love renew.
RUSSELL SCHULZ- WIDMAR (b.1944) [Hymn 353, v.2]

With food the celebration of a couple who are about to be married is a time to indulge in favorites and fantasies. When I am preparing a meal for such an occasion, I banish the idea of heavy traditional and head in the direction of light and the unusual. In honoring this new bond and covenant of husband and wife, the food should be light and elegant with a contrast of color, shape and texture. It is a time in life when thoughts are turned to romance and love.

Celebrations like these call for professions of love and passion. Invite other couples who will be willing to speak of their love, their faith together, their times of struggle and disappointment, times of joy and mystical union. I once attended such a party where an older gentleman who had been married for many years stood up, wished the couple well, and quoted the following Elizabeth Barrett Browning sonnet to describe the love he and his wife still shared:

How do I love thee? Let me count the ways.
I love thee to the depth and breadth and height
My soul can reach, when feeling out of sight...
-and if God choose,
I shall but love thee better after death.

THE REVEREND BRIAN S. SUNTKEN, ASSOCIATE RECTOR

Oriental Chicken Wontons – page 27
Chilled Squash Soup – page 38
Make–Ahead Buffet Shrimp Casserole – page 186
Microwaved Asparagus – page 95
Poppy Seed Bread – page 77
Cammie's Layer Cake with Caramel Frosting – page 193

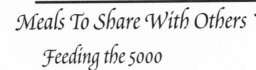

Meals To Share With Others
Feeding the 5000

Now come, most worthy Lord, God's Son, Incarnate Word,
Alleluia!
We follow all and heed your call
to come into the banquet hall.
PHILIPP NICOLAI (1556-1608), German Lutheran pastor [Hymn 61, v.2]
tr. CARL P. DAW, JR. (b.1944), Priest; contemporary American hymn writer

Since its founding in 1943, Christ Church has had many mouths to feed. Banquets for hundreds commemorating parish anniversaries or program initiatives...New members' dinners...Casual on-the-grounds picnics for Parish Day celebrations...Midweek luncheons for many commissions and committees...Receptions to honor people and occasions.

We also feed those who come to Christ Church from the greater church and community: Lenten suppers for area Episcopalians, meals for visiting choirs, receptions for St. Francis Jobs Program graduates to name but a few.

And many of our members work in the soup kitchen or provide casseroles and sandwiches for citizens of God's kingdom who do not have the means to provide for themselves.

Cooking for a crowd requires the same love and care with each and every dish as the most intimate gathering at home. But it also helps to have experienced staff and lots of willing volunteers as we do at Christ Church.

Jesus often used meal times and parties as occasions for celebration, for teaching, for outreaching, and he had a wide diversity of dining companions. So must we.

ANNE B. TOMLINSON, SENIOR WARDEN

In Order To Serve

House Blessing

O let thy table honored be, and furnished well with joyful guests;
and may each soul salvation see, that here its sacred pledges tastes.
PHILIP DODDRIDGE (1702-1751) English independent theologian, writer and poet
[Hymn 321, v. 2]

The church's occasional liturgy for the blessing of a house reminds us of the sacredness of the homes in which God's people dwell. The service includes carrying a lighted candle and sprinkling water in each room of the house, with a blessing for each according to its unique purpose. It is a lovely occasion for inviting neighbors and friends in to celebrate a new home.

"There is no place like home," in Dorothy's immortal words after her adventures in Oz. To be human is to search for home like Dorothy and her companions. Our restlessness and searching can only be satisfied by God, by the vision of that place where, in the words of the marriage service, "the saints feast forever in your heavenly home."

For now our earthly homes are sacramental signs of our eternal home. They are places to savor life. They are spaces for gathering with those we love. They are havens of hospitality for others. Other than the altar in the church, there is no more sacred place than the table in our homes where we break bread and share God's board and bounty. There with the psalmist we can *"Taste and see that the Lord is good; happy are they who trust in him!"*

Open the windows and doors of this house
that the light and love of your
Holy Spirit may shine within,
a light in the world for warmth and welcome.
[New Zealand Prayer Book]

THE REVEREND HENRY NUTT PARSLEY, JR., RECTOR

242

Meals To Share With Others
House Blessing

Brie Cheese with Chutney – page 18
Chicken Paella – page 169
Cranberry Salad – page 61
Marinated Green Beans – page 97
Rolls
Pears Baked in Cream – page 224

SPICE SIMMERING BOUQUET

Yield: 1/2 gallon
Mary Redding

Large cinnamon stick
Cloves
Pine needles, preferably
Douglas spruce
1 nutmeg, crushed
1 teaspoon cinnamon
1/2 gallon water

† In a triple thickness bag of cheesecloth, boil all ingredients.

Wonderful holiday smell in your home.

243

In Order To Serve

A Visit with the Elderly

Every task, however simple, sets the soul that does it free;
every deed of human kindness done in love is done for thee.
HENRY VAN DYKE (1852-1933), Presbyterian minister; English professor; Navy chaplain
[Hymn 586, v.3]

Along with the gift of a meal, go to visit with the elderly with the intention of sharing some of yourself and your time.

Listening to one another and valuing the gems of their life experience, the wisdom of their years, is the heart of good ministry.

Expect to receive as well as give, with an openness to the uniqueness of this person and the life that he or she has lived. It is in such encounters that we meet Christ.

Remember, O Lord, we pray,
the men and women who reach the summit of their years.
Teach them to lay aside former responsibilities without regret
and to enjoy new leisure with delight.
Keep their minds open and make their hearts young.
Sustain them in health, surround them with love,
and crown their days with such a living sense of your presence
that they may be prepared to see you face to face
in your heavenly kingdom;
through Jesus Christ our Lord. Amen.

[Prayers, Thanksgivings and Litanies]

THE REVEREND DOCTOR RACHEL HAYNES, ASSOCIATE RECTOR

Meals To Share With Others

A Meal for those in Mourning

Come, my Way, my truth, my life:
such a way as gives us breath;
such a truth as ends all strife;
such a life as killeth death.
GEORGE HERBERT (1593-1633), Priest; village parson; metaphysical poet
[Hymn 487, v.1]

One of the first questions that comes to mind when visiting with someone who has recently experienced the death of a loved one is, "What can I say?"

Just being there is often far more important than saying the "right" thing. Your ministry of presence can be far more meaningful than words.

If you feel the need to say something, simply saying, "I'm sorry," may be all that you need to say. The fact that you took the time to prepare something for them to eat, and were with them in their grief often says more than words could ever express.

Come, my Light, my feast, my Strength:
such a light as shows a feast;
such a feast as mends in length;
such a strength as makes his guest.
GEORGE HERBERT (1593-1633), Priest; village parson; metaphysical poet
[Hymn 487, v.2]

THE REVEREND FRED W. PASCHALL, JR., ASSOCIATE RECTOR

Beef Tenderloin – page 150
Zoe's Rice Casserole – page 113
Green Beans Gruyere – page 98
Sour Cream Muffins – page 84
Irwin's Super Brownies – page 202

Index

Index

Index

Index

255

Notes: